# 1,000,000 Books

are available to read at

# Forgotten Books

www.ForgottenBooks.com

Read online
Download PDF
Purchase in print

ISBN 978-1-330-94719-7
PIBN 10124966

This book is a reproduction of an important historical work. Forgotten Books uses state-of-the-art technology to digitally reconstruct the work, preserving the original format whilst repairing imperfections present in the aged copy. In rare cases, an imperfection in the original, such as a blemish or missing page, may be replicated in our edition. We do, however, repair the vast majority of imperfections successfully; any imperfections that remain are intentionally left to preserve the state of such historical works.

Forgotten Books is a registered trademark of FB &c Ltd.
Copyright © 2018 FB &c Ltd.
FB &c Ltd, Dalton House, 60 Windsor Avenue, London, SW19 2RR.
Company number 08720141. Registered in England and Wales.

For support please visit www.forgottenbooks.com

# 1 MONTH OF
# FREE READING

## at
## www.ForgottenBooks.com

By purchasing this book you are eligible for one month membership to ForgottenBooks.com, giving you unlimited access to our entire collection of over 1,000,000 titles via our web site and mobile apps.

To claim your free month visit: www.forgottenbooks.com/free124966

\* Offer is valid for 45 days from date of purchase. Terms and conditions apply.

English
Français
Deutsche
Italiano
Español
Português

# www.forgottenbooks.com

**Mythology** Photography **Fiction**
Fishing Christianity **Art** Cooking
Essays **Buddhism** Freemasonry
Medicine **Biology** Music **Ancient Egypt** Evolution Carpentry Physics
Dance Geology **Mathematics** Fitness
Shakespeare **Folklore** Yoga Marketing
**Confidence** Immortality Biographies
Poetry **Psychology** Witchcraft
Electronics Chemistry History **Law**
Accounting **Philosophy** Anthropology
Alchemy Drama Quantum Mechanics
Atheism Sexual Health **Ancient History**
**Entrepreneurship** Languages Sport
Paleontology Needlework Islam
**Metaphysics** Investment Archaeology
Parenting Statistics Criminology
**Motivational**

# THE CAMBRIDGE, ELY, AND KING'S LYNN ROAD

## WORKS BY THE SAME AUTHOR.

**The Brighton Road:** Old Times and New on a Classic Highway.

**The Portsmouth Road,** and its Tributaries: To-day and in Days of Old.

**The Dover Road:** Annals of an Ancient Turnpike.

**The Bath Road:** History, Fashion, and Frivolity on an Old Highway.

**The Exeter Road:** The Story of the West of England Highway.

**The Great North Road:** The Old Mail Road to Scotland. Two Vols.

**The Norwich Road:** An East Anglian Highway.

**The Holyhead Road:** The Mail-Coach Road to Dublin. Two Vols.

**Cycle Rides Round London.**

**The Oxford, Gloucester, and Milford Haven Road.** [*In the Press.*

# LYNN ROAD THE GREAT FENLAND HIGHWAY
## BY CHARLES G. HARPER

AUTHOR OF "THE BRIGHTON ROAD" "THE PORTSMOUTH ROAD" "THE DOVER ROAD" "THE BATH ROAD" "THE EXETER ROAD" "THE GREAT NORTH ROAD" "THE NORWICH ROAD" "THE HOLYHEAD ROAD" AND "CYCLE RIDES ROUND LONDON"

ILLUSTRATED BY THE AUTHOR, AND FROM OLD-TIME PRINTS AND PICTURES

(*All Rights Reserved*)

DA
600
H3

# Preface

*IN the course of an eloquent passage in an eulogy of the old posting and coaching days, as opposed to railway times, Ruskin regretfully looks back upon "the happiness of the evening hours when, from the top of the last hill he had surmounted, the traveller beheld the quiet village where he was to rest, scattered among the meadows, beside its valley stream." It is a pretty, backward picture, viewed through the diminishing-glass of time, and possesses a certain specious attractiveness that cloaks much of the very real discomfort attending the old road-faring era. For not always did the traveller behold the quiet village under conditions so ideal. There were such things as tempests, keen frosts, and bitter winds to make his faring highly uncomfortable; to say little of the snowstorms that half smothered him and pre-*

vented his reaching his destination until his very vitals were almost frozen. Then there were MESSIEURS the highwaymen, always to be reckoned with, and it cannot too strongly be insisted upon that until the nineteenth century had well dawned they were always to be confidently expected at the next lonely bend of the road. But, assuming good weather and a complete absence of those old pests of society, there can be no doubt that a journey down one of the old coaching highways must have been altogether delightful.

In the old days of the road, the traveller saw his destination afar off, and—town or city or village—it disclosed itself by degrees to his appreciative or critical eyes. He saw it, seated sheltered in its vale, or, perched on its hill-top, the sport of the elements; and so came, with a continuous panorama of country in his mind's eye, to his inn. By rail the present-day traveller has many comforts denied to his grandfather, but there is no blinking the fact that he is conveyed very much in the manner of a parcel or a bale of goods, and is delivered at his journey's end oppressed with a sense of detachment never felt by one who travelled the road in days of old, or even by the cyclist in the present age. The railway traveller is set down out of the void in a strange place, many leagues from his base;

*the country between a blank and the place to which he has come an unknown quantity. In so travelling he has missed much.*

*The old roads and their romance are the heritage of the modern tourist, by whatever method he likes to explore them. Countless generations of men have built up the highways, the cities, towns, villages and hamlets along their course, and have lived and loved, have laboured, fought and died through the centuries. Will you not halt awhile and listen to their story — fierce, pitiful, lovable, hateful, tender or terrible, just as you may hap upon it; flashing forth as changefully out of the past as do the rays from the facets of a diamond? A battle was fought here, an historic murder wrought there. This way came such an one to seek his fortune and find it; that way went another, to lose life and fortune both. In yon house was born the Man of his Age, for whom that age was ripe; on yonder hillock an olden malefactor, whom modern times would call a reformer, expiated the crime of being born too early — there is no cynic more consistent in his cynicism than Time.*

*All these have lived and wrought and thought to this one unpremeditated end — that the tourist travels smoothly and safely along roads once rough and dangerous beyond belief and that as he goes every place has a story to tell, for him to hear if he will. If he have no ears for such, so much the worse for him, and by so much the poorer his faring.*

CHARLES G. HARPER.

PETERSHAM, SURREY,
*October* 1902.

# LIST OF ILLUSTRATIONS

## SEPARATE PLATES

| | PAGE |
|---|---|
| THE "CAMBRIDGE TELEGRAPH" STARTING FROM THE WHITE HORSE, FETTER LANE . . . . *Frontispiece* | |
| *From a Print after J. Pollard.* | |
| THE "STAR OF CAMBRIDGE" STARTING FROM THE BELLE SAUVAGE YARD, LUDGATE HILL, 1816 . . | 17 |
| *From a Print after T. Young.* | |
| "KNEE-DEEP": THE "LYNN AND WELLS MAIL" IN A SNOWSTORM . . . . . . . . | 23 |
| *From a Print after C. Cooper Henderson.* | |
| A LONDON SUBURB IN 1816: TOTTENHAM . . . | 39 |
| *From a Drawing by Rowlandson.* | |
| WALTHAM CROSS . . . . . . . | 61 |
| THE "HULL MAIL" AT WALTHAM CROSS . . . | 65 |
| *From a Print after J. Pollard.* | |
| CHESHUNT GREAT HOUSE . . . . . . | 77 |
| HODDESDON . . . . . . . . | 83 |
| WARE . . . . . . . . . | 89 |
| BARLEY . . . . . . . . . | 105 |
| FOWLMERE: A TYPICAL CAMBRIDGESHIRE VILLAGE . | 113 |
| MELBOURN . . . . . . . . | 129 |

## List of Illustrations

|  | PAGE |
|---|---|
| Trumpington Mill | 137 |
| Trumpington Street, Cambridge | 145 |
| Hobson, the Cambridge Carrier | 159 |
| A Wet Day in the Fens | 203 |
| Aldreth Causeway | 219 |
| A Fenland Road: the Akeman Street near Stretham Bridge | 245 |
| Stretham Bridge | 249 |
| Ely Cathedral . *After J. M. W. Turner, R.A.* | 271 |
| Ely, from the Ouse | 277 |
| Joseph Beeton in the Condemned Cell | 311 |
| The Town and Harbour of Lynn, from West Lynn | 317 |
| "Clifton's House" | 320 |
| The Custom-House, Lynn | 323 |
| The Ferry Inn, Lynn | 327 |

# ILLUSTRATIONS IN TEXT

|  | PAGE |
|---|---|
| VIGNETTE: EEL-SPEARING | *Title-page* |
| PREFACE | vii |
| LIST OF ILLUSTRATIONS: TAKING TOLL | xi |
| THE CAMBRIDGE, ELY, AND KING'S LYNN ROAD | 1 |
| THE GREEN DRAGON, BISHOPSGATE STREET, 1856 | 8 |
| *From a Drawing by T. Hosmer Shepherd.* | |
| THE FOUR SWANS, BISHOPSGATE STREET, 1855 | 9 |
| *From a Drawing by T. Hosmer Shepherd.* | |
| TOTTENHAM CROSS | 38 |
| BALTHAZAR SANCHEZ' ALMSHOUSES, TOTTENHAM | 41 |
| WALTHAM CROSS A HUNDRED YEARS AGO | 59 |
| THE ROMAN URN; CHESHUNT | 76 |
| CHARLES THE FIRST'S ROCKING-HORSE | 79 |
| CLARKSON'S MONUMENT | 99 |
| A MONUMENTAL MILESTONE | 111 |
| THE CHEQUERS, FOWLMERE | 115 |
| WEST MILL | 118 |
| A QUAINT CORNER IN ROYSTON | 125 |
| CAXTON GIBBET | 127 |
| THE FIRST MILESTONE FROM CAMBRIDGE | 139 |
| HOBSON'S CONDUIT | 141 |
| HOBSON | 162 |
| *From a Painting in Cambridge Guildhall.* | |
| MARKET HILL, CAMBRIDGE | 167 |
| THE FALCON, CAMBRIDGE | 168 |

## List of Illustrations

|  | PAGE |
|---|---|
| Interior of St. Sepulchre's Church | 169 |
| Cambridge Castle a hundred years ago | 171 |
| Landbeach | 181 |
| The Fens | 191 |
| *After Dugdale.* | |
| The Isle of Ely and district | 215 |
| Aldreth Causeway and the Isle of Ely | 218 |
| Upware Inn | 237 |
| Wicken Fen | 241 |
| Hodden Spade and Becket | 248 |
| Stretham | 254 |
| The West Front, Ely Cathedral | 265 |
| Ely Cathedral, from the Littleport Road | 289 |
| Littleport | 291 |
| The River Road, Littleport | 293 |
| The Ouse | 295 |
| Southery Ferry | 296 |
| Kett's Oak | 300 |
| Denver Hall | 301 |
| The Crown, Downham Market | 302 |
| The Castle, Downham Market | 303 |
| Hogge's Bridge, Stow Bardolph | 305 |
| The Lynn Arms, Setchey | 306 |
| The South Gates, Lynn | 308 |
| The Guildhall, Lynn | 314 |
| The Duke's Head, Lynn | 321 |
| Islington | 329 |

# THE ROAD TO CAMBRIDGE, ELY, AND KING'S LYNN

London (Shoreditch Church) to—

| | MILES |
|---|---|
| Kingsland | $1\frac{1}{2}$ |
| Stoke Newington | $2\frac{1}{2}$ |
| Stamford Hill | $3\frac{1}{4}$ |
| Tottenham High Cross | $4\frac{1}{4}$ |
| Tottenham | $5\frac{1}{4}$ |
| Upper Edmonton | 6 |
| Lower Edmonton | $6\frac{3}{4}$ |
| Ponder's End | $8\frac{1}{2}$ |
| Enfield Highway | $9\frac{1}{4}$ |
| Enfield Wash | 10 |
| Waltham Cross | $11\frac{1}{4}$ |
| Crossbrook Street | 12 |
| Turner's Hill | 13 |
| Cheshunt | $13\frac{1}{4}$ |
| Cheshunt Wash | $13\frac{3}{4}$ |
| Turnford | 14 |
| Wormley (cross New River) | $14\frac{3}{4}$ |
| Broxbourne | $15\frac{3}{4}$ |
| Hoddesdon | 17 |
| Great Amwell (cross New River and the Lea) | $19\frac{1}{4}$ |
| Ware | 21 |
| Wade's Mill (cross River Rib) | 23 |
| High Cross | $23\frac{1}{2}$ |
| Collier's End | 25 |
| Puckeridge (cross River Rib) | $26\frac{3}{4}$ |
| Braughing | $27\frac{3}{4}$ |
| Quinbury | $28\frac{3}{4}$ |
| Hare Street | $30\frac{3}{4}$ |
| Barkway | 35 |
| Barley | $36\frac{3}{4}$ |
| Fowlmere | 42 |
| Newton | $44\frac{1}{4}$ |
| Hauxton (cross River Granta) | $47\frac{3}{4}$ |

|  | MILES |
|---|---|
| Trumpington | 48½ |
| Cambridge (Market Hill) | 50¾ |

To Cambridge, through Royston—

|  | MILES |
|---|---|
| Puckeridge (cross River Rib) | 26¾ |
| West Mill | 29¾ |
| Buntingford | 31 |
| Chipping | 32½ |
| Buckland | 33¾ |
| Royston | 37¾ |
| Melbourn | 41¼ |
| Shepreth | 43¼ |
| Foxton Station and Level Crossing | 44 |
| Harston | 45½ |
| Hauxton (cross River Granta) | 46½ |
| Trumpington | 48¾ |
| Cambridge (Market Hill) | 51 |
| Milton | 54 |
| Landbeach | 54¾ |
| Denny Abbey | 58 |
| Chittering | 58¾ |
| Stretham Bridge (cross Great Ouse River) | 61¾ |
| Stretham | 63¼ |
| Thetford Level Crossing | 64½ |
| Ely | 67½ |
| Chettisham Station and Level Crossing | 69½ |
| Littleport | 72½ |
| Littleport Bridge (cross Great Ouse River) | 73½ |
| Brandon Creek (cross Little Ouse River) | 76¾ |
| Southery | 78¾ |
| Modney Bridge (cross Sams Cut Drain) | 80¼ |
| Hilgay (cross Wissey River) | 81¾ |
| Fordham | 82¾ |
| Denver | 84 |
| Downham Market | 85¼ |
| Wimbotsham | 86½ |
| Stow Bardolph | 87¼ |
| South Runcton (cross River Nar) | 89¼ |
| Setchey | 92¼ |
| West Winch | 93¾ |
| Hardwick Bridge | 95¼ |
| King's Lynn | 97¼ |

# THE CAMBRIDGE ELY AND KING'S LYNN ROAD

## I

"SISTER ANNE, Sister Anne, do you see anyone coming?" asks Fatima in the story of Bluebeard. Clio, the Muse of History, shall be my Sister Anne. I hereby set her down in the beginnings of the Cambridge Road, bid her be retrospective, and ask her what she sees.

"I see," she says dreamily, like some medium or clairvoyant,—"I see a forest track leading from the marshy valley of the Thames to the still more marshy valley of the Lea. The tribes who inhabit the land are at once fierce and warlike, and greedy for trading with merchants from over the narrow channel that separates Britain from Gaul. They are fair-haired and blue-eyed, they are dressed in the skins of wild animals, and their chieftains wear many ornaments of red gold." Then she is silent, for Clio, like her eight sisters, is a very ancient personage, and like the aged, although she knows much, cannot recall sights and scenes without a deal of mental fumbling.

"And what else do you see?"

"There comes along the forest track a great concourse of soldiers. Never before were such seen in the land. They form the advance-guard of an invading army, and the tribes presently fly from them, for these are the conquering Romans, whose fame has come before them. There are none who can withstand those soldiers."

"Many a tall Roman warrior, doubtless, sleeps where he fell, slain by wounds or disease in that advance?"

Clio is indignant and corrective. "The Romans," she says, "were not a race of tall men. They were undersized, but well built and of a generous chest-development. They are, as I see them, imposing as they march, for they advance in solid phalanx, and their bright armour, their shields and swords, flash like silver in the sun.

"I see next," she says, "these foreign soldiers as conquerors, settled in the land. They have an armed camp in a clearing of the forest, where a company of them keep watch and ward, while many more toil at the work of making the forest track a broad and firm military way. Among them, chained together like beasts, and kept to their work by the whips and blows of taskmasters, are gangs of natives, who perform the roughest and the most unskilled of the labour.

"And after that I see four hundred years of Roman power and civilisation fade like a dream, and then a dim space of anarchy, lit up by the fitful glare of fire, and stained and running red with blood. Many strange and heathen peoples come and go in this period along the road, once so broad and flat and straight, but now grown neglected. The strange peoples call themselves by many names,—Saxons, Vikings, Picts, and Scots and Danes,—but their aim is alike: to plunder and to slay. Six hundred years pass before they bring back something of that civilisation the Romans planted, and the land obtains a settled Christianity and an approach to rest. And then, when things have come to this pass, there comes a stronger race to make the land its own. It is the coming of the Normans.

"I see the Conqueror, lord of all this land but the Isle of Ely, coming to vanquish the English remnant. I see him, his knights and men-at-arms, his standard-bearers and his bowmen, marching where the Romans marched a thousand years before, and in three years I see the shrunken remains of his army return, victorious, but decimated by those conquered English and their allies, the agues and fevers, the mires and mists of the Fens."

"And then—what of the Roman Road, the Saxon 'Ermine Street'? tell me, why does it lie deserted and forgot?"

But Clio is silent. She does not know; it is a question rather for archæology, for which there is no Muse at all. Nor can she tell much of the history of the road, apart from the larger national concerns in which it has a part. She is like a wholesale trader, and deals only in bulk. Let us in these pages seek to recover something from the past to illustrate the description of these many miles.

## II

THE coach-road to Cambridge, Ely, and King's Lynn —the modern highway—follows in general direction, and is in places identical with, two distinct Roman roads. From Shoreditch Church, whence it is measured, to Royston, it is on the line of the Ermine Street, the great direct Roman road to Lincoln and the north of England, which, under the names of the "North Road" and the "Old North Road," goes straight ahead, past Caxton, to Alconbury Hill, sixty-eight miles from London, where it becomes identical with our own Great North Road, as far as Stamford and Casterton.

From Royston to Cambridge there would seem never to have been any direct route, and the Romans apparently reached Cambridge either by pursuing the Ermine Street five miles farther, and thence turning to the right at Arrington Bridge; or else by Colchester, Sudbury, and Linton. Those, at anyrate, are the ways obvious enough on modern maps, or in the Antonine Itinerary, that Roman road-book made about A.D. 200–250. We have, however, only to exercise our own observation to find that the Antonine Itinerary is a very inaccurate piece of work, and that the Romans almost certainly journeyed to *Camboricum*, their Cambridge, by way of Epping, Bishop's Stortford, and Great Chesterford, a route taken by several coaches sixty years ago.

From Cambridge to Ely and King's Lynn the

coach-road follows with more or less exactness the Akeman Street, a Roman way in the nature of an elevated causeway above the fens.

The Ermine Street between London and Lincoln is not noted by the Antonine Itinerary, which takes the traveller to that city by two very indirect routes: the one along the Watling Street as far as High Cross, in Warwickshire, and thence to the right, along the Fosse Way past Leicester; the other by Colchester. The Ermine Street, leading direct to Lincoln, is therefore generally supposed to be a Roman road of much later date.

We are not to suppose that the Romans knew these roads by the names they now bear; names really given by the Saxons. Ermine Street enshrines the name of Eorman, some forgotten hero or divinity of that people; and the Akeman Street, running from the Norfolk coast, in a south-westerly direction through England, to Cirencester and Bath, is generally said to have obtained its name from invalids making pilgrimage to the Bath waters, there to ease them of their aches and pains. But a more reasonable theory is that which finds the origin of that name in a corruption of *Aquæ Solis*, the name of Bath.

No reasonable explanation has ever been advanced of the abandonment of the Ermine Street between Lower Edmonton and Ware, and the choosing of the present route, running roughly parallel with it at distances ranging from half a mile to a mile, and by a low-lying course much more likely to be flooded than the old Roman highway.

The change must have been made at an early period, far beyond the time when history dawns on the road, for it is always by the existing route that travellers are found coming and going.

Few know that the Roman road and the coaching road are distinct; and yet, with the aid of a large-scale Ordnance map, the course of the Ermine Street can be distinctly traced. Not only so, but a day's exploration of it, as far as its present condition, obstructed and diverted in places, will allow, is of absorbing interest.

It makes eleven miles of, in places, rough walking, and often gives only the satisfaction of being close to the actual site, and not actually on it. A straight line drawn from where the modern road swerves slightly to the right at Northumberland Park, Edmonton, to Ware, gives the direction the ancient road pursued.

The exact spot where the modern road leaves the Roman way is found at Lower Edmonton, where a Congregational Church stands in an open space, and the houses on the left hand are seen curving back to face a lane that branches off at this point. This, bearing the significantly ancient name of "Langhedge Lane," goes exactly on the line of the Ermine Street; but it cannot be followed for more than about a hundred yards, for it is cut through by railways and modern buildings, and quite obliterated for some distance. Where lanes are found near Edmonton Rectory on the site of the ancient way, names that are eloquent of an antiquity closely allied with Roman times begin to appear. "Bury

Hall," and, half a mile beyond it, "Bury Farm," neighboured by an ancient moat, are examples. "Bury" is a corruption of a Saxon word meaning anything, from a fortified camp to a settlement, or a hillock; and when found beside a Roman road generally signifies (like that constantly recurring name "Coldharbour") that the Saxons found deserted Roman villas by the wayside. Beyond Bury Farm the cutting of the New River in the seventeenth century obscured some length of the Ermine Street. A long straight lane from Forty Hill Park, past Bull's Cross, to Theobalds, represents it pretty accurately, as does the next length, by Bury Green and Cheshunt Great House. Cold Hall and Cold Hall Green mark its passing by, even though, just here, it is utterly diverted or stopped up. "Elbow Lane" is the name of it from the neighbourhood of Hoddesdon to Little Amwell. Beyond that point it plunges into narrower lanes, and thence into pastures and woods, descending steeply therefrom into the valley of the Lea by Ware. In those hillside pastures, and in an occasional wheatfield, a dry summer will disclose, in a long line of dried-up grass or corn, the route of that ancient paved way below the surface. A sepulchral barrow in one of these fields, called by the rustics "Pennyloaf Hill," is probably the last resting-place of some prehistoric traveller along this way. A quarter of a mile from Ware the Ermine Street crossed the Lea to "Bury Field," now a brickfield, where many Roman coins have been found. Thenceforward it is one with the present highway to Royston.

## III

ALTHOUGH Shoreditch Church marks the beginning of the Cambridge Road, of the old road to the North, and of the highways into Lincolnshire, it was always to and from a point somewhat nearer the City of

THE GREEN DRAGON, BISHOPSGATE STREET, 1856.
[*From a Drawing by T. Hosmer Shepherd*]

London that the traffic along these various ways came and went. Bishopsgate Street was of old the great centre for coaches and vans, and until quite modern times — until, in fact, after railways had come — those ancient inns, the Four Swans, the Vine, the Bull, the Green Dragon, and many another, still faced upon the street, as for many centuries they had done. Coaches were promptly withdrawn on the opening of the railways, but the lumbering old road-waggons, with their vast tilts, broad wheels, swinging horn-lanterns, and long teams of horses, survived for some years later. Now everything is changed; inns, coaches, waggons are all gone. You will look in vain for them; and of

THE FOUR SWANS, BISHOPSGATE STREET, 1855.
[*From a Drawing by T. Hosmer Shepherd.*]

the most famous inn of all—the Bull, in Bishopsgate Street Within—the slightest memory survives. On its site rises that towering block of commercial offices called "Palmerston House," crawling abnudantly, like some maggoty cheese, with companies and secretaries, clerks and office-boys, who seem, like mites, to writhe out of the interstices of the stone and plaster. Overhead, on the dizzy roof, are the clustered strands of the telegraph-wires, resembling the meshes of some spider's web, exquisitely typical of much that goes forward in those little cribs and hutches of offices within. It is a sorry change from the old Bull — the Black Bull, as it was originally named — with its cobble-stoned courtyard and surrounding galleries, whence audiences looked down upon the plays of Shakespeare and others of the Elizabethans, and so continued until the Puritans came and stage-plays were put under interdict. When plays were not being enacted in that old courtyard, it was crowded with the carriers' vans out of Cambridgeshire and the Eastern Counties generally. "The Black Bull," we read in a publication dated 1633, "'is still looking towards Shoreditch, to see if he can spy the carriers coming from Cambridge." Would that it still looked towards Shoreditch!

It was to the Bull that old Hobson, the Cambridge carrier of such great renown, drove on his regular journeys, between 1570 and 1631. Hobson was the precursor, the grand original, of all the Pickfords and Carter Patersons of this crowded age, and lives immortal, though his body be long resolved to dust, as the originator of a proverb. That is immortality indeed! No deed of chivalry, no great achievement in the arts of peace and war, shall so surely render your name imperishable as the linking of it with some proverb or popular saying. Who has not heard of "Hobson's

Choice"? Have you never been confronted with that "take it or leave it" offer yourself? For, in truth, Hobson's Choice is no choice at all; and is, and ever was, "that or none." The saying arose from the livery-stable business carried on by Thomas Hobson at Cambridge, in addition to his carrying trade. He is, indeed, rightly or wrongly, said to have been the first who made a business of letting out saddle-horses. His practice, invariably followed, was to refuse to allow any horse in his stables to be taken out of its proper turn. "That or none" was his unfailing formula, when the Cambridge students, eager to pick and choose, would have selected their own fancy in horseflesh. Every customer was thus served alike, without favour. Hobson's fame, instead of flickering out, has endured. Many versified about him at his death, but one of the best rhymed descriptions of his stable practice was written in 1734, a hundred and three years later, by Charles Waterton, as a translation from the Latin of Vincent Bourne—

> "In his long stable, Cambridge, you are told,
> Hobson kept studs for hire in days of old,
> On this condition only—that the horse
> Nearest the door should start the first on course,
> Then next to him, or none: so that each beast
> Might have its turn of labour and of rest;
> This granted, no one yet, in college dress,
> Was ever known this compact to transgress.
> Next to the door—next to the work; say, why
> Should such a law, so just, be doomed to die?
> Remember then this compact to restore,
> And let it govern as it did before.
> This done, O happy Cambridge! you will see,
> Your Hobson's stud just as it ought to be."

## IV

WHO was that man, or who those associated adventurers, to first establish a coach between London and Cambridge, and when was the custom first introduced of travelling by coach, instead of on horseback, along this road? No one can say. We can see now that he who first set up a Cambridge coach must of necessity have been great and forceful: as great a man as Hobson, in whose time people were well content to hire horses and ride them; but although University wits have sung the fame of Hobson, the greater innovator and the date of his innovation alike remain unknown. It is vaguely said that the first Cambridge coach was started in the reign of Charles the Second, but Pepys, who might have been trusted to mention so striking a novelty, does not refer to such a thing, and, as on many other roads, we hear nothing definite until 1750, when a Cambridge coach went up and down twice a week, taking two whole days each way, staying the night at Barkway going, and at Epping returning. The same team of horses dragged the coach the whole way. There was in this year a coach through to Lynn, once a week, setting out on Fridays in summer and Thursdays in winter.

In 1753 a newer era dawned. There were then two conveyances for Cambridge, from the Bull and the Green Dragon in Bishopsgate: one leaving Tuesdays and Fridays, the other Wednesdays and Saturdays, reaching the Blue Boar and the Red Lion, Cambridge, the same night and returning the following day, when that day did not happen to be Sunday.

Each of these stage-coaches carried six passengers, all inside, and the fares were about twopence-halfpenny a mile in summer and threepence in winter. The cost of a coach journey between London and Cambridge was then, therefore, about twelve shillings.

Hobson's successors in the carrying business had by this time increased to three carriers, owning two waggons each. There were thus six waggons continually going back and forth in the mid-eighteenth century. They took two and a half days to perform the fifty-one miles, and "inned" at such places as Hoddesdon, Ware, Royston, and Barkway, where they would be drawn up in the coachyards of the inns at night, and those poor folk who travelled by them at the rate of three-halfpence a mile would obtain an inexpensive supper, with a shakedown in loft or barn.

The coaches at this period did by much effort succeed in performing the journey in one day, but it was a long day. They started early and came late to their journey's end; setting out at four o'clock in the morning, and coming to their destination at seven in the evening; a pace of little more than three miles an hour.

In 1763, owing partly to the improvements that had taken place along the road, and more perhaps to the growing system of providing more changes of horses and shorter stages, the "London and Cambridge Diligence" is found making the journey daily, in eight hours, by way of Royston, "performed by J. Roberts of the White Horse, Fetter Lane;

Thomas Watson's, the Red Lyon, Royston; and Jacob Brittain, the Sun, Cambridge." The "Diligence" ran light, carrying three passengers only, at a fare of thirteen shillings and sixpence. There were in this same year two other coaches; the "Fly," daily, from the Queen's Head, Gray's Inn Lane, by way of Epping and Chesterford, to the Rose on the Market Hill, Cambridge, at a fare of twelve shillings; and the "Stage," daily, to the Red Lion, Petty Cury, carrying four passengers at ten shillings each.

We hear little at this period of coaches or waggons on to Ely and King's Lynn. Cambridgeshire and Norfolk roads were only just being made good, after many centuries of neglect, and Cambridge town was still, as it always had been (strange though it may now seem), something of a port. The best and safest way was to take boat or barge by Cam and Ouse, rather than face the terrors of roads almost constantly flooded. Gillam's, Burleigh's, and Salmon's waggons, which at this time were advertised to ply between London and Cambridge, transferred their loads on to barges at the quays by Great Bridge. Indeed it was not until railways came that Cambridge ceased to depend largely upon the rivers, and the coals burnt, the wine drank, and the timber used were water-borne to the very last. Hence we find the town always in the old days peculiarly distressed in severe winters when the waterways were frozen; and hence, too, the remonstrance made by the Mayor and Corporation when Denver Sluice was rebuilt in 1745, " to the hindering of the navigation to King's Lynn."

In 1796, the roads now moderately safe, a stage-coach is found plying from Cambridge to Ely and back in one day, replacing the old "passage-boats"; but Lynn, as far as extant publications tell us, was still chiefly approachable by water. In this year Cambridge enjoyed a service of six coaches between the town and London, four of them daily; the remaining two running three times a week. The Mail, on the road ten years past, started at eight o'clock every night from the Bull and Mouth, London, and, going by Royston, arrived at the Sun, Cambridge, at 3.30 the following morning. The old "Diligence," which thirty-three years before had performed the journey in eight hours, now is found to take nine, and to have raised its fares from thirteen shillings and sixpence to one guinea, going to the Hoop instead of the Sun. The "Fly," still by Epping and Great Chesterford, has raised its fares from twelve shillings to eighteen shillings, and now takes "outsides" at nine shillings. It does not, however, fly very swiftly, consuming ten hours on the way. "Prior's Stage" is one of the new concerns, leaving the Bull, Bishopsgate Street, at eight in the morning on Tuesdays, Thursdays, and Saturdays, and, going by Barkway, arriving at some unnamed hour at the Red Lion, Petty Cury. It conveys six passengers at fifteen shillings inside and eight shillings out, like its competitor, "Hobson's Stage," setting out on Mondays, Wednesdays, and Saturdays from the Green Dragon, Bishopsgate Street, for the Blue Boar, Cambridge. "Hobson's" is another new-comer, merely trading on the glamour of the old name.

The "Night Post Coach" of this year, starting from the Golden Cross, Charing Cross, every afternoon at 5.30, went by Epping and Great Chesterford. It carried only four passengers inside, at fifteen shillings each, and a like number outside at nine shillings. Travelling all night, and through the dangerous glades of Epping Forest, the old advertisement especially mentions it to be "guarded." Passing through many nocturnal terrors, the "Night Post Coach" finally drew up in the courtyard of the still-existing Eagle and Child (now called the Eagle) at Cambridge, at three o'clock in the morning.

The next change seems to have been in 1804, when the "Telegraph" was advertised to cover the fifty-one miles in seven hours,—and made the promise good. People said it was all very well, but shook their heads and were of opinion that it would not last. In 1821, however, we find the "Telegraph" still running, and actually in six hours, starting every morning at nine o'clock from the White Horse in Fetter Lane, going by Barkway, and arriving at the Sun at Cambridge at 3 p.m. This is the coach shown in Pollard's picture in the act of leaving the White Horse. In the meanwhile, however, in 1816 another and even faster coach, the "Star of Cambridge," was established, and, if we may go so far as to believe the statement made on the rare old print showing it leaving the Belle Sauvage Yard on Ludgate Hill in that year, it performed the journey in four hours and a half! Allowing for necessary stops for changing on the way, this would give a pace of over eleven miles an hour; and we may

THE "STAR OF CAMBRIDGE" STARTING FROM THE BELLE SAUVAGE YARD, LUDGATE HILL, 1816.
[*From a Print after T. Young.*]

perhaps, in view of what both the roads and coaching enterprise were like at that time, be excused from believing that, apart from the special effort of any one particular day, it ever did anything of the kind; even in 1821, five years later, as already shown, the "Telegraph," the crack coach of the period on this road, took six hours!

Let us see what others there were in 1821. To Cambridge went the "Safety," every day, from the Boar and Castle, Oxford Street, and the Bull, Aldgate, leaving the Bull at 3 p.m. and arriving at Cambridge, by way of Royston, in six hours; the "Tally Ho," from the Bull, Holborn, every afternoon at two o'clock, by the same route in the same time; the "Royal Regulator," daily, from the New Inn, Old Bailey, in the like time, by Epping and Great Chesterford; the old "Fly," daily, from the George and Blue Boar, Holborn and the Green Dragon, Bishopsgate, at 9 a.m., by the same route, in seven hours; the "Cambridge Union," daily, from the White Horse, Fetter Lane and the Cross Keys, Wood Street, at 8 a.m., by Royston, in eight hours, to the Blue Boar, Cambridge; the "Cambridge New Royal Patent Mail," still by Royston, arriving at the Bull, Cambridge, in seven and a half hours; the "Cambridge and Ely" coach, every evening at 6 p.m., from the Golden Cross and the White Horse, arriving at the Eagle and Child, Cambridge, in ten hours; and the "Cambridge Auxiliary Mail," and two other coaches, which do not appear to have borne any distinctive names, the duration of whose pilgrimage is not specified.

Cambridge was therefore provided in 1821 with no fewer than twelve coaches a day, starting from London at all hours, from a quarter to eight in the morning until half-past six in the afternoon. There were also the "Lynn and Wells Mail," every evening, reaching Lynn in twelve hours thirty-three minutes; and the "Lynn Post Coach," through Cambridge, starting every morning from the Golden Cross, Charing Cross, and reaching Lynn in thirteen hours. The "Lynn Union" ran three days a week, in thirteen and a half hours, through Barkway. Other Lynn stages were the "Lord Nelson," "Lynn and Fakenham Post Coach," and two not dignified by specific names.

By 1828 the average speed was greatly improved, for although no coach reached Cambridge in less than six hours, there was, on the other hand, only one that took so long a time as seven hours and a half. The Mail had been accelerated by one hour, throughout to Lynn, and was, before driven off the road, further quickened, the post-office schedule of time for the London, Cambridge, King's Lynn, and Wells Mail in 1845 standing as under:—

| | |
|---|---|
| London (G.P.O.) | 8.0 p.m. |
| Wade's Mill | 10.32 „ |
| Buckland | 11.43 „ |
| Melbourn | 12.32 a.m. |
| Cambridge | 1.36 „ |
| Ely | 3.31 „ |
| Brandon Creek | 4.27 „ |
| Downham Market | 5.21 „ |
| Lynn | 6.33 „ |
| Wells | 10.43 „ |

In the 'forties, up to 1846 and 1847, the last

years of coaching on this road, the number of coaches does not seem to have greatly increased. The "Star" was still, meteor-like, making its swift daily journey to the Hoop at Cambridge, and the "Telegraph," "Regulator," "Times," and "Fly," and the "Mail," of course, were old-established favourites; but new names are not many. The "Regulator," indeed,—the daily "Royal Regulator" of years before,—is found going only three times weekly. The "Red Rover," however, was a new-comer, between London and Lynn daily; with the "Norfolk Hero" (which was probably another name for Nelson) three days a week between London, Cambridge, Ely, Lynn, and Wells. Recently added Cambridge coaches were the Tuesday, Thursday, and Saturday "Bee Hive," and the daily "Rocket"; while one daily and two tri-weekly coaches through Cambridge to Wisbeach—the daily "Rapid"; the Tuesday, Thursday, and Saturday "Day"; and the Monday, Wednesday, and Friday "Defiance," make their appearance.

How do those numbers compare with the number of trains run daily to Cambridge in our own time? It is not altogether a fair comparison, because the capacities of a coach and of a railway train are so radically different. Twenty-nine trains run by all routes from London to Cambridge, day by day, and they probably, on an average, set down five hundred passengers between them at the joint station. Taking the average way-bill of a coach to contain ten passengers, the daily arrivals at Cambridge were a hundred and sixty, or, adding twenty post-chaises daily with two passengers each, a hundred and eighty. These are only speculative figures, but, unsupported by exact data though they must be, they give an approximation to an idea of the growth of traffic between those times and these. The imagination refuses to picture this daily host being conveyed by road. It would have meant some thirty-five coaches, fully laden, and as for goods and general merchandise, the roads could not possibly have sufficed for the carrying of them.

## V

COACHING on the road from London to Lynn has found some literary expression in the *Autobiography of a Stage Coachman*, the work of Thomas Cross, published in 1861. Cross was a remarkable man. Born in 1791, he may fairly be said to have been born to the box-seat, his father, John Cross, having been a mail-contractor and stage-coach proprietor established at the Golden Cross, Charing Cross. The Cross family, towards the end of the eighteenth century, claimed to rank with the county families of Hampshire, and John Cross was himself a man of wealth. He had inherited some, and had made more by fetching and carrying for the Government along the old Portsmouth Road in the romantic days of our long wars with France. He not only had his establishment in London and a town house in Portsmouth, but also the three separate and distinct country seats of Freeland House and Stodham, near

"KNEE-DEEP": THE "LYNN AND WELLS MAIL" IN A SNOWSTORM.
[*From a Print after C. Cooper Henderson.*]

Petersfield, and the house and grounds of Qualletes, at Horndean, purchased in after years by Admiral Sir Charles Napier, and renamed by him "Merchistoun." John Cross was always headstrong and reckless, and made much money—and lost much. The story of how he would fill his pockets with gold at his bank at Portsmouth and then ride the lonely twenty miles thence to Horndean explains his making and his losing. No cautious traveller in those times went alone by that road, and the highwaymen tried often to bag this particularly well-known man, who carried such wealth on him. "Many a shot I've had at old John Cross of Stodham," said one of these gentry when lying, cast for execution, in Portsmouth Gaol; adding regretfully, "but I couldn't hit him: he rode like the devil."

This fine reckless character lived to dissipate everything in ill-judged speculations, and misfortunes of all kinds visited the family. We are told but little of them in the pages of his son's book, but it was entirely owing to one of these visitations that Thomas Cross found his whole career changed. Destined by his father for the Navy, he was entered as a midshipman, but he had been subject from his birth to fits, and coming home on one occasion and going into the cellars of a wine business his father had in the meanwhile taken, he was seized by one of these attacks, and falling on a number of wine-bottles, was so seriously injured that the profession of the Navy had to be abandoned. We afterwards find him as a farmer in Hampshire, and then, involved in the financial disasters that overtook the family, reduced to seeking an engagement as coachman in the very yard his father had once owned. It is curious that, either intentionally or by accident, he does not mention the name of the coach he drove between London and Lynn, but calls it always "the Lynn coach." There were changes on the road between 1821, when he first drove along it, and 1847, when he was driven off, but he is chiefly to be remembered as the driver of the "Lynn Union." He tells how he came to the box-seat, how miserably he was shuttlecocked from one to the other when in search of employment, and how, when the whip who drove the "Lynn coach" on its stage between Cambridge and London had taken an inn and was about to relinquish his seat, he could obtain no certain information that the post would be vacant. The bookkeeper of the coach-office said it would; the coachman himself told a lie and said he was not going to give up the job. In this condition of affairs Cross did not know what to do, until a kindly acquaintance gave him the date upon which the lying Jehu must take possession of his inn and of necessity give up coaching, and advised him to journey down to Cambridge, meet the up coach there as it drove into the Bull yard, and present himself as the coachman come to take it up to London. Cross scrupulously carried out this suggestion, and when he made his appearance, with whip and in approved coaching costume, at the Bull, and was asked who he was and what he wanted, replied as his friend had indicated. No one offered any objection, and no other coachman had appeared by the time he drove away, punctual to the very second we may be quite sure. An old resident of Lynn, who has written his recollections of bygone times in that town, tells us that Thomas Cross "was not much of a whip," a criticism that seems to be doubly underscored in Cross's own description of this first journey to London, when he drove straight into the double turnpike gates that then stretched across the Kingsland Road, giving everyone a good shaking, and cause, in many bruises, to remember his maiden effort.

Cross had a long and varied experience, extending to twenty-eight years, of this road. At different times he drove between London and Cambridge, on the middle ground between Cambridge and Ely, and for a while took the whole distance between Ely and Lynn. He drove in his time all sorts and conditions of men, and instances some of his experiences. Perhaps the most amusing was that occasion when he drove into Cambridge with a choleric retired Admiral on the box-seat. The old sea-dog was come to Cambridge to inquire into the trouble into which a scapegrace son had managed to place himself. He confided the whole story to the coachman. By this it seemed that the Admiral had two sons. One he had designed to make a sailor; the other was being educated for the Church. It was the embryo parson who had got into trouble: very serious trouble, too, for he had knocked down a Proctor, and was rusticated for that offence. The Admiral, in fact, had made a very grave error of judgment. His sons had very opposite characters:

the one was wild and high-spirited, and the other was meek and mild to the last degree of inoffensiveness. Unfortunately it was this good young man whom he had sent to sea, while his devil's cub he had put in the way of reading for Holy Orders.

"I have committed a great mistake, sir," he said. "I ought to have made a sailor of him and a parson of the other, who is a meek, unassuming youth aboard ship, with nothing to say for himself; while this, sir, would knock the devil down, let alone a Proctor, if he offended him."

The Admiral was a study in the mingled moods of offended dignity and of parental pride in this chip of the old block; breathing implacable vengeance one moment and admiration of a "d——d high-spirited fellow" the next. When Thomas Cross set out on his return journey to London, he saw the Admiral and his peccant son together, the best of friends.

Cross was in his prime when railways came and spoiled his career. In 1840, when the Northern and Eastern line was opened to Broxbourne, and thence, shortly after, to Bishop Stortford, he had to give up the London and Cambridge stage and retire before the invading locomotive to the Cambridge and Lynn journey. In 1847, when the Ely to Lynn line was opened, his occupation was wholly gone, and all attempts to find employment on the railway failed. They would not have him, even to ring the bell when the trains were about to start. Then, like many another poor fellow at that time, he presented an engrossed petition to Parliament, setting forth how hardly circumstances had dealt with him, and hoping that "your honourable House" would do something or another. The House, however, was largely composed of members highly interested in railways, and ordered his petition, with many another, to lie on the table: an evasive but well-recognised way of utterly ignoring him and it and all such troublesome and inconvenient things and persons. Alas! poor Thomas! He had better have saved the money he expended on that engrossing.

What became of him? I will tell you. For some years he benefited by the doles of his old patrons on the "Union," sorry both for him and for the old days of the road, gone for ever. He then wrote a history of coaching, a work that disappeared —type, manuscript, proofs and all—in the bankruptcy proceedings in which his printers were presently involved. Then he wrote his *Autobiography*. He was, you must understand, a gentleman by birth and education, and if he had little literary talent, had at least some culture. Therefore the story of his career, as told by himself, although discursive, is interesting. He had some Greek and more Latin, and thought himself a poet. I have, however, read his epic, *The Pauliad*, and find that in this respect he was mistaken. That exercise in blank verse was published in 1863, and was his last work. Two years later he found a place in Huggens' College, a charitable foundation at Northfleet, near Gravesend; and died in 1877, in his eighty-sixth year, after twelve years' residence in that secure retreat. He lies in Northfleet churchyard, far away from that place where he would be,—the little churchyard of Catherington beside the Portsmouth Road, where his father and many of his people rest.

## VI

FEW and fragmentary are the recollections of the old coachmen of the Cambridge Road. A coloured etching exists, the work of Dighton, purporting to show the driver of the "Telegraph" in 1809; but whether this represents that Richard Vaughan of the same coach, praised in the book on coaching by Lord William Pitt-Lennox as "scientific in horseflesh, unequalled in driving," is doubtful, for the hero of Dighton's picture seems to belong to an earlier generation. Among drivers of the "Telegraph" were "Old Quaker Will" and George Elliott, just mentioned by Thomas Cross; himself not much given to enlarging upon other coachmen and their professional skill. Poor Tommy necessarily moved in their circle; but although with them, he was not of them, and nursed a pride both of his family and of his own superior education that grew more arrogant as his misfortunes increased. As for Tommy himself, we have already heard much of him and his *Autobiography of a Stage Coachman*. The "Lynn Union," however, the coach he drove down part of the road one day and up the next, was by no means one of the crack "double" coaches, but started from either end only three times a week, and although upset every now and again, was a jog-trot affair that averaged but seven miles an hour, including stops. That the "Lynn Union" commonly carried a consignment of shrimps one way and the returned empty baskets another was long one of Cross's minor martyrdoms. He drove along the road, his head full of poetry and noble thoughts, and yearning for cultured talk, while the shrimp-baskets diffused a penetrating odour around, highly offensive to those cultured folk for whose society his soul longed. People with a nice sense of smell avoided the "Lynn Union" while the shrimp-carrying continued.

Contemporary with Cross was Jo Walton, of the "Safety," and later of the "Star." He was perhaps one of the finest coachmen who ever drove on the Cambridge Road, and it was possibly the knowledge of this skill, and the daring to which it led, that brought so many mishaps to the "Star" while he wielded the reins. He has been described as "a man who swore like a trooper and went regularly to church," with a temper like an emperor and a grip like steel. This fine picturesque character was the very antithesis of the peaceful and dreamy Cross, and thought nothing of double-thonging a nodding waggoner who blocked the road with his sleepy team. Twice at least he upset the "Star" between Royston and Buntingford when attempting to pass another coach. He, at last, was cut short by the railway, and his final journeys were between Broxbourne and Cambridge. "Here," he would say bitterly, as the train came steaming into Broxbourne Station, "here comes old Hell-in-Harness!"

Of James Reynolds, of Pryor, who drove the

"Rocket," of many another, their attributes are lost and only their names survive. That William Clark, who drove the "Bee Hive," should have been widely known as "the civil coachman" is at once a testimonial to him and a reproach to the others; and that memories of Briggs at Lynn should be restricted to the facts that he was discontented and quarrelsome is a post-mortem certificate of character that gains in significance when even the name of the coach he drove cannot be recovered.

## VII

BISHOPSGATE STREET WITHIN and Without, and Norton Folgate of to-day, would astonish old Hobson, not only with their press of ordinary traffic, but with the vast number of railway lorries rattling and thundering along, to and from the great Bishopsgate Goods Station of the Great Eastern Railway; the railway that has supplanted the coaches and the carriers' waggons along the whole length of this road. That station, once the passenger terminus of Shoreditch, before the present huge one at Liverpool Street was built, remains as a connecting-link between the prosperous and popular "Great Eastern" of to-day and the reviled and bankrupt "Eastern Counties" of fifty years ago. The history of the Great Eastern Railway is a complicated story of amalgamations of many lines with the original Eastern Counties Railway. The line to Cambridge, with which we are principally concerned, was in the first instance the project of an independent company calling itself the Northern and Eastern Railway, opened after many difficulties as far as Broxbourne in 1840, and thence, shortly afterwards, to Bishop Stortford. Having reached that point and the end of its resources simultaneously, it was taken over by the Eastern Counties and completed in 1847, the line going, as the Cambridge expresses do nowadays, *viâ* Audley End and Great Chesterford.

Having thus purchased and completed the scheme of that unfortunate line, the Eastern Counties' own difficulties became acute. Locomotives and rolling stock were seized for debt, and it fell into bankruptcy and the Receiver's hands. How it emerged at last, a sound and prosperous concern, this is not the place to tell, but many years passed before any passenger whose business took him anywhere along the Eastern Counties' "system" could rely upon being carried to his destination without vexatious delays, not of minutes, but of hours. Often the trains never completed their journeys at all, and came back whence they had started. Little wonder that this was then described as "that scapegoat of companies, that pariah of railways."

"On Wednesday last," said *Punch* at this time, "a respectably-dressed young man was seen to go to the Shoreditch terminus of the Eastern Counties Railway and deliberately take a ticket for Cambridge. He has not since been heard of. No motive has been assigned for the rash act."

The best among the Great Eastern Cambridge

expresses of to-day does the journey of 55¾ miles in 1 hour 13 minutes. Onward to Lynn, 97 miles, the best time made is 2 hours 25 minutes.

## VIII

It is a far cry from Shoreditch Church to the open country. Cobbett, in 1822, journeying from London to Royston, found the suburbs far-reaching even then. "On this road," he says, "the enormous Wen" (a term of contempt by which he indicated the Metropolis) "has swelled out to the distance of above six or seven miles." But from the earliest times London exhibited a tendency to expand more quickly in this direction than in others, and Edmonton, Waltham Cross, and Ware lay within the marches of Cockaigne long before places within a like radius at other points of the compass began to lose their rural look. The reason is not far to seek, and may be found in the fact that this, the great road to the North, was much travelled always.

But where shall we set the limits of the Great Wen in recent times? Even as these lines are written they are being pushed outwards. It is not enough to put a finger on the map at Stamford Hill and to say, "here, at the boundary of the London County Council's territory," or "here at Edmonton, the limit of the 'N' division of the London Postal Districts," or, again, "here, where the Metropolitan Police Area meets the territories of the Hertfordshire and the Essex Constabulary at Cheshunt"; for those are but arbitrary bounds, and, beyond their own individual significances, tell us nothing. Have you ever, as a child, looking, large-eyed and a little frightened it may be, out upon the bigness of London, wondered where the houses ended and God's own country began, or asked where the last house of the last street looked out upon the meadows, and the final flag-stone led on to the footpath of the King's Highway?

I have asked, and there was none to tell, and if you in turn ask me where the last house of the ultimate street stands on this way out of London—I do not know! There are so many last houses, and they always begin again; so that little romantic mental picture does not exist in plain fact. The ending of London is a gradual and almost insensible process. You may note it when, leaving Stoke Newington's continuous streets behind, you rise Stamford Hill and perceive its detached and semi-detached residences; and, pressing on, see the streets begin again at Tottenham High Cross, continuing to Lower Edmonton. Here at last, in the waste lands that stretch along the road, you think the object of your search is found. As well seek that fabled pot of gold at the foot of the rainbow. The pot and the gold may be there, but you will never, never reach the rainbow.

The houses begin again, absurdly enough, at Ponder's End. You will come to an end of them at last, but only gradually, and when, at fifteen and three-quarter miles from Shoreditch Church, Broxbourne and the first glimpse of "real country" are reached, the original quest is forgotten.

Very different was the aspect of these first miles out of London in the days of Izaak Walton, Cowper, and Lamb. Cowper's Johnny Gilpin rode to Edmonton and Ware, and Walton and Lamb—the inspired Fleet Street draper and the thrall of the Leadenhall Street office—are literary co-parceners in the valley of the Lea.

"You are well overtaken, gentlemen," says Piscator, in the *Compleat Angler*, journeying from London; "a good morning to you both. I have stretched my legs up Tottenham Hill to overtake you, hoping your business may occasion you towards Ware, whither I am going this fine, fresh May morning." He meant that suburban eminence known as Stamford Hill, where, in the beginning of May 1603, the Lord Mayor and Sheriffs of London, having ridden out in State for the purpose, met James the First travelling to London to assume the Crown of England.

Stamford Hill still shadows forth a well-established prosperity. It was the favoured suburban resort of City merchants in the first half of the nineteenth century, and is still intensely respectable and well-to-do, even though the merchants have risen with the swelling of their bankers' pass-books to higher ambitions, and though many of their solid, stolid, and prim mansions know them no more, and are converted not infrequently into what we may bluntly call "boys' and girls' schools," termed, however, by their respective Dr. Blimber's and Miss Pinkerton's "scholastic establishments for young ladies and young gentlemen." The old-time City merchant who resided at Stamford Hill when the nineteenth century was young (a period when people began to "reside" in "desirable residences" instead of merely living in houses), used generally, if he were an active man, to go up to his business in the City on horseback, and return in the same way. If not so active, he came and went by the "short stage," a conveyance between London and the adjacent towns, to all intents and purposes an ordinary stage-coach, except that it was a two-horsed, instead of a four-horsed, affair. The last City man who rode to London on horseback has probably long since been gathered to his fathers, for the practice naturally was discontinned when railways came and revolutionised manners and customs.

As you top Stamford Hill, you glimpse the valley of the Lea and its factory-studded marshes, and come presently to Tottenham High Cross. No need to linger nowadays over the scenery of this populous road, lined with shops and villas and crowded with tramways and omnibuses; no need, that is to say, except for association's sake, and to remark that it was here Piscator called a halt to Venator and Auceps, on their way to the Thatched House at Hoddesdon, now going on for two hundred and fifty years ago. "Let us now" (he said) "rest ourselves in this sweet, shady arbour, which Nature herself has woven with her own fine fingers; it is such a contexture of woodbines, sweet briars, jessamine, and myrtle, and so interwoven as will secure us both from the sun's violent heat and from the approaching shower." And so they sat and discussed a bottle of sack, with oranges and milk.

So gracious a "contexture" is far to seek from Tottenham nowadays. If you need shelter from

TOTTENHAM CROSS.

the approaching shower you can, it is true, obtain it more securely in the doorway of a shop than under a hedgerow in May, when Nature has not nearly finished her weaving; but there is something lacking in the exchange.

Tottenham High Cross that stands here by, over against the Green, is a very dubious affair indeed;

A LONDON SUBURB IN 1816: TOTTENHAM.
[*From a Drawing by Rowlandson.*]

an impostor that would delude you if possible into the idea that it is one of the Eleanor Crosses; with a will-o'-wisp kind of history, from the time in 1466, when it is found mentioned only as existing, to after ages, when it was new-built of brick and thereafter horribly stuccoed, to the present, when it is become a jibe and a jeer in its would-be Gothic.

Much of old Tottenham is gone. Gone are the " Seven Sisters," the seven elms that stood here in a circle, with a walnut-tree in their midst, marking, as tradition would have you believe, the resting-place of a martyr; but in their stead is the beginning of the Seven Sisters' Road; not a thoroughfare whose romance leaps to the eye. What these then remote suburbs were like in 1816 may be seen in this charming sketch of Rowlandson's, where he is found in his more sober mood. The milestone in the sketch marks four and three-quarter miles from Shoreditch: this is therefore a scene at Tottenham, where the tramway runs nowadays, costermongers' barrows line the gutters, and crowds press, night and day. Little enough traffic in Rowlandson's time, evidently, for the fowls and the pigs are taking their ease in the very middle of the footpath.

Yet there are still a few vestiges of the old and the picturesque here. Bruce Grove, hard by, may be but a name, reminiscent of Robert Bruce and other Scottish monarchs who once owned a manor and a castle where suburban villas now cluster plentifully, and where the modern so-called " Bruce Castle " is a school; but there are dignified old red-brick mansions here still, lying back from the road behind strong walls and grand gates of wrought iron. The builder has his eye on them, an Evil Eye that has already blasted not a few, and with bulging money-bags he tempts the owners of the others: even as I write they go down before the pick and shovel.

Old almshouses there are, too, with dedicatory

BALTHAZAR SANCHEZ' ALMSHOUSES, TOTTENHAM.

tablet, complete. The builder and his money-bags cannot prevail here, you think. Can he not? My *good* sirs, have you never heard of the Charity Commissioners, whose business it is to sit in their snug quarters in Whitehall and to propound "schemes" whereby such old buildings as these are torn down, their sites sold for a mess of pottage, and the old pensioners hustled off to some new settlement? "But look at the value of the land," you say: "to sell it would admit of the scope of the charity being doubled." No doubt; but what of the original testator's wishes? I think, if it were proposed to remove these old almshouses, the shade of Balthazar Sanchez, the founder, somewhere in the Beyond, would be grieved.

One Bedwell, parson of Tottenham High Cross *circa* 1631, and a most diligent Smelfungus, tells us Balthazar was "a Spanyard born, the first confectioner or comfit-maker, and the grand master of all that professe that trade in this kingdome"; and the tablet before-mentioned, on the front of the old almshouses themselves, tells us something on its own account, as thus—

> "1600
> BALTHAZAR SANCHEZ, Borne in Spayne
> in the Cittie of Sherez in Estremadu-
> ra, is the Fownder of these Eyght
> Almeshowses for the Releefe of
> Eyght poor men and women of the
> Towne of Tattenham High Crasse."

Long may the queer old houses, with their monumental chimney-stalks and forecourt gardens remain: it were not well to vex the ghost of the good comfit-maker.

"Scotland Green" is the name of an odd and haphazard collection of cottages next these almshouses, looking down into Tottenham Marshes. Its name derives from the far-off days when those Scottish monarchs had their manor-house near by, and though the weather-boarded architecture of the cottages by no means dates back to those times, it is a queer survival of days before Tottenham had become a suburb; each humble dwelling a law to itself, facing in a direction different from those of its neighbours, and generally approached by crazy wooden footbridges over what was probably at one time a tributary of the Lea, now an evil-smelling ditch where the children of the neighbourhood enjoy themselves hugely in making mud-pies, and by dint of early and constant familiarity become immune from the typhoid fever that would certainly be the lot of a stranger.

## IX

EDMONTON, to whose long street we now come, has many titles to fame. John Gilpin may not afford the oldest of these, and he may be no more than the purely imaginary figure of a humorous ballad, but beside the celebrity of that worthy citizen and execrable horseman everything else at Edmonton sinks into obscurity.

> "John Gilpin was a citizen
> Of credit and renown,
> A train-band captain eke was he
> Of famous London town."

Izaak Walton himself, of indubitable flesh and blood, forsaking his yard-measure and Fleet Street counter and tramping through Edmonton to the fishful Lea, has not made so great a mark as his fictitious fellow-tradesman, the draper of Cheapside.

Who has not read of John Gilpin's ride to Edmonton, in Cowper's deathless verse? Cowper, most melancholy of poets, made the whole English-speaking world laugh with the story of Gilpin's adventures. How he came to write the ballad it may not be amiss to tell. The idea was suggested to him at Olney, in 1782, by Lady Austen, who, to rouse him from one of his blackest moods, related a merry tale she had heard of a London citizen's adventures, identical with the verses into which he afterwards cast the story. He lay awake all that night, and the next morning, with the idea of amusing himself and his friends, wrote the famous lines. He had no intention of publishing them, but his friend, Mrs. Unwin, sent a copy to the *Public Advertiser.* Strange to say, it did not attract much attention in those columns, and it was not until three years later, when an actor, Henderson by name, recited the ballad at Freemasons' Hall that (as modern slang would put it) it "caught on." It then became instantly popular. Every ballad-printer printed, and every artist illustrated it; but the author remained unknown until Cowper included it in a collection of his works.

There are almost as many originals of John Gilpin as there are of Sam Weller. There used to be numbers of respectable and ordinarily dependable people who were convinced they knew the original of Sam Weller, in dozens of different persons and in widely-sundered towns, and the literary world is even now debating as to who sat as the model for Squeers. So far back as the reign of Henry the Eighth the ludicrous idea of a London citizen trying to ride horseback to Edmonton made people laugh, and on it Sir Thomas More based his metrical "Merry Jest of the Serjeant and the Frère." It would be no surprise to discover that Aristophanes or another waggish ancient Greek had used the same idea to poke fun at some clumsy Athenian, and that, even so, it was stolen from the Egyptians. Indeed, I have no doubt that the germ of the story is to be found in the awkwardness of one of Noah's sons in trying to ride an unaccustomed animal into the Ark.

The immediate supposititious originals of John Gilpin were many. Some identified him with a Mr. Beger, a Cheapside draper, who died in 1791, aged one hundred. Others found him in Commodore Trunnion, in *Peregrine Pickle*, and a John Gilpin lies in Westminster Abbey. The *Gentleman's Magazine* in 1790, five years after Cowper's poem became the rage, records the death at Bath of a Mr. Jonathan Gilpin, "the gentleman who was so severely ridiculed for bad horsemanship under the title of 'John Gilpin.'" All accidental resemblances and odd coincidences, without doubt.

But if John had no corporeal existence, the Bell at Edmonton — at Upper Edmonton, to be precise—was a very real place, and, in an altered form, still is. Who could doubt of the man who ever saw the house? Is not the present Bell real enough, and, for that matter, ugly enough? and is not the picture of John, wigless and breathless, and his coat-tails flying, sufficiently prominent on the sign? The present building is the third since Cowper's time, and is just an ordinary vulgar London " public," standing at the corner of a shabby street (where there are *no* trees), called, with horrible alliteration, " Gilpin Grove."

Proceed we onwards, having said sufficient of Gilpin. Off to the right hand turned old Izaak, to Cook's Ferry and the Bleak Hall Inn by the Lea, that " honest ale-house, where might be found a cleanly room, lavender in the windows, and twenty ballads stuck about the wall." Ill questing it would be that should seek nowadays for the old inn. Instead, down by Angel Road Station and the Lea marshes, you find only factories and odours of the Pit, horrent and obscene. We have yet to come to the kernel, the nucleus of this Edmonton. Here it is, at Lower Edmonton, at the end of many houses, in a left-hand turning—Edmonton Green; the green a little shorn, perhaps, of its old proportions, and certainly by no means rural. On it they burnt the unhappy Elizabeth Sawyer, the Witch of Edmonton, in 1621, with the full approval of king and council: Ahriman perhaps founding one of his claims to Jamie for that wicked deed. It was well for Peter Fabell, who at Edmonton deceived the devil himself, that he practised his conjuring arts before Jamie came to rule over us, else he had gone the way of that unhappy Elizabeth; for James was of a logical turn of mind, and would have argued the worst of one who could beat the Father of Lies at his own game. Peter flourished, happily for him, in the less pragmatical days of Henry the Seventh. We should call him in these matter-of-fact days a master of legerdemain, and he would dare pretend to no more; but he was honoured and feared in his own time, and lies somewhere in the parish church, his monument clean gone. On his exploits Elizabethan dramatists founded the play of the *Merry Devil of Edmonton.*

The railway and the tramway have between them played the very mischief with Edmonton Green and the Wash—

". . . the Wash
Of Edmonton so gay"—

that here used to flow athwart the road, and does actually still so flow, or trickle, or stagnate; if not always visible to the eye, at least making its presence obvious at all seasons to the nose. In the first instance, the railway planted a station and a level crossing on the highway, practically in the Wash; and then the Tramway Company, in order to carry its line along the road to Ponder's End, constructed a very steeply rising road over the railway. Add to these objectionable details, that of another railway crossing over the by-road where Lamb's Cottage and the church are to be found, and enough will have been said to prove that the Edmonton of old is sorely overlaid with sordid modernity.

Charles Lamb would scarce recognise his Edmonton if it were possible he could revisit the spot, and it seems—the present suburban aspect of the road before us—a curious ideal of happiness he set himself: retirement at Edmonton or Ponder's End, "toddling about it, between it and Cheshunt, anon stretching on some fine Izaak Walton morning to Hoddesdon or Amwell, careless as a beggar, but walking, walking ever, till I fairly walked myself off my legs, dying walking."

Everyone to his taste, of course, but it does not seem a particularly desirable end. It is curious, however, to note that this aspiration was, in a sense, realised, for it was in his sixtieth year that, taking his customary walk along the London road one day in December 1834, he stumbled against a stone and fell, cutting his face. It seemed at the time a slight injury, but erysipelas set in a few days later, and on the twenty-seventh of the same month he died. It was but a fortnight before, that he had pointed out to his sister the spot in Edmonton churchyard where he wished to be buried.

Lamb's last retreat—"Bay Cottage" as it was named, and "Lamb's Cottage" as it has since been re-christened, "the prettiest, compactest house I ever saw," says he—stands in the lane leading to the church; squeezed in between old mansions, and lying back from the road at the end of a long narrow strip of garden. It is a stuccoed little house, curiously like Lamb himself, when you come to consider it: rather mean-looking, undersized, and unkempt, and overshadowed by its big neighbours, just as Lamb's little talents were thrown into insignificance by his really great contemporaries. The big neighbours of the little cottage are even now on the verge of being demolished, and the lane itself, the last retreat of old-world Edmonton, is being modernised; so that those who cultivate their Lamb will not long be able to trace these, his last landmarks. Already, as we have seen, the Bell has gone, where Lamb, "seeing off" his visitors on their way back to London, took a parting glass with them, stutteringly bidding them hurry when the c-cu-coach c-came in.

One of the most curious of literary phenomena is this Lamb worship. Dingy, twittering little London sparrow that he was, diligent digger-up of Elizabethan archaisms with which to tune his chirpings, he seems often to have inspired the warmest of personal admiration. As the "gentle Elia" one finds him always referred to, and a halo of romance has been thrown about him and his doings to which neither he nor they can in reality lay much claim. Romance flies abashed before the picture of Lamb and his sister diluting down the poet of all time in the *Tales from Shakespeare*: Charles sipping gin between whiles, and Mary vigorously snuffing. Nor was his wit of the kindly sort readily associated with the epithet "gentle." It flowed the more readily after copious libations of gin-and-water, and resolved itself at such times into the offensive, if humorous, personalities that were the stock in trade of early nineteenth-century witlings. His famous witticism at a card-party on one who had hands not of the cleanest ("If dirt were trumps, what a hand you'd have") must have been bred of the juniper berry.

Stuttering and blue-lipped the next morning, he was an object of pity or derision, just according to the charity of those who beheld him. Carlyle, who knew Lamb in his latter days, draws him as he was, in one of those unmerciful pen-portraits he could create so well :—" Charles Lamb and his sister came daily once or oftener ; a very sorry pair of phenomena. Insuperable proclivity to gin in poor old Lamb. His talk contemptibly small, indicating wondrous ignorance and shallowness, even when it was serious and good-mannered, which it seldom was, usually ill-mannered (to a degree), screwed into frosty artificialities, ghastly make-believe of wit, in fact more like 'diluted insanity' (as I defined it) than anything of real jocosity, humour, or geniality. A most slender fibre of actual worth in that poor Charles, abundantly recognisable to me as to others, in his better times and moods; but he was Cockney to the marrow ; and Cockneydom, shouting 'glorious, marvellous, unparalleled in nature!' all his days had quite bewildered his poor head, and churned nearly all the sense out of the poor man. He was the leanest of mankind, tiny black breeches buttoned to the knee-cap, and no further, surmounting spindle-legs also in black, face and head fineish, black, bony, lean, and of a Jew type rather; in the eyes a kind of smoky brightness or confused sharpness ; spoke with a stutter; in walking tottered and shuffled ; emblem of imbecility bodily and spiritual (something of real insanity I have understood), and yet something too of human, ingenuous, pathetic, sportfully much enduring. Poor Lamb! he was infinitely astonished at my wife and her quiet encounter of his too ghastly London wit by a cheerful native ditto. Adieu, poor Lamb!"

Edmonton Church has lain too near London in all these years to have escaped many interferences, and the body of it was until recently piteous with the doings of 1772, when red brick walls and windows of the factory type replaced its ancient architecture. These have now in their turn been swept away, and good modern Gothic put in their stead, already densely covered with ivy. The ancient tower still rises grandly from the west end, looking down upon a great crowded churchyard; a very forest of tombstones. Near by is the grave of Charles and Mary Lamb, with a long set of verses inscribed upon their headstone.

There was once in this churchyard of Edmonton a curious epitaph on one William Newberry, ostler to the Rose and Crown Inn, who died in 1695 from the effects of unsuitable medicine given him by a fellow-servant acting as an amateur doctor. The stone was removed by some clerical prude—

"Hic jacet Newberry, Will
Vitam finivet cum Cochiæ Pill
Quis administravit? Bellamy, Sue
Quantum quantitat nescio, scisne tu?
Ne sutor ultra crepidam."

The feelings of Sue Bellamy will not be envied, but Sue, equally with William, has long reached beyond all such considerations, and the Rose and Crown of that day is no more. There is still, however, a Rose and Crown, and a very fine building it is, with eleven windows in line and wearing a noble and dignified air. It is genuine Queen Anne architecture; the older house being rebuilt only ten years after the ostler was cut off untimely, as may be seen by the tablet on its front, dated not only 1705, but descending to the small particular of actual month and day of completion.

## X

The tramway line, progressing through Edmonton in single track, goes on in hesitating fashion some little distance beyond Edmonton Green, and terminates in a last feeble, expiring effort on the open road, midway between Edmonton and Ponder's End; like the railhead of some African desert line halting on the edge of a perilous country. Where it ends there stands, solitary, a refreshment house, so like the last outpost of civilisation that the wayfarer whimsically wonders whether he had not better provision himself liberally before adventuring into the flats that lie so stark and forbidding before him.

It is indeed an uninviting waste. On it the gipsy caravans halt; here the sanguine speculative builder projects a street of cheap houses and generally leaves derelict "carcases" of buildings behind him; here the brick-maker and the market-gardener contend with one another, and the shooters of rubbish bring their convoys of dust, dirt, and old tins from afar. On the skyline ahead are factory chimneys, and to the east—the only gracious note in the whole scene—the wooded hills of Essex, across the malodorous Lea.

This desolate tract is bounded by the settlement of Ponder's End, an old roadside hamlet. "Ponder's End," says Lamb, "emblematic name, how beautiful!" Sarcasm that, doubtless, for of what it is emblematic, and where lies the beauty of either place or name, who shall discover? The name has a heavily ruminative or contemplative sound, a little out of key with its modern note. For even Ponder's End has been rudely stirred up by the pitchfork of progress and bidden go forward, and new terraces of houses and shops—no, not *shops*, nothing so vulgar; "business premises" if you please—have sprung up, and the oldest inhabitant is distraught with the changes that have befallen. Where he plodded in the mud there are pavements; the ditch into whose unsavoury depths he has fallen many a time when returning late from the old Two Brewers is filled up, and the Two Brewers itself has changed from a roadside tavern to something resplendent in plate-glass and brilliant fittings. Our typical ancient and his friends, the market-gardening folk and the loutish waggoners, are afraid to enter. Nay, even the name of the village or hamlet, or urban district, or whatever the exact slang term of the Local Government Board for its modern status may be, is not unlikely to see a change, for to the newer inhabitants it sounds derogatory to be a Ponder's Ender.

To this succeeds another strip of sparsely-settled land, and you think that here, at last, the country is gained. Vain thought! Enfield Highway, a populous mile-length, dispels all such ideas, and even Enfield Wash, where the travellers of old were content to be drenched in the frequent floods, so long as they actually escaped with their lives, is suburban and commonplace. The stretch of road between the Wash and Waltham Cross still goes by the shivery name of Freezywater.

Enfield Highway, like Ponder's End, was until quite recently stodged in sloughs, and resolutely old-world; almost as old world indeed as when, in 1755, Mr. Spencer, the Lord Spencer of a few years later, came up from the shires in great state with his bride. Their procession consisted of three chariots, each drawn by six horses and escorted by two hundred horsemen. At sight of this cavalcade the whole neighbourhood was up in arms. The timid fled, the Jacobites rejoiced and ran off to ring the church bells in a merry peal, while loyal folks and brave armed themselves with pitchforks, pokers, and spades; for all thought the Pretender had come again and was marching on London.

At Waltham Cross, formerly entered through a toll-gate, Middlesex is left behind and Hertfordshire gained. The name of Waltham Cross probably does not at this period inspire anyone with dread, but that was the feeling with which travellers approached it at any time between 1698 and 1780; for this was in all those years a neighbourhood where highwaymen robbed and slew with impunity. Here was the favourite lurk of those desperate disbanded soldiers who on the Peace of Ryswick, finding pay and occupation gone, banded together, and, building huts in the coverts of Epping Forest, came forth even in broad daylight, and, to the number of thirty, armed with swords and pistols, held up the traffic on this and the surrounding roads. Even when that formidable gang was disposed of by calling out the Dragoon Guards in a regular campaign against them, there were others, for in 1722 a London morning paper stated that the turnpike-men from Shoreditch to Cheshunt had been furnished with speaking-trumpets, " as well to give notice to Passengers as to each other in case any Highwaymen or footpads are out," and the satisfactory report is added, " we don't find that any robbery has been committed in that quarter since they have been furnished with them, which has been these two months." Was it not hereabouts, too, that Turpin first met Tom King, and, taking him for an ordinary citizen, proposed to rob him? Ay, and in that self-same Epping Forest, whose woodlands may even yet be seen, away to the right-hand, Turpin had his cave. Even so late as 1775 the Norwich stage was attacked one December morning by seven highwaymen, three of whom the guard shot dead. He would perhaps have finished the whole of them had his ammunition not failed and he in turn been shot, when the coach was robbed at leisure by the surviving desperadoes.

## XI

If the traveller does not know what to expect on approaching Waltham Cross, then the cross, standing in the centre of the road, must needs be a pleasant surprise to him, even though he presently discovers that they have done a great deal in recent times to spoil it; "they" meaning the usual pastors and masters, the furbishers and titivators of things ancient and worshipful, applying to such things their own little nostrums and programmes. But, woefully re-restored though it be, its crockets and pinnacles and panellings patched with a stone whose colour does not match with that of the old work, one can still find it possible to look upon it with reverence, for among the ancient wayside memorials of our storied land the beautiful Eleanor Crosses stand foremost, both for their artistic and their historic interest. More than any others, they hold the sentiment and the imagination of the wayfarer, and their architecture is more complex. The story that belongs to them is one long since taken to the warm hearts of the people, and cherished as among the most touching in all the history of the realm—a realm rich in stories of a peculiarly heart-compelling kind.

It is that of Eleanor of Castile, Queen of Edward the First, who accompanied him to Palestine in 1270, on his Crusade against the Infidel. History tells how, on the evening of June 17, 1272, the King was seated alone and unarmed in a tent of the camp before Acre. It was his birthday, but birthdays find scant celebration in the tented field, and Edward on that day was engaged in the sterner business of receiving proposals of surrender from the besieged. He had given audience to a messenger from the Emir of Jaffa, who, having delivered the letter he had brought, stood waiting. Bending low, in answering a question the King had put to him, he suddenly put his hand to his belt, as though to produce other letters; but, instead, drew a poisoned dagger and struck at the King with it. Edward endeavoured to shield himself, but received a deep wound in the arm; then, as the man endeavoured to strike again, giving him a kick that felled him to the ground, he wrenched away the would-be assassin's dagger and plunged it into his body. When the King's attendants came rushing in, the man was dead. Fortunate for him it was that he died so simply, for the imaginations of those who dispensed the rough justice of the time were sufficiently fertile to have devised many novel and exquisitely painful variations of torture for such an one.

The King's wound was serious, and although all the drugs and balsams in the limited pharmacopœia of those times were administered, it grew worse. Then it was, according to the pretty story universally received, that the Queen, finding the efforts of physicians vain, sucked the poison from the wounded arm of her lord to such good purpose that he recovered, and sat his charger again within fifteen days.

Medical criticism on this recorded action of the

poison could scarce fail of being destructive, and indeed it is not to be expected that the story of Eleanor of Castile would be left unassailed in these days, when history is treated scientifically, and when all the old and gracious stories are being explained away or resolved into something repellent and utterly commonplace. Modern historians have told us that William Tell is a myth, and that, consequently, the famous incident of the apple could never have occurred. Robin Hood, they say, was equally imaginary, or if any real person existed on whom that figure of endearing romance was built up, he had more the attributes of a footpad than those of the chivalrous outlaw those legends have made him. They would even take from us Dick Whittington and his cat. In fact, all these romantic people are classed with King Arthur, Jack the Giant Killer, and Little Red Riding Hood. It is not a little cruel thus to demolish these glamorous figures, but historians since Macaulay have been merciless. It is, therefore, not surprising to read that Eleanor, instead of being heroic was a very woman, and was led "weeping and wailing" from the scene when the surgeons declared that the King's hurt was incurable, unless the whole of the poisoned flesh were cut away. The cure, says an old chronicler, was effected by the surgeons, and the romantic story has in recent times been declared "utterly unworthy of credit."

Alas! too, for the gentle and tender character that has ever been ascribed to Eleanor of Castile; for we read that "though pious and virtuous, she was rather grasping," causing scandal by taking part with Jewish usurers in cozening Christians out of

WALTHAM CROSS A HUNDRED YEARS AGO.

their estates.  Ancient records, done on rolls of sheepskin in mediæval dog-Latin, and preserved in the Record Office for all men to see—and read if they can—tell how hard a landlord she was, and how Archbishop Peckham interfered on behalf of her unfortunate tenants, telling her that reparation for wrongs done must precede absolution.

And yet, although we allow this to be truth, to some she must have been winsome and gracious. Not to the lower herd, almost certainly, for people below the rank of knights or dames were never, in those times, thought worthy the least consideration. To those who more nearly approached her own rank she may have been the generous personality she has ever been pictured, although for a true Castilian to be other than insufferably haughty and arrogant would seem, if traditions do not lie, to be against nature. To the King she was evidently all in all, or how explain the existence of so long and elaborate a series of crosses raised to the memory of his *chère reine*? Eighteen years after the famous incident of the poisoned wound the Queen died, on November 28, 1290. She breathed her last on the evening of that day at the village of Harby, in Nottinghamshire, whither she had accompanied the King on a royal progress he had been making through the Eastern Counties during the three preceding months. Parliament in those times was a perambulating body of lawgivers, following of necessity the footsteps of the monarch. The King, therefore, having arranged to stay at his Royal Palace of Clipstone, in Sherwood Forest, at the end of October, Parliament was summoned to meet there on the twenty-seventh of that month. Meanwhile, however, the Queen fell ill of a lingering fever, and

WALTHAM CROSS.

for sake of the quiet that could not be obtained in the neighbourhood of the Court she was housed at Harby, twenty miles distant. But not all the care that was hers, nor the syrups and other medicines detailed in the old accounts, procured in haste from the city of Lincoln, five miles away, availed to avert the fatal conclusion of that wasting sickness.

The Queen's body was at once removed to Lincoln Cathedral, and the funeral procession seems to have set out from Lincoln city for Westminster on the fourth day of December. London was not reached until eleven days later, and the entombment at Westminster did not take place until the seventeenth of the month. Travelling was a slow and tedious process then, but not necessarily so slow as this. The reasons for the length of time consumed between Lincoln and Westminster were two, and are found both in the pompous circumstances of the journey and in the circuitous route taken. The ordinary route was by Stamford, Huntingdon, Royston, Puckeridge, and Cheshunt; but it was determined that the august procession should pass through a more frequented part of the country, and through districts where the Queen had been better known. Another object was to take some of the great religious houses on the way, and thus have suitable places at which to rest. The route chosen, therefore, included Grantham, Stamford, Geddington, Northampton, Stony Stratford, Woburn, Dunstable, St. Albans, Waltham Abbey, West Cheap, and Charing. At each of these places the Queen's body rested, and at each one was subsequently erected a memorial cross. This is no place for recounting the almsgiving, the endowments of charities and monasteries, and the payments for tapers and masses for the repose of her soul. Let it be understood that all these things were done on a scale of the greatest magnificence, and that the erection of these twelve great crosses was but one feature among many in the means employed to keep her memory alive and her soul in bliss unending. This last, indeed, was the principal reason of their building. In these days one regards the three crosses, that the rage of rabid men and the slower but scarce less sure fury of the elements between them have alone left us of the twelve, as merely beautiful specimens of the wedded arts of Sculpture and Architecture; or as affecting memorials of conjugal love. Those, however, would be erroneous regards. The crosses were to attract by their beauty, no doubt; but their higher purpose was to inspire the devotional sentiment; their presence by the wayside was to implore the passers-by to remember the "Queen of Good Memory," as documents of the time call her, that they might pray for her. Although they bore no inscription, they silently bade the traveller "*Orate pro animâ*," and were, accordingly, consecrated with full religious ceremonies.

The crosses were not of a uniform pattern, although many of them seem to have borne strong likenesses to each other. Nine have so utterly disappeared that not a single stone of them is discoverable at this day, but old prints serve to show, in conjunction with the still existing building

THE "HULL MAIL" AT WALTHAM CROSS.
[*From a Print after J. Pollard.*]

accounts, their relative size and importance. The three remaining are those of Geddington, Hardingstone near Northampton, and this of Waltham. Waltham Cross stands seventy feet in height. It cost £95, equal to £1000 of our present money, and was originally built of stone from the quarries of Caen, in Normandy, as the lower stage of the work still shows. The two upper stages and the spirelet were restored and reconstructed in 1832 at a cost of £1200, and again, as recently as 1885-92, at an almost equal expense.

The beautiful old engraving of 1806, reproduced here, proves into what a dilapidated condition the Cross had at that time fallen. It would appear to have been even worse in 1720, when Dr. Stukeley was commissioned by the Society of Antiquaries to see that posts were placed round for its protection; and in 1757 it was in danger of falling, for Lord Monson, the then Lord of the Manor of Cheshunt, was petitioned to build some brickwork round the base and to set up some other posts. A later Lord of the Manor, a certain Sir George Prescott, in 1795, with colossal impudence endeavoured to remove it to his park at Theobalds, and would have done so had not his workmen found the stone too decayed to be displaced.

In the old print already referred to, and in the coaching print of some thirty years later, it will be noticed that a portion of that old coaching hostelry, the Falcon, actually abutted upon the Cross. The inn, indeed, occupied the site of a chantry chapel adjoining, where prayers for the soul of the Queen had been said for some two hundred and fifty years after her death. It may be suspected that those prayers, endowments notwithstanding, had grown somewhat perfunctory after that lapse of time, and the Queen herself little more than a legend; and so, when all Chantries were dissolved under Edward the Sixth, their revenues seized and the mumbling priests ejected, the world was well rid of a hoary piece of humbug. The Falcon was demolished when the latest restoration was brought to a conclusion, and a portion of its site thrown into the roadway, so that the Cross stands once more free from surrounding buildings.

In choosing a stone for those parts to be restored, the gross mistake was made of selecting a brownish-red stone from the Ketton quarries, in Northants. The reason for making this selection was that Caen stone is perishable and that of Ketton particularly durable; but in the result the restored Cross wears to-day a sadly parti-coloured appearance.

## XII

THE already named Falcon was not the only hostelry at Waltham Cross. The Four Swans, whose great gallows sign still straddles across the highway, with the four swans themselves represented in effigy against the sky, was the other house. There is always Another in everything, even in Novelettes and on the Stage, where he or she, as the case may happen, is generally accorded a capital letter. That there should always be a rival, that is to say, Another, shows, I suppose, that competition is a heaven-sent condition of affairs, and incidentally that "Trusts" and "Combines" are immoral and a direct challenge to Providence. That, however, is another matter. But, in this case, which is "the other" it would be difficult, if not impossible, to determine. Whether the Falcon or the Four Swans was established first cannot be told with certainty, although if it be true that the Four Swans is built on the site of the ancient manor-house of Cheshunt, it seems likely that to this queer rambling old coaching-inn must be given the honour.

A story used to be told of an adventure here that might have had unpleasant consequences, had it not been for the ready wit of the guard attached to the "York Mail." When the Mail reached the village and drew up in front of the inn, shortly after nine o'clock, a quiet, gentlemanly-looking man took a vacant seat inside, and remained silent and inoffensive until the coach started on its way to Ware, when he suddenly became very talkative. Addressing a lady present with some absurd remarks, the other gentlemen turned upon him and said, if he did not cease they would put him in the road. This was no sooner said than he began to adopt a threatening tone; but no notice was taken of him, as Ware was being neared, when he could be better dealt with than by stopping the coach. When it came to a halt, the guard was beckoned to and told quietly what an odd customer was seated within.

The guard looked inside, and at once recognised the strange person as a gentleman of that neighbourhood who had been consigned to a lunatic asylum, and must have escaped. "Ah! Mr. F——," he said, "how are you? Are you going far down the road?" "I'm going," said Mr. F——, "to Stamford to catch that rascal C——, who has stolen my estates." "Why," rejoined the guard, with the well-known promptitude of his class, "you needn't go any farther, I've just seen him in the back parlour, behind the bar." "Have you?" shouted the madman. "By Jove! let me find him," and he leapt out of the coach. "Right away, Bill," sang out the guard, and the Mail was off. How the people at Ware dealt with the poor wretch is not recorded.

As this, so far as Royston, was a part of the original great post-road to Scotland, many royal and noble processions, besides that attendant on the obsequies of Queen Eleanor, passed of necessity through Waltham Cross, and the coaching and posting traffic was of huge dimensions, up to the last days of the road.

Royal processions and progresses have a way, as you read them, of being insufferably dull; hedged about with formula and rule and precedent surrounding the gilded and be-crowned fetish for the time being, who, generally wrapped up warm in selfishness and greed, and dealing out lies and condescension, passes by and affords no interest or amusement to later generations, who merely yawn when they read of the dusty old properties, the tinsel and the gold lace. It is otherwise when the faults and foibles of the fetish are known and can be displayed to show that a monarch is, after all, human; and sometimes even a very poor specimen of humanity. James the First (of England and Sixth of Scotland, as the tender susceptibilities of Scots put it) came up this way to his Kingdom of England, on Elizabeth's death in 1603. He had set out from Edinburgh on the 5th of April, and only arrived in London on the 7th of May. Abundant and overbrimming loyalty had kept him long on the road. The noblemen and gentry of the shires lavished attentions on James and his following, and festive gatherings enlivened every manor-house on the way. Many a squire loaded his estates with encumbrances, in his anxiety to royally entertain the new sovereign and his numerous suite, and the story told of one of their halting-places very eloquently illustrates the sacrifices made. After staying some days with his host, the King remarked upon the disappearance of a partienlarly fine herd of cattle he had noticed in the park on his arrival, and asked what had become of them? As a matter of fact, they had been all slaughtered for the use of James's hungry Scots, and his host unwillingly told him so. "Then," said the King ungraciously, it is time we were going"; and so, when the food was exhausted, they went.

So prodigal was the display made for him that James might almost have thought the country tired of Elizabeth's long rule, and glad to welcome a new monarch. He conferred titles with a lavish hand as he went, and knights-bachelors sprouted up in every town and village like mustard-and-cress after a dewy evening. He came across the Border mild enough, but by degrees rid himself of the humility proper to a King of Scots, and as King of England assumed an imperious air not even inferior to that of Henry the Eighth himself. Such an air sat ill upon James, at once constitutionally weak in body and simultaneously timid and braggart in disposition. The "British Solomon" his toadies called him, and indeed he was in many ways the Superior Person. Educated in all the 'ologies, and accounting himself in especial a master of theology and demonology, he was learned and superstitious at once. Witchcraft he firmly believed possible, and made it a capital offence, and was thus the prime cause of many an ill-favoured old woman or eccentric person being cruelly put to death as warlocks and wizards. The Duke of Sully, better informed than James's satellites, or more candid, pronounced him "the wisest fool in Europe."

At no place was the new monarch so lavishly entertained as at Theobalds, the princely residence of Lord Burleigh, whose estates bordered the road between Waltham Cross and Cheshunt. Who was the original owner of Theobalds, history does not tell us. Doubtless some Saxon notable, Theobald by name, thus immortalised in unilluminative fashion. In the late Elizabeth's time it had been acquired by the great Cecil, dead some six years before the coming of this northern light. Cecil's son, only less great than his father, now ruled, and received James right nobly in those magnificent halls his sire had added, where Elizabeth herself had been royally entertained. Four days he stayed, hunting and feasting, and left with so profound an admiration of the place that he never rested until he had exchanged the Royal Palace of Hatfield for it. Cecil made no bad bargain in the transfer, and in addition secured much favour and many added dignities, ending as Earl of Salisbury.

James's passion for the chase explains his eagerness to secure Theobalds, surrounded in those times by far-reaching and ancient woodlands. Epping Forest and the woods of Waltham lay for miles to the east, and the green alleys of Enfield Chase and Northaw (really "north holt," *i.e.* north wood) to the south and the north-west.

The figure of James is thus prominent on this part of the road. By no means an imposing figure, this King, as he reels in his saddle, or shambles rather than walks, his weak knees threatening a collapse, his thin yellow beard scarce disguising a chin striking the mean between obstinacy and weak irresolution; his wide-staring, watery, light-blue eyes rimmed with red eyelids; and lips running with the thin slobber of the drunkard, or rather of the inveterate tippler, not honestly drunken but grown maudlin, babbling and bubbling like a spring. This poor creature, who pretends to Right Divine, has the tense nerves of a hare; a hunted, hare-like glance too, when not primed and blusterous with Greek wine. He has a ludicrously acute sense of personal danger, and yet chases the deer a-horseback, seated on a padded saddle and plentifully equipped with drink. I see him very plainly, though much of the great domain of Theobalds be disparked, and landmarks grown dim and confused, hunting and halloing in the greenwood, and cursing and raving like a madman when the quarry escapes him—forgetful, in the excitement of the moment, of the Solomonic character he has to sustain—and falling out of his saddle and biting the grass in frenzy.

But James's domestic character bears more scrutiny than that of many of his predecessors. He would have pleased Mr. Squeers, for his "morrils" (in the common and restricted sense) were distinctly good—much better than those of the Hebrew Solomon.

It is quite evident that James delighted in his nickname and failed to discover any hidden vein of sarcasm in it, for in one of the extravagant masques he gave in honour of his father-in-law, Christian the Fourth of Denmark, at Theobalds, he took the part of that incarnation of Wisdom. Conceive the gorgeousness and the scandal of the occasion. Royal James as Solomon, and no less royal Christian, *his* part not stated, seated on a throne awaiting the Queen of Sheba, coming to offer precious gifts: attendant upon her, Faith, Hope, and Charity. The Queen of Sheba, sad to say, had taken too much to drink, and, there being no one to advise her to "Mind the step!" she tripped over the throne and shot all the gifts, some very treacly and sticky, into the lap of his Danish majesty, who rose and essayed a dance with her, but fell down and had to be taken off to bed, like many a jolly toper before and since. Then the Three Virtues, hiccoughing and staggering, tried their parts, but nature forbade, and they retired very sick. The spectacle of the drunken endeavouring to carry off the drunk must have been vastly entertaining to His Majesty, himself too well seasoned to be quite helpless. It seems probable that, picking an unsteady way among the courtiers who strewed the floor, he saw himself to bed without the aid of chamberlains and grooms-in-waiting and their kind.

James the First and Sixth died at Theobalds in 1625, in the fifty-ninth year of his age, cut off in part by the agency of Greek wine. The halls where he revelled, and where between whiles he piously translated the Psalms, are gone, dismantled under the rule of the Commonwealth, a period especially fatal to Royal Palaces. The site of the Palace is commemorated by "Theobalds Square." The modern mansion of Theobalds is a mile distant.

## XIII

An inn bearing the odd name of the Roman Urn stands by the wayside on entering the hamlet of Cheshunt called Crossbrook Street. An urn in a niche of the wall over the front door bears the inscription " Via Una," and is witness to the finds of Roman remains close by. It gives point to the old belief that Cheshunt itself was a station on that Roman road, the Ermine Street.

Turner's Hill, Cheshunt, and Cheshunt Wash are all one loosely-joined stretch of houses : recent houses,

houses not so recent, dignified old mansions, and undignified second- and third-rate shops. It is an effect of shabbiness, of a halting two ways, between remaining as it was and developing into a modern suburb. The road itself shares this uncertainty, for it is neither a good country highway nor a decent town street, being bumpy macadam and gravel alternating, and full of holes. Cheshunt's modern fame is for roses, and the nurseries where they are cultivated spread far and wide. Its ancient fame

THE ROMAN URN, CHESHUNT.

was not so pleasing, for the Wash, when the Lea was in flood, made Cheshunt a place to be dreaded, as we learn from the diary of Ralph Thoresby, who travelled prayerfully this way between 1680 and 1720. Coming up from Yorkshire to London on one occasion, he found the washes upon the road near Ware swollen to such a height that travellers had to swim for their lives, one poor higgler being drowned. Thoresby prudently waited until some country-

CHESHUNT GREAT HOUSE.

people came and conducted him over the meadows, to avoid the deepest part of Cheshunt Wash. Even so, he tells how "we rode to the saddle-skirts for a considerable way, but got safe to Waltham Cross."

Cheshunt possesses a local curiosity in the shape of "Cheshunt Great House," a lonely mansion of red brick, standing in a meadow within what was once a moated enclosure. It is a gloomy old place belonging to the time of Henry the Seventh, but altered and patched to such a degree that even the genuine parts of it look only doubtfully authentic. A large central hall with hammer-beam carved roof is the feature of the interior, hung with tapestry, suits of armour, and portraits of historic personages, in which are mixed together real antiquities and forgeries of such age that *they* even are antique. Among them is a rude and battered rocking-horse, said to have been used by Charles the First when an infant.

CHARLES THE FIRST'S ROCKING-HORSE.

Obviously Cheshunt Great House should be haunted, and is! Cardinal Wolsey's is the unquiet shade that disturbs the midnight hours beneath this roof, lamenting the more or less authentic murders he is said to have perpetrated here. There is not, of course, the slightest foundation for these wild stories, and the great Cardinal, so far as Cheshunt is concerned, leaves the court without a stain on his character.

But we must hasten onward to Ware, halted, however, in half a mile, at Turnford, a place forgotten by most map-makers. Writers of guide-books, too, pass it coldly by. And indeed, if you be of the hurrying sort, you may well pass and never know the individual existence of the hamlet; so close are Cheshunt on the one hand and Wormley on the other. As the poet remarks—

> "Full many a flower is born to blush unseen
> And waste its sweetness on the desert air";

and Turnford is a modest place, consisting, all told, of an old residence or so, a farmstead, and the Bull Inn: the sign showing a bull's head with a remarkably coy expression. One no longer splashes through the ford that gave the place its name; a bridge has long since replaced it.

Why, it may be asked, linger over Turnford? Because here, in some lowly cot not now to be identified, somewhere about the year 1700, was born, of the usual poor but honest parents, one who might have been truly great in his profession had not the accursed shears of Fate cut him off before he had time to develop himself. I speak of "Dr." William Shelton, apothecary and highwayman. William was at an early age apprenticed to an apothecary at Enfield, and presently distinguished himself in an endeavour to elope with the apothecary's sister, an elderly charmer by no means averse from being run away with. The attempt miscarried, and our poor friend was soundly cudgelled for his pains. His second enterprise, the carrying off of a widow's daughter, was more fortunate. The runaways were married at the Fleet, and afterwards settled at Enfield, where, with the aid of his wife's fortune, Shelton eked out a living while trying to develop a practice. Tiring, after a while, of this, he obtained an appointment as surgeon in Antigua, but although generally liked in that island, he was obliged to return home on account of some wild escapades. He then settled in succession at Buntingford and Braughing, but doctors were at a discount at those places, and so, like many another wild spirit, he took to the road. A good horse and a reliable pair of pistols did more for him than his dispensary, and he prospered for a little while. There is no knowing to what eminence he might have risen—for he robbed with grace and courtesy—had not the authorities seized him one evil day. He made a dignified exit at Tyburn in 1732.

At Wormley, a roadside village of nondescript character, the New River is crossed, bringing us into Broxbourne, lying in a dip of the road, with that famous Cockney resort, Broxbourne Gardens, off to the right, by the river Lea. The Gardens themselves are as popular as ever, but the medicinal spring—the "rotten-egg water" is the eloquently descriptive name of it—has fallen into neglect.

The traveller along the highroad has left Broxbourne behind before he has quite discovered he has reached it, and comes into Hoddesdon unawares. Broxbourne, where the "brocks," or badgers, were once plentiful enough to give a name to the little stream running into the Lea, is indeed a much more shy and retiring place than those who on Saturdays, Sundays, and Mondays visit the tea-gardens aforesaid have any idea of. This is by way of a testimonial. Hoddesdon, too, which to be sure is not a tiny village like Broxbourne, but quite a little town, is altogether delightful. It has not been modernised, and its inhabitants still obtain their water in pailsful from the public pump in the middle of the broad street, which remains much as it was when the Cambridge "Telegraph" came through, and when the Newmarket and Bishop Stortford traffic branched off to the right in the midst. To this day most of its old inns remain, clustering round the fork of the roads: the Bull, its gabled porch and projecting sign quickening the traveller's pace as he sees it afar; the Salisbury Arms, the Maiden's Head, the Swan.

The Bull is a famous house, finding, as it does, a mention in Prior's "Down Hall." It was in 1715 that Matthew Prior, one of the most notable poets of his day, and sometime Ambassador at the Court of Versailles, travelled this road to Down Hall, near Hatfield Broadoak. His "chariot" halted at the Bull, as he tells us—

> "Into an old inn did this equipage roll,
>   At a town they call Hodsdon, the sign of the Bull,
>   Near a nymph with an urn that divides the highway,
>   And into a puddle throws mother of tea."

HODDESDON.

Nymph and urn and puddle are gone long since, and where they were placed there stands at this day the ugly modern building that Hoddesdon folk call the "Clock House": really a fire-engine house with a clock-tower; the tower surmounted by a weather-vane oddly conjoining the characteristics of a fiddler, a sagittarius, and a dolphin. Inquiry fails to discover what it symbolises. Before ever the nymph or the present building occupied this site, there stood here the wayside chapel of St. Catherine, whose ancient bell hangs in the clock-tower.

Prior writes as though the Bull had long been familiar to him, but his intimate touches of the life and character of an inn came, doubtless, from his own youthful observation; for his uncle had been landlord of the Rummer at Charing Cross, where as a boy he had been a waiter and general help. Doubtless he had heard many an old frequenter of the Rummer put questions similar to these he asks:—

"'Come here, my sweet landlady! how do you do?
Where's Cic'ly so cleanly, and Prudence, and Sue?
And where is the widow that lived here below?
And the other that sang, about eight years ago?
And where is your sister, so mild and so dear,
Whose voice to her maids like a trumpet was clear?'

'By my troth,' she replies, 'you grow younger, I think.
And pray, sir, what wine does the gentleman drink?
But now, let me die, sir, or live upon trust,
If I know to which question to answer you first,
For things since I saw you most strangely have varied—
The ostler is hanged, and the widow is married;

And Prue left a child for the parish to nurse ;
And Cic'ly went off with a gentleman's purse ;
And as to my sister, so mild and so dear,
She has lain in the churchyard full many a year.'"

What a sorry catalogue of changes and disasters!

A mile or more distant, along the Bishop Stortford road, is the gatehouse of the famous Rye House, its clustered red-brick chimneys and thick walls still left to remind the historically-minded of that Rye House Plot of 1681 which was to have ended Charles the Second, and his brother, the Duke of York, on their way past from Newmarket to London. Although the Bishop Stortford road does not concern us, the house is alluded to in these pages because it now contains that notorious piece of furniture, the Great Bed of Ware.

Hoddesdon gives place to Amwell, steeply downhill. The village is properly "Great Amwell," but no one who knows his Lamb would think of calling it so, although there is a "Little Amwell" close at hand. To the Lambs it was just "Amwell," and that is sufficient for us. Moreover, like so many places named "Great," it is now really very small. It is, however, exceedingly beautiful, with that peculiarly park-like beauty characteristic of Hertfordshire. The old church, also of the characteristically Hertfordshire type, stands, charmingly embowered amid trees, on a bank overlooking the smoothly-gliding stream of the New River, new-born from its source in the Chadwell Spring, and hurrying along on its beneficent mission toward the smoke and fog of London. Two islands divide the stream; one of them containing a monument to Sir Hugh Myddelton, and a stone with lines from Scott, the "Quaker poet of Amwell," commencing—

> "Amwell, perpetual be thy stream,
> Nor e'er thy spring be less."

An aspiration which, let us hope, will be fulfilled.

## XIV

ALTHOUGH to hurry past spots so interesting and so beautiful looks much like the act of a Vandal, our business is with the road, and linger we must not; and so, downhill again, by the woods of Charley —or "Charl-eye" as the country folk insist on calling them—we come to a vantage-point overlooking Ware; an old town of many maltings, of the famous Bed aforesaid, and of Johnny Gilpin's ride. Fortunate are those who come thus in view of Ware upon some still golden afternoon of summer, when the chimes from the old church-tower are spelling out the notes of that sentimental old song, "Believe me, if all those endearing young charms." Time and tune conspire to render Ware romantic.

The town takes its name from the weir or dam built across the Lea by invading Danes in the year 896. Coming up the Lea in a great flotilla of what historians call ships, more correctly perhaps to be named sailing-barges, they halted here, and, designing a fort beside the dam they built, imagined themselves secure. Around them in the Lea valley between Ware and Hertford stretched the great lake their dam had created, and all King Alfred's men could not by force dislodge them.

Can you not find it possible to imagine that great King—that King truly great in counsels both of war and peace, that contriver and man of his hands—on these Amwell heights and looking down upon that Danish fortress and its ceinture of still water, with twice a hundred prows lying there, proudly secure? Truly, despite the dark incertitude of history on these doings, we may clearly see that monarch. He knits his brows and looks upon the country spread out beneath him: just as you may look down to-day upon the valley where the Lea and the railway run, side by side. He—we have said it with meaning—is a contriver; has brains of some quality beneath that brow; will not waste his men in making glorious but wasteful attacks upon the foe: they shall work—so he wills it—not merely fight; or, working, fight the better for King and Country. Accordingly, his army is set to digging a great channel down this selfsame valley; a channel whose purport those Danes, lying there, do by no means comprehend; nor, I think, many even in this host of the great Alfred himself; for the spy has ever watched upon the doings of armies, and he who keeps his own counsel is always justified of his reticence.

This great ditch, then, excavated over against

WARE.

the camp and harbour of the sea-rovers, is therefore inexplicable, and doubtless the subject of much jest among the enemy : jesting that dies away presently, when, the excavation completed, it is found to touch the river above and below the weir, and indeed to be designed to drain away the Lea from its old channel and so steal away those cherished water-defences.

With what rejoicings Alfred turned the stream into this artificial course we know not, nor anything of the Saxon advance when the old channel ran dry and the Danish war-fleet presently lay stranded; the black hulls canted in all manner of ridiculous and ineffective angles; the sails with the cognisance of the raven on them flapping a farewell to the element they were to know no more. Only this we know, that the Danish host were forced to fly across the country to Cambridge and the fens; those unfailing resorts of fugitives in the long ago.

Alfred probably burnt the deserted fleet; but there may yet lie, somewhere in this pleasant valley between Hertford and Ware, deep down in immemorial ooze and silt, the remains of those hapless craft.

Ware, seen from a distance, is a place of singular picturesqueness ; its Dutch-like mass of mellow red roofs endowed with a skyline whose fantastic appearance is due to the clustered cowls of the four-score malthouses that give the old town a highly individual character. Here, as elsewhere, the sunset hour touches the scene to an unearthly beauty : only here those slanting cowls assume the last note of melodramatic significance, to which, ordinarily, in the broad eye of day, they are by no means entitled; being just so many ventilators to buildings in whose dark recesses is carried on the merely commercial work of drying the malt of which it is fondly assumed our beer is made.

The town, when you come to it, resolves itself into zigzag streets, coal-dust, and bargees. It is a very back-door kind of entrance you find, coming downhill, past a railway goods-yard and a smelly waterside with wharves and litter, where solemn horses stolidly drag barges and railway-trucks, and modern Izaak Waltons, sublime in faith, diligently "fysshe with an angle," with ill results. What they seek, these hapless sportsmen, is known only to themselves. Is it the festive ·tiddler, dear to infantile fisherfolk, or do they whip the water for the lordly trout, the ferocious pike, the grey mullet, or the carp? I know not; but what they find is the Old Boot, the discarded hat, the derelict gamp; in short, the miscellaneous floatable refuse of Hertford. To see one of these brothers of the angle carefully playing what ultimately discloses itself as a ragged umbrella affords one of the choicest five minutes that life has to offer.

Crossing an iron bridge over this fishful stream, you are in Ware. To the left stands the old Saracen's Head, now a little out of date and dreamy, for it is the veritable house where the principal coaches changed horses, and it has remained outwardly the same ever since. Here it was that the Great Bed of Ware stood for many years, conferring fame upon the town until 1869, when it was spirited away to the Rye House, there to be made a show of.

He who would correctly rede the riddle of the Great Bed would be a clever man, for its history is so confounded with legend that to say where the one begins and the other ends is now impossible. The Bed is a huge four-poster of black oak, elaborately carved with Renaissance designs, and is now twelve feet square, having been shorn of three feet of its length by a former landlord of the Saracen's Head. The date, 1463, painted on the head is an ancient and impudent forgery intended to give verisimilitude to the legend of this monumental structure's origin. This story tells how it was the work of one Jonas Fosbrooke, a journeyman carpenter, who presented it to Edward the Fourth "for the use of the royal family or the accommodation of princes, or nobles, or for any great occasion." The King, we are told, was highly pleased with this co-operative bedstead, and pensioned the ingenious Fosbrooke for life; but history, curiously, fails to tell us of royal or any other families herding together in this way. The legend then goes on to tell how, not having been used for many years by any noble persons, it was put to use when the town was very full of strangers. These unfortunate plebeian persons found it anything but a bed of roses, for they were tormented throughout the night by the snobbish and indignant ghost of Jonas, who objected to anyone beneath the rank of a knight-bachelor sleeping in his bed, and savagely pinched all who could not claim gentility. This weird ghost-story was probably invented by the landlords of the several inns in which the Bed has been housed to account for a vigorous and hungry race of fleas that inhabited the old four-poster, and must have been originated at a very early date, for on it hangs the story of Harrison Saxby, Master of Horse to Henry the Eighth. Saxby fell violently in love with the daughter of a miller near Ware, and swore he would do anything to win her from her many other suitors. The King, passing through the town, heard of this and promised to give her (those were autocratic times!) to him who should sleep in the Great Bed, and, daring all that the ferocious apparition of Fosbrooke could do, should be found there in the morning. All save the valorous Saxby held back, but he determined that no disembodied spirit should come between him and his love, and, duly tucked in, was left to sleep—no, not to sleep, for the powers of darkness were exalted to considerable purpose in the night, and when day dawned the rash Saxby was discovered on the floor, covered with bruises. If we seek rather the practical joker than the supernatural visitant to poor Saxby, we shall probably be on the right quest.

The Great Bed was not always housed at the Saracen's Head. Coming originally from Ware Priory, it was next at the Crown, where it remained until that old house was pulled down, in 1765, being in turn transferred to the Bull.

Ware was always a place of great traffic in the long ago. Railways have altered all that, and it is now a gracious old town, extraordinarily rich in the antique entries of ancient hostelries disappeared so long since that their very signs are forgot. As you go along its High Street there are between twenty and thirty of these arched entries countable, most of them relics of that crowded era of road-faring when Ware was a thoroughfare town at the end of a day's journey from London on the main road to the North. It was, in the words of an Elizabethan poet, "the guested town of Ware," and so remained for centuries, even when day's journeys grew longer and longer, and until the road became an obsolete institution. Some of these entries, on the other hand, always were, and others early became, features in the warehouse premises of the old maltsters, for Ware has ever been a place dedicated to the service of John Barleycorn.

Long centuries ago, ere railways were dreamt of, this was the great warehousing place of the malt from five neighbouring counties. It came in vast quantities by road and by river from up country, and was stored here, over against the demands of the London brewers; being sent to town chiefly by the river Lea. The Lea and its ready passage to London built up this distinctive trade of Ware: the railway destroyed it, and the maltsters' trade exists here nowadays only because it always has been here and because to utterly kill its local habitation would be perhaps impossible. But it is carried on with a difference, and malt is not so much brought and warehoused here as made on the spot. Many of the old houses in which the old-established maltsters reside, adjoining their own warehouses, in the good old style absolutely obsolete in other places, are of early eighteenth century date, and rich in exquisite moulded plaster ceilings and carved oak panelling. One at least dates back to 1625, and is nothing less in appearance than the home of an old prince of commerce.

To have an opportunity of inspecting this is a privilege not lightly to be valued. On one side of the entry, and over the archway, is the residence, and on the other the old-world counting-house, with a narrow roadway between for the waggons to and from the maltings at the farther end. The maltings themselves are rebuilt and fitted with modern appliances, but they strike the only note out of key with the general harmony of the place, and, even so, they are not altogether unpleasing, for they are earnest of trade still brisk and healthy, in direct descent from days of old. Beyond the maltings are old walled gardens where peaches ripen, and velvet lawns and queer pavilions overhanging the river Lea : the whole, from the entry in the High Street, down the long perspective to the river, embowered in flowers.

For the rest, Ware commands much interest, not greatly to be enlarged upon here. The church-tower, rising nobly above the roof-tops of the town, amid a thickly clustered group of oast-house cowls, the interior of the building, noble beyond the common run ; the so-called "John Gilpin's House" ;

the river scenery up the delightful valley to Hertford: all these things are to be seen and not adequately written about in this place.

## XV

UPHILL goes the road out of Ware, passing the Royston Crow Inn and some old cottages on the outskirts. The two miles between this and Wade's Mill form the dividing-line between the valleys of the Lea and the Rib, and consequently the way, after climbing upwards, has to go steeply down again. The Sow and Pigs is the unusual name of an inn standing on the crest of the hill before descending into Wade's Mill. Who was Wade of the mill that stands to this day in the hollow where the little stream called the Rib runs beneath the highway? History, imperial, national, or parochial, has nothing to tell us on this head. Perhaps—nay, probably—there never was a Wade, a person so-named; the original mill, and now the hamlet that clusters in the bottom, taking its name from the ford—the ford, or watersplash, or "wade"—that was here before ever a bridge was built. The parish of St. Nicholas-at-Wade, beside the channel that formerly divided the Isle of Thanet from Kent, obtained its name from the ford at that point, and in like manner derives the name of Iwade, overlooking the King's Ferry entrance to Sheppey.

The hamlet of Wade's Mill is a product of the coaching age. Before folks travelled in any large numbers there stood only the mill in the hollow; but, as road-faring progressed, there at length rose the Feathers Inn beside the way, and by degrees a dozen or so cottages to keep it company. Here they are still; standing, all of them, in the parish of Thundridge, whose old church, a mile distant, is now in ruins. The new church is built on the height overlooking Wade's Mill, and may be noticed in the illustration on the following page.

Steeply rising goes the road out of this sleepy hollow; passing, when half-way up the hill, a mean little stone obelisk perched on a grassy bank. This is a memorial to Thomas Clarkson, a native of Wisbeach, and marks the spot where in his youth he knelt down and vowed to dedicate his life to the abolition of the slave trade. It was placed here in 1879 by Arthur Giles Puller, of Youngsbury, in the neighbourhood. Clarkson was born in 1760, the son of the Rev. John Clarkson, Headmaster of Wisbeach Free Grammar School. He graduated at Cambridge in 1783, and two years later gained the first prize in the Latin Essay competition on the subject of "Slavery and Commerce of the Human Species, particularly the African." This success finally fixed his choice of a career, and he forthwith set afoot an agitation against the slave trade. In an introduction to the wealthy William Wilberforce, he succeeded in enlisting the support of that philanthropist, to whom the credit of abolishing the nefarious traffic is generally given. A Committee was formed to obtain the passing of an Abolition Bill through Parliament; an object secured after twenty years' continued agitation and strenuous work on the platform. Clarkson's health and substance were alike expended in the effort, but he was not eventually without reward for his labours,

CLARKSON'S MONUMENT.

a recompense in subscriptions to which he seems to have looked forward in quite a business-like way; more soothing than Wordsworth's pedestrian sonnet beginning—

"Clarkson, it was an obstinate hill to climb;
How toilsome, nay, how dire it was."

Doubtless he argued the labourer was worthy of his hire.

Abolition in the West Indian Islands followed, and then the Emancipation Act of 1833, liberating 800,000 slaves and placing the sum of twenty millions sterling, as compensation, into the pockets of Liverpool, Bristol, and Glasgow slave-owners. That sturdy beast of burden, the British taxpayer, of course paid for this expensive burst of sentiment. Clarkson, already an old man, and weary with his long labours, received the Freedom of the City of London in 1839, and died in his eighty-seventh year, in 1846.

Midway between the hamlets of High Cross and Collier's End, at the second of the two left-hand turnings sign-posted for "Rowney Abbey and the Mundens," is the other hamlet of Standon Green End—if the two cottages and one farmhouse in a by-lane may so be dignified. Some three hundred yards along this lane, in the centre of a meadow, stands the singular monument known in all the country round about as the "Balloon Stone," a rough block of sandstone, surrounded by an iron railing, placed here to record the alighting on this spot of the first balloon that ever ascended in England. Tradition still tells of the terror that seized the rustics when they saw "a summat" dropping out of the sky, and how they fled for their lives.

On lifting a hinged plate, the astonishing facts of this antique æronautical adventure may be found duly set out in an amusingly grandiloquent inscription, engraved on a bronze tablet let into the upper part of the stone—

"Let Posterity Know
And Knowing be Astonished
That
On the 15 Day of September 1784
Vincent Lunardi of Lucca in Tuscany
The first Aerial Traveller in Britain
Mounting from the Artillery Ground
in London
And
Traversing the Regions of the Air
For Two Hours and Fifteen Minutes,
In this Spot
Revisited the Earth.
On this Rude Monument
For Ages be Recorded
That Wondrous Enterprise
Successfully atchieved
By the Powers of Chemistry
And the Fortitude of Man
That Improvement in Science
Which
The Great Author of all Knowledge
Patronising by His Providence
The Invention of Mankind
Hath graciously permitted
To their Benefit
And
His own Eternal glory."

---

"This Plate
A facsimile of the Original
One was placed here
in the month of November
1875 by Arthur Giles
Puller of Youngsbury."

Collier's End is a wayside hamlet of a few timber-framed and plaster cottages, leading to Puckeridge, where the ways to Cambridge divide: one going by Buntingford, Royston, and Melbourn; the other by Braughing, Barkway, Barley, and Fowlmere, meeting again at Harston in another nineteen miles. Away to the left, between Collier's End and Puckeridge, is St Edmund's College, a Roman Catholic seminary.

Puckeridge itself, standing where the roads branch, grew in the old road-faring days from a tiny hamlet to be considerably larger than its mother-parish of Standon, a village nearly two miles distant, to the right-hand. That it developed early is quite evident in its two old inns, the fifteenth century Falcon, and the Old George, scarcely a hundred years younger.

## XVI

WE will first take the right-hand road to Cambridge, by Barkway, for that would appear in early days to have been the favourite route. Braughing, the first village on this route, is soon reached, lying down below the highway beside the river Rib, with the usual roadside fringe of houses. The local pronunciation of the place-name is "Braffing."

The road now begins to climb upwards to the crest of the Chilterns at Barley, passing the small hamlets of Quinbury and Hare Street, and through a bold country of rolling downs to Barkway, whose name, coming from Saxon words meaning "a way over the hill," is descriptive of its situation. Few signs of habitation are seen on the way, and those at great distances; Great and Little Hormead and Ansty peering down upon the road from distant hillsides.

Since the coaches left the road, Barkway has gone to sleep, and dreams still of a bygone century. At the beginning of its broad street there stands the old toll-house, with the clock even yet in its gable that marked the flight of time when the Cambridge "Telegraph" passed by every day, at two o'clock in the afternoon; and old houses that once were inns still turn curiously gabled frontages to the street. The Wheatsheaf, once the principal coaching house, still survives; outside it a milestone of truly monumental proportions, marking the thirty-fifth mile from London. It stands close upon six feet in height, and besides bearing on its face a bold inscription, setting forth that it is thirty-five miles from London and sixteen from Cambridge, shows two shields of arms, one of them bearing a crescent, the other so battered that it is not easily to be deciphered. This is one of a series of milestones stretching between this point and Cambridge; a series that has a history. It seems that Dr. William Mouse, Master of Trinity Hall, and a Mr. Robert Hare, left between them in 1586 and 1599 the sum of £1600 in trust to Trinity Hall, the interest to be applied to mending the highway along these sixteen miles; as the Latin of the original document puts it, "*in et circa villam nostram Cantabrigiæ præcipue versus Barkway.*" Whatever Trinity Hall may have done for the repair of the road in the hundred and twenty-six years following the bequest, there were certainly no milestones along its course until 1725, when Dr. William Warren, the then Master, set up on October 20th the first five, starting from the church of Great St. Mary in Cambridge Market Square. On the 25th June, in the following year, another five stones were placed in continuation, and the next year another five. The sixteenth was not placed until 29th May 1728. Of this series the fifth, tenth, and fifteenth were about six feet in height, with the Trinity Hall arms carved on them; in heraldic jargon described as "sable, a crescent in fess ermine, with a bordure engrailed of the second." The others were originally small, with merely the number of miles engraved on them, but were replaced between 1728 and 1732 by larger stones, each bearing the black crescent; as may be seen to this day.

These stones, very notable in themselves, and more so from the open and exposed character of the road, have not only the interest of the circumstances already narrated, but gain an additional notability in the fact that, excluding those set up by the Romans, they are the earliest milestones in England. Between Roman times and the date of these examples the roads knew no measurement, and miles were a matter of repute. It was not until the Turnpike Act of 1698 that, as part of their statutory obligations, Turnpike Trusts were always bound not only to maintain the roads on which they collected tolls, but to measure them as well, and to set up a stone at every mile.

The road between Barkway and Barley is a

BARLEY.

constant succession of hills; steep descents, and correspondingly sharp rises, with the folds of the Chilterns, bare in places and in others heavily wooded, rising and falling for great distances on either hand. It was while ascending Barkway Hill on the up journey that the "Lynn Union," driven by Thomas Cross, was involved in a somewhat serious affair. Three convicts were being taken to London in charge of two warders, and the whole party of five had seats on the roof. As the coach slowed to a walking pace up the ascent, one of the gaol-birds quietly slipped off at the back, and was being followed by the other two when attention was drawn to their proceedings. The principal warder, who was on the box-seat, was a man of decision. He drew a pistol from his pocket, and, cocking it, said, "If you do not immediately get up I'll shoot you!" The one who had already got down, thereupon, with a touching faith in the warder's marksmanship, returned to his place, and the others remained quiet. They finished the remainder of the journey handcuffed. It is, indeed, surprising that they were not properly secured before.

The road on to Barley is of a switchback kind, finally rising to the ridge where Barley is perched, overlooking a wild treeless country of downs. Barley is a little village as thoroughly agricultural as its name hints, and consists of but a few houses, mostly thatched, with a not very interesting church on a by-way, and a very striking inn, the Fox and Hounds, on the main road. It is the sign of the inn, rather than the house itself, that is so notable, for it is one of those gallows signs, stretching across the road, that are now becoming so few. The illustration sufficiently describes its quaint procession of fox, hounds, and huntsmen, said to have been placed here in allusion to a fox that took refuge in a dog-kennel of the inn.

If the name of Barley hints strongly of agricultural pursuits, it does not by any means derive it from that kind of grain. Its earliest Saxon name is "Berle," coming from the words "beorh" and "lea," and meaning a cleared space in a forest. Barley, in fact, stands on the final ridge where the Chiltern Hills end and the East Anglian heights and the forest of Essex begin, overlooking a valley between the two where the trees fell back and permitted a way through the primeval woods.

The restored and largely rebuilt church contains little of interest, but in the churchyard lies one whose career claims some notice. There the passing stranger may see a simple stone cross, bearing the words, "Heinrich, Count Arnim. Born May 10th, 1814. Died October 8th, 1883." Beside him lies his wife, who died in 1875. The story of Count Arnim is one of political enthusiasms and political and personal hatreds. One of the greatest nobles in conservative Germany, he early developed Radical ideas, and joined Kossuth in his struggle for Hungarian liberty, refusing to desert that ill-fated cause, and disregarding the call of his own country to arms. The neglect of this feudal duty rendered his vast estates liable to forfeiture, and placed him in danger of perpetual confinement in a military prison; a danger aggravated by the personal and bitter animosity of the all-powerful Bismarck, and the hatred of the relatives of two antagonists whom he had slain in duels. To escape this threatened lifelong imprisonment he fled to England, and, after much privation, established a school of fencing and physical exercise, under the assumed name of Major Loeffler. In the meanwhile he had married a German governess. His association with Barley arose from the then Rector resorting to his school for a course of exercise, and becoming in time a fast friend, to whom the Count disclosed his identity. The Rector interested himself in Arnim's fortunes, and went so far as to write to the German Emperor on behalf of his son, then growing to manhood. As a result of these efforts young Arnim was permitted to enter the German Army and to enjoy his father's estates. Unfortunately his mother accompanied him, and as, according to the savage notions of German society, she was not of noble birth and not ennobled by marriage, she was restricted to the servants' hall at every place her son visited, while he was received in the highest circles. Count Arnim had, in his long residence in England, adopted the sensible views prevailing here, and indignantly recalled his son. "I would rather," he said in a noble passage, "I would rather have my son grow up a poor man in England, in the service of his adopted country, than as a rich man in the service of his Fatherland, where he would have to be ashamed of his mother."

It was his friendship with the Rector that made

the Count choose this as the resting-place of his wife and himself. His body was brought by train to Buntingford, and thence by road, being buried by the light of torches at midnight, after the old German custom.

## XVII

A MILE beyond Barley the road leaves Hertfordshire and enters Essex, but passes out of that county again and enters Cambridgeshire in another two miles. Midway, amid the solemn emptiness of the bare downs, the Icknield Way runs as a rugged chalk-and-grass track athwart the road, neighboured by prehistoric tumuli. Amidst all these reminders of the dead-and-gone Iceni, at the cross-roads to Royston and Whittlesford, and just inside the Cambridgeshire border, stands a lonely inn once known as the Flint House. Beside it is one of the Trinity Hall milestones, with the crescent badge of the college, and hands with fingers like sausages pointing down the weirdly straight and empty roads.

The two miles of road through Essex long bore the name of the "Recorder's Road." It seems that when in 1725 an Act of Parliament was obtained for mending the then notoriously bad way from Cambridge to Fowlmere and Barley "in the counties of Cambridgeshire and Hertfordshire," the fact that two miles lay in Essex was overlooked. In consequence of this omission nothing was done to the Essex portion, which became almost impassable for carriages until the then Recorder of Cambridge, Samuel Pont, obtained the help of several of the colleges, and at last mended it.

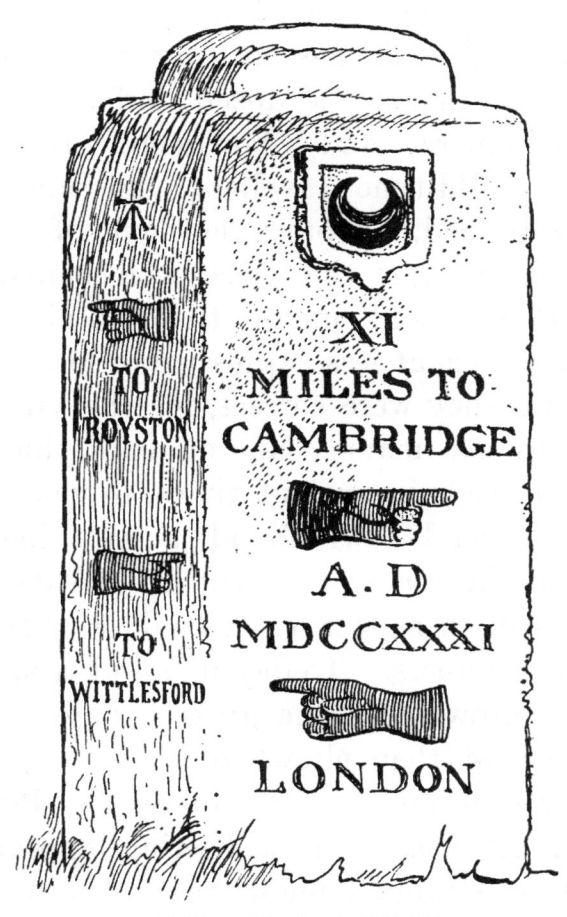

A MONUMENTAL MILESTONE.

It is a good enough road now, though passing through very exposed and open country, with tumuli, the solemn relics of a prehistoric race, forming striking objects on the bare hillsides and the skyline. In cosy and sheltered contrast with these comes the village of Fowlmere, snugly nestled amid the elms and poplars aptly named "Crows' Parlour."

Fowlmere is a very Proteus in the spelling of its name. In Domesday Book it is set down as "Fugelesmare," and has at any time since then been written in half a dozen different ways, in which "Foulmere" and "Fowlmere" are the most prominent. Old-time travellers, who found the road inexpressibly bad, adopted the first of these two styles, and thought the place well suited with a name: others—and among them local patriots—adopted the variant less expressive of mud and mire. In so doing they were correct, for the village takes its name from a marshy lake or mere, thickly overgrown with reeds in ancient times, in whose recesses myriads of wild-fowl found a safe harbourage. Even when the nineteenth century had dawned the mere was still in existence, and wild-fowl frequented it in some numbers. To-day it is but a spot where watercress grows and the grass springs a thought more luxuriant than elsewhere.

Here we are on the track of Samuel Pepys, who makes in his Diary but a fleeting appearance on this road,—a strange circumstance when we consider that he was a Cantab. It is, however, an appearance of some interest. In February 1660, then, behold him rising early, taking horse from London, and setting out for Cambridge, in company with a Mr. Pierce, at seven o'clock in the morning, intending to make that town by night. They rode

FOWLMERE: A TYPICAL CAMBRIDGESHIRE VILLAGE.

twenty-seven miles before they drew rein, baiting at Puckeridge,—doubtless at that old house the Falcon,—the way "exceeding bad" from Ware. "Then up again and as far as Fowlmere, within six miles of Cambridge, my mare almost tired."

Almost! Good Heavens! he had ridden the poor beast forty-six miles. At anyrate, if the mare was not quite tired, Samuel at least was, and at Fowlmere he and Mr. Pierce stayed the night, at

THE CHEQUERS, FOWLMERE.

the Chequers. An indubitable Chequers still stands in the village street, but it is not the house under whose roof the old diarist lay, as the inscription, "W.T., Ano Dom. 1675," on the yellow-plastered front sufficiently informs us. The next morning Samuel was up betimes, and at Cambridge by eight o'clock.

Thriplow Heath once stretched away between Fowlmere and Newton, our next village, but it is all enclosed now, and cultivated fields obscure that historic portion of the Heath where, in June 1647, Cromwell's troops, victorious over the last struggles of the Royalists, assembled and sent demands to the Parliament in London for their long overdue pay. A striking position, this. The Parliament had levied war upon the King and had brought him low, and now the hammer that had shattered his power was being threatened against itself. Cromwell and a military dictatorship loomed ominous before my lords and gentlemen of Westminster, and they hastily sent down two months' pay, with promises of more, to avert Cromwell's threat that he would seize the captive King, and, placing him at the head of the army, march upon London. That payment and those promises did not suffice, and how Cornet Joyce was sent across country from this point, with a troop of horse, to seize Charles from the custody of the Parliamentary Commissioners at Holmby House is a matter of history, together with the military usurpation that did actually follow.

Newton village itself has little interest, but a small hillside obelisk on the right calls for passing notice. It marks the spot where two friends were in the habit of meeting in the long ago. The one lived at Newton and the other at Little Shelford. Every day for many years they met at this spot, and when one died the survivor erected this memorial. The left-hand hillside also has its interest, for the commonplace brick building on the hilltop is all that remains of one of a line of semaphore telegraph stations in use between London and Cambridge over a hundred years ago. A descending road brings us from this point to a junction with the Royston route to Cambridge, at Harston.

## XVIII

The Royston route to Cambridge now demands attention. Harking back to Puckeridge, we have by this road certainly the most difficult way, for eight of the eleven miles between Puckeridge and Royston lead, with few and unimportant intervals, steadily uphill, from the deep valley of the Rib up to the tremendous and awe-inspiring climax of Royston Downs; from whose highest point, on Reed Hill, the road drops consistently for three miles in a staggering descent into Royston town.

At West Mill, where the valley opens out on the left, the road continues on the shoulder of the hill, with the village and the railway lying down below; a sweetly pretty scene. West Mill is a name whose sound is distinctly modern, but the place is of a venerable age, vouched for by its ancient church, whose architecture dates back to the early years of the thirteenth century. It is the fashion to spell the place-name in one word — Westmill — an ugly and altogether objectionable form.

Buntingford succeeds to West Mill. A brick bridge crossing a little river, an old red-brick chapel bulking large on the left hand, a long, long street of rustic cottages and shops and buildings of more urban pretensions, and over all a sleepy half-holiday air: that is Buntingford. It is difficult to take Buntingford seriously, even though its street be half a mile in length, for its name recalls that hero of nursery rhyme, that Baby Bunting whose father went a-hunting, and went to buy a rabbit-skin to put the Baby Bunting in. Buntingford, for all the

WEST MILL.

length of its long street and the very considerable age of it, is but a hamlet of Layston, close upon a mile distant. That is why Buntingford has no old parish church, and explains the building of the red-brick chapel aforesaid in 1615, to the end that the ungodly might have no excuse for not attending public worship and the pious might exercise their piety without making unduly long pilgrimage. " Domus Orationis " is inscribed on the gable-wall of the chapel, lest perhaps it might be mistaken for some merely secular building; an easy enough matter. Behind it, stands the little group of eight almshouses built in 1684 by Dr. Seth Ward, "born in yis town," as the tablet over the principal door declares; that Bishop of Salisbury who lent his carriage-horses to King James's troops to drag the ordnance sent against the Monmouth rebels on Sedgemoor.

Layston Church stands in a meadow, neglected, and with daylight peering curiously through its roof; and the village itself has long disappeared.

The fifteen miles between Wade's Mill and Royston, forming the "Wade's Mill Turnpike Trust," continued subject to toll long after the railway was opened. With the succeeding trusts on through Royston to Kirby's Hut and Caxton, on the Old North Road, and so on to Stilton, it was one of the earliest undertakings under the general Turnpike Act of 1698, and, like them, claimed direct descent from the first turnpike gates erected in England in 1663, under the provisions of the special Act of that year, which, describing this "ancient highway and post-road" to the North as almost impassable, proceeded to give powers for toll-gates to be erected at Stilton and other places.

To this particular Trust fell the heavy task of lowering the road over the London Road hill, the highest crest of the Downs; a work completed in 1839, at a cost of £1723, plus £50 compensation paid to a nervous passenger on one of the coaches who jumped off the roof while it was crossing a temporary roadway and broke his leg. The tolls at this time were let for £4350 per annum.

Reed Hill, to which we now come, passing on the way the hamlets of Buckland and Chipping, commands the whole of Royston Downs, a tract of country whose bold, rolling outlines are still impressive, even though the land be enclosed and brought under cultivation in these later years. This chalky range is a continuation of the Chiltern Hills, and gives Royston, lying down below in the deep hollow, a curiously isolated and remote appearance. Indeed, whether it be the engineering difficulties in tunnelling these heights, or whether the deterrent cause lies in rival railway politics, or in its not being worth while to continue, the branch of the Great Eastern Railway to Buntingford goes no farther, but comes ingloriously to a terminus in that little town; while the Great Northern Railway reaches Royston circuitously, by way of Hitchin and Baldock, and artfully avoids the heights.

A wayside inn — the Red Lion — crowns the summit of Reed Hill, and looks out upon vast distances. The Red Lion himself, a very fiercely-whiskered vermilion fellow projecting over the front door of the house, and looking with an agonised expression of countenance over his shoulder—*passant regardant*, as the heralds say—hails from Royston itself, where he occupied a similar position in front of the old coaching-inn of the same name. Alas! when old coaching days ended and those of railways dawned, the Red Lion at Royston, ever in the forefront of coaching affairs in the town, was doomed. The

High Street knows it no more, and the Bull reigns in its stead as the principal house.

These windy downs, now robbed of much of their wildness of detail, but losing nothing of their bold outline, long harboured two forms of wild life not commonly found elsewhere. The Royston Crow, indeed, still frequents this range of hills; and on some undisturbed slopes of turf the wandering botanist is even yet rewarded in his Eastertide search for the *Anemone Pulsatilla*, the Pasque Flower. The Royston Crow, the *Corvus cornix* of ornithologists, is a winter visitor from Sweden and Norway, and is known in other parts of the country as the "hooded crow." He is distinguished from his cousin corvi by his grey head and back, giving him an ancient and venerable appearance. He is not a sociable bird, and refuses to mix with the blackbirds, the thrushes, and his kindred crows, who, for their part, are content to leave him alone, and doubtless rejoice when in April he wings his way to northern latitudes.

The Pasque Flower, so named from the paschal season of its blossoming, affects the windiest and most unlikely situations in chalk and limestone pastures, and thrives where it might be supposed only the coarsest grasses would grow. In these exposed places its purple blooms flourish. They nestle close to the ground, and are only to be easily discovered by the expert. Do not attempt to transplant this wild beauty of the downs. You may dig roots with the greatest care, and cherish them as tenderly as possible; but, torn from its stern surroundings and lapped in botanical luxury, the Pasque Flower droops and dies.

## XIX

ROYSTON stands where the Ermine Street and the Icknield Way intersect one another. To old Cobbett, travelling with a censorious eye upon men and things and places in the early years of the nineteenth century, it appeared to be "a common market-town. Not mean, but having nothing of beauty about it." This is not a very shrewd or illuminating opinion, because, while it is true that Royston is not beautiful on the one hand, nor exactly mean on the other, this description is not quite descriptive, and fails to explain where the town stops short of beauty or of meanness. Royston, in fact, is a little grim, and belies the preconceived notion of the expectant traveller, who, doubtless with some wild idea of a connection between Royston and roystering, is astonished at the grave, almost solemn, look of its narrow streets. The grim shadow of the Downs is thrown over the little town, and the houses huddle together as though for company and warmth.

There are those to whom the place-name suggests a Norman-French derivation—Roy's ton, or the King's Town,—but although the name arose in Norman times, it had a very different origin from anything suggested by royal patronage. Eight hundred years ago, when this part of the country remained little but the desolate tract the fury of the Conqueror had made it, the Lady Rohesia, wife of the Norman lord of the manor, set up a wayside cross where the roads met. The object of this cross does not clearly appear, but it probably filled the combined purpose of a signpost and wayside oratory, where those who fared the roads might pray for a happy issue from the rigours of their journey. At anyrate, the piety of the Lady Rohesia (or Roesia, for they were very uncertain about their h's in those times) has kept her name from being quite forgot, preserved as it is in Royston's designation; but it is not to be supposed that the pilgrims, the franklins, and the miscellaneous wayfarers along these roads tortured their tongues much with this awkward word, and so Rohesia's Cross speedily became known as "Roise's," just as to the London 'bus-conductors High Holborn has become "'iobun." A town gathered in course of time round the monastery—"Monasterium de Cruce Roesiæ"—founded here a century after this pious lady had gone her way. Monastery and cross are alike gone, but the parish church is the old priory church, purchased by the inhabitants for public worship when the monastic establishment was dissolved, and Royston Fair, held on 7th July in every year, is a reminiscence of that old religious house, for that day is the day of St. Thomas à Becket, in whose honour it was dedicated. As "Becket's Fair" this annual celebration is still known.

For centuries afterwards Royston was a town and yet not a parish, being situated in portions of the five adjoining parishes of Melbourn, Bassingbourn, Therfield, Barley, and Reed; and for centuries more, after it had attained parochial dignity, its chief cross street, Melbourn Street, divided the place into two Roystons—Royston, Hertfordshire, and Royston, Cambridgeshire. The doings of one with the other afford amusing reading: how a separate workhouse was established and separate assessments made for each parish, and how at length, in 1781, an Act was passed for consolidating the two for local government purposes; all these inconvenient and absurdly conflicting jurisdictions of parishes and counties being eventually swept away in 1895, when the Cambridgeshire portion of Royston was transferred to Hertfordshire, the whole of the town now being in that county.

They still cherish the memory of King James the First at Royston, though the open Heath where he hunted the hare is a thing of the past, and the races and all the ancient jollifications of that time are now merely matters for the antiquary. Where the four roads from the four quarters of the compass still meet in the middle of the town stood the old Palace. Its remains, of no very palatial appearance, are there even yet, and form private residences. Close by is that prime curiosity, Royston Cave. James and his courtiers and all their gay world at this corner never knew of the Cave, which was only discovered in 1742. It is a bottle-shaped excavation in the chalk, situated immediately under the roadway. Its age and original purpose are still matters in dispute. Whether it was excavated to serve the purpose of dust-bin to a Roman villa, or was a flint quarry, we shall never know, but that it certainly was in use by some religious recluse in the twelfth century is assured by the curious rough carvings in the chalk, representing St. Catherine, the Crucifixion, mitred abbots, and a variety of subjects of a devotional character. The hermit whose singular piety led him to take up his abode in this dismal hole must have had great difficulty in entering or leaving, for it was then only to be approached by plunging as it were into the neck of the bottle.

A QUAINT CORNER IN ROYSTON.

The staircase by which visitors enter was only made in modern times.

The old Red Lion at Royston has already been mentioned as having ceased to be. It was kept for many years in the eighteenth century by Mrs. Gatward, a widow, assisted in the posting and coaching business attached to the house by her two sons. One of them came to a terribly tragic end. What induced him to turn highwayman we shall never know; but he took to the road, as many a roving blade in those times did. Perhaps his life lacked excitement. If that were so, he took the readiest means of adding variety to existence, for he waylaid the postboy carrying His Majesty's Mails on the North Road, between Royston and Huntingdon, and robbed the bags. There was in those times no method of courting death with such success as robbing the mails, and accordingly young Gatward presently found himself convicted and cast for execution. They hanged him in due course and gibbeted his body, pursuant to the grim old custom, near the scene of his crime. The story of this unhappy amateur highwayman is told—and, a tale of horror it is—by one Cole, a diligent antiquary on Cambridgeshire affairs, whose manuscript collections are in the British Museum. Hear him: "About 1753-54, the son of Mrs. Gatward, who kept the Red Lion at Royston, being convicted of robbing the mail, was hanged in chains on the Great Road. I saw him hanging, in a scarlet coat, and after he had hung about two or three months it is supposed that the screw was filed which supported him, and that he fell in the first high wind after. Mr. Lord, of Trinity, passed by as he lay on the ground, and, trying to open his breast, to see what state his body was in, not being offensive, but quite dry, a button of brass came off, which he preserves to this day, as he told me at the Vice-Chancellor's, Thursday, June 30th, 1779. I sold this Mr. Gatward, just as I left college in 1752, a pair of coach horses, which was the only time I saw him. It was a great grief to his mother, who bore a good character, and kept the inn for many years after."

This account of how a malefactor's body might lie by the roadside, the sport of any wayfarer's idle curiosity, gives no very flattering glimpse of this England of ours a hundred and fifty years ago. Yet these were the " good old times."

The story goes that the agonised mother of the gibbeted man secretly conveyed his body to the inn

CAXTON GIBBET.

and gave it decent, if unconsecrated, burial in the cellar. His brother, James Gatward, was for many years afterwards part proprietor of the London, Royston, and St. Ives coach, running past the gibbet.

Caxton Gibbet, where Gatward's body hung in chains, is still marked by a tall post standing on a mound by the wayside, on the North Road, thirteen miles from Royston. It is a singularly lonely spot, even though a public-house with the gruesome name of the Gibbet Inn stands close by. A mile distant is the village of Caxton, with its old coaching-inns converted into farmhouses; the only other places on the twelve miles being the old Hardwicke Arms Posting House and the gates of Wimpole Park at Arrington Bridge, and the solitary "Old North Road" railway station.

Royston's old inns have lost much of their old-time air. Among them, the George possessed one of those old "gallows" signs crossing the road in a fashion similar to that of the Fox and Hounds at Barley, but, somewhere towards the close of the eighteenth century, it fell at the moment when a London-bound waggoner was passing beneath, and killed him. Since then such signs have not been in favour in the town.

## XX

Royston has of late years spread out largely to the north, over those grassy heaths where James hunted. Looking back when midway between the town and Melbourn, this modern growth is readily noted, for the houses of it are all of Cambridgeshire white brick. At this distance they give a singularly close imitation of a tented military camp.

Melbourn—why not spelled with a final 'e,' like other Melbournes, is a mystery no inquiry can satisfy —is a large village of much thatch. Especially is the grey-green velvety moss on the thatch of a row of yellow plaster cottages beyond the church a thing

MELBOURN.

of beauty, however rotten the thatch itself may be. Melbourn has a beautiful church and church-tower, seen in the accompanying picture, but its other glory, the Great Elm that for many centuries spread a shade over the road by the church, is now only a memory,—a memory kept green by the sign of the inn opposite. Everyone in Melbourn lives on fruit. In other words, this is a great fruit-growing district. This village and its neighbour, Meldreth, specialise in greengages, and from the railway station that serves the two, many hundreds of tons of that fruit are despatched to London in the season. These terms are perhaps vague, but they are reduced to a more definite idea of the importance of the greengage harvest when some returns are noted. From Melbourn station, then, thirty tons a day is an average consignment. Little wonder, then, that when one has come down from the bleak downs and heaths of Royston to these sheltered levels, the swelling contours of the windy pastures and breezy cornfields give place to long lines of orchards.

Cambridgeshire very soon develops its flat and fenny character along this route, and Melbourn left behind, the road on to Cambridge is a dead level. The low church-tower just visible to a keen eye, away to the left, among some clustered trees, is that of Shepreth. Shepreth hides its modest self from the road: let us take the winding by-way that leads to it and see what a purely agricultural Cambridgeshire village, set down in this level plain, and utterly out of touch with the road, may be like. It needs no great exercise of the deductive faculty to discover, on the way to Shepreth, that it is not a place of great or polite resort, for the lane is a narrow and winding way, half muddy ruts and half loose stones. Beside it crawls imperceptibly in its deep, ditch-like bed, overhung by pollard willows, a stream that takes its rise in the bogs of Fowlmere. By what lazy, snakish windings it ultimately finds its way into the Cam does not concern us. Here and there old mud-walled cottages, brilliantly whitewashed and heavily thatched, dot the way; the sum total of the village, saving indeed the church, standing adjoining a farmyard churned into a sea of mud.

The appearance of Shepreth Church is not altogether prepossessing. The south aisle has been rebuilt in white brick, in a style rivalling the worst efforts of the old-time chapel-builder; and the old tower, whose upper stages have long fallen in ruin, shows in the contorted courses of its stonework how the building has sunk and settled in the waterlogged soil.

Beyond this soddened village, coming to the highroad again, the station and level-crossing of Foxton are reached; the situation of Foxton itself clearly fixed by the church-tower, rising from the flat fields on the right, half a mile away. There is something of a story belonging to this line of railway from Royston to Shepreth, Foxton, Shelford, and Cambridge. As far as Shepreth it is a branch of the Great Northern, anxious in the long ago to find a way into Cambridge and so cut up the Great Eastern's trade. The Great Eastern could not defeat the scheme altogether, but stopped it at Shepreth, to which point that line was opened in 1848. This was awkward for the Great Northern, brought to a halt seven miles from Cambridge, at a point which may, without disrespect to Shepreth, well be called "nowhere in particular." But the Great Northern people found a way out of the difficulty. Parliament, in the interests of the Great Eastern, would not permit them to build a railway into Cambridge, but no one could forbid them conveying passengers by coach along these last few miles. And so, for close upon four years, Great Northern passengers left the trains at Shepreth and were conveyed by a forty minutes' coach journey the rest of the way. Thus, along these few miles at anyrate, coaching survived on the Cambridge road until 1851, when the Great Eastern built a short line from Shelford to Foxton and Shepreth, to join the Great Northern branch, allowing running-powers to that Company into Cambridge station.

Harston village succeeds to Foxton. Its present name is a corruption of "Harleston," which itself was a contraction of "Hardeliston." It stands at a bend of the road, with a very small village green and a very large church to the left, and the long village street of small cottages and large gardens following the high road, and bringing the traveller presently to an inn—the Old English Gentleman—where the Barkway route to Cambridge meets this; both thenceforward joining forces for the remaining four miles and a half. Hauxton Church starts up on the right, by the Granta, which comes down from Audley End and is crossed here, over a little bridge, the only striking object in what has now become a very desolate road, so lonely and empty that an occasional thorn-tree, rising from the dwarf hedges of the immense flat fields, becomes quite companionable, and a distant clump of leafy elms a landmark. Those distant trees mark where Trumpington village church lies hid, and, if the horizon ahead be closely scanned, the long line of King's College Chapel will presently be seen. We are coming at last into Cambridge.

## XXI

THE entrance to Cambridge town through Trumpington is singularly noble and dignified. This is an age when almost every ancient town or city is approached through a ring of modern suburbs, but Cambridge is one of the few and happy exceptions. You cannot enter Oxford by the old coach road from London without passing through the modern suburb of St. Clements, whose mean street pitifully discounts the approach to the city over Magdalen Bridge; but at first, when nearing Cambridge, nothing breaks the flat landscape save the distant view of King's College Chapel, that gigantic pile of stone whose long flat skyline and four angle-turrets so wrought upon Ruskin's feelings that he compared it with a billiard-table turned upside down. It is not because of the great Chapel that the entrance to Cambridge is noble: it will add nothing to the beauty of the scene until that day—perhaps never to come—when the building shall be completed with a stately belltower after the design contemplated by its founder, Henry the Sixth. No; it is rather by reason, firstly, of the broad quiet rural village street of Trumpington, set humbly, as it were, in the gates of learning, and secondly of the still broad and quiet, but more urban, Trumpington Road that follows it, that Cambridge is so charmingly entered. A line of old gabled cottages with old-fashioned gardens occupies either side of the road; while an ancient mansion or two, together with the village church, are hid, or perhaps glimpsed for a moment, off to the left, where a by-road goes off, past the old toll-house, to Grantchester. This is Trumpington. In that churchyard lies a remarkable man : none other, indeed, than Henry Fawcett—we will not call him by his title of "Professor," for that seems always so blatant a dignity —who died at Cambridge in 1884, thus ending a life that had risen triumphant above, surely, the keenest affliction Fate can inflict. Completely blinded in youth by an accident of the most deplorable kind, he yet lived to fill a career in life and politics apparently denied by loss of sight. The text on his gravestone — a garbled passage from Exodus, chap. xiv. ver. 15—is singularly appropriate : "Speak unto the people, that they go forward."

It is down this leafy by-way, past the church, that one finds Grantchester Mill, a building generally thought to occupy the site of that "Trumpington Mill" made famous in one of Chaucer's *Canterbury Tales.*

For Trumpington has a certain literary fame, in association with Chaucer's "Reeve's Tale":—

> "At Trompington, not fer fro Cantebrigge,
> Ther goth a brook, and over that a brigge,
> Upon the whiche brook ther stout a melle."

The "Reeve's Tale" is not precisely a part of Chaucer to be discussed in every drawing-room, and is indeed a story well calculated to make a satyr laugh and the judicious grieve. Therefore, it is perhaps no great pity that the mill stands no longer, so that you cannot actually seek it out and say, "Here the proud Simon, the 'insolent Simkin,' ground the people's corn, taking dishonest toll of it, and hereabouts those roystering blades of University scholars, Allen and John, played their pranks." Grantchester Mill is a building wholly modern.

It is a grave and dignified road, tree-shaded and echoing to the drowsy cawing of rooks (like tired professors weary of lecturing to inattentive classes), that conducts along the high road through Trumpington village to the beginnings of the town. Here, by the bridge crossing the little stream called the "Vicar's Brook," one mile from Great St. Mary's Church, the very centre of Cambridge, stands the eight-foot high milestone, the first in the series set up between Cambridge and Barkway in the early years of the eighteenth century, and paid for out of "Dr. Mouse's and Mr. Hare's Causey Money." This initial stone cost £5, 8s. The arms of Dr. Mouse may still be traced, impaling those of Trinity Hall.

Beyond this hoary but little-noticed relic begin

TRUMPINGTON MILL.

the Botanic Gardens, and beside them runs or creeps that old Cambridge water-supply, the "little new river," brought in 1610 from the Nine Wells under yonder gentle hills that break the flatness of the landscape away on the right.

The idea of bringing pure water into Cambridge

THE FIRST MILESTONE FROM CAMBRIDGE.

originated, in 1574, with a certain Dr. Perne, Master of Peterhouse; its object both to cleanse the King's Ditch, "which," says Fuller, "once made to defend Cambridge by its strength, did in his time offend it with its stench," and to provide drinking water for the University and town. This clear-running stream has an interest beyond its local use, for the cutting of its course was designed by Edward Wright, of Gonville and Caius College, who also drew the plans for Sir Hugh Myddleton's "New River," whose course so closely neighbours this old road between Ware and London.

The Conduit — "Hobson's Conduit," as it is called—that once stood on Market Hill, was removed in 1854, and now stands at the very beginning of Cambridge, where Trumpington "Road" becomes "Street," at the head of this open stream.

The Nine Wells are not easy to find. They are situated near the village of Great Shelford, under a shoulder of the Gog Magog Hills, and are approached across two rugged pastures, almost impracticable in wet weather. The term "wells" is misleading. They are springs, found trickling feebly through the white clay in the bed of a deep trench with two branches, cut in the hillside. Above them stands a granite obelisk erected by public subscription in 1861, and setting forth all the circumstances at great length. The term "Nine Wells" is not especially applied to this spot, but is used throughout Cambridgeshire for springs, whatever their number. A similar custom obtained in classic Greece, but the evidence by which our Cambridgeshire practice might possibly be derived from such a respectable source, and so be linked with the Pierian spring and the Muses Nine, is entirely lacking.

The Gog Magogs—"the Gogs," as the country-

folk irreverently abbreviate their mysterious name—
are the Cambridgeshire mountains. They are not
particularly Alpine in character, being, indeed, just
a series of gently rising grassy downs, culminating
in a height of three hundred feet above sea-level.

HOBSON'S CONDUIT.

No one will ever be able to explain how these very
mild hills obtained their terrific title; and Gog and
Magog themselves, mentioned vaguely in Revelations,
where the devil is let loose again after his thousand

years' imprisonment in the bottomless pit, are equally inexplicable.

The crowning height of the Gog Magogs was in Roman times the summer camp of a cohort of Vandals, quartered in this district to overawe the conquered British. It was then the policy of Rome, as it is of ourselves in India and elsewhere at the present day, to enrol into her service the strange tribes and alien nations she had conquered, and to bring them from afar to impress her newest subjects with the far-reaching might and glory of the Empire. This Vandalian cohort was formed from the barbarian prisoners defeated on the Danube by Aurelian, and enlisted by the Emperor Probus. The earthworks of their camp are still traceable within the grounds of the mansion and estate of Vandlebury, on the hilltop, once belonging to the Duke of Leeds. From this point of view Cambridge is seen mapped out below, while in other directions the great rolling fields spread downwards in fold upon fold. Immense fields they are, enclosed in the early years of last century, when Cambridgeshire began to change its immemorial aspect of open treeless downs, where the sheep grazed on the short grass and the bustard still lingered, for its present highly cultivated condition. Fields of this comparatively recent origin may generally be recognised by their great size, in striking contrast with the ancient enclosures whose area was determined by the work of hand-ploughing. These often measure over half a mile square, and mark the advent of the steam-plough.

## XXII

THE old Cambridge water-supply, meandering down from the hills, has induced a similar discursiveness in these last pages. Onward from Trumpington Road it runs in a direct line to the Conduit, and our course shall, in sympathy, be as straight.

The Fitzwilliam Museum is the first public building to attract notice on entering the town: a huge institution in the classic style, notable for the imposing Corinthian columns that decorate its front; its effect marred by the stone screen that interrupts the view up the noble flights of steps. "The Fitzbilly," as all Cambridge men know it, derives from the noble collections of art objects and antiquities, together with great sums of money, left to the University in 1816 by a Lord Fitzwilliam for the establishment of a museum and art gallery. It was completed some forty years ago, and has since then been the great architectural feature in the first glimpse of Cambridge. The coloured marble decorations and the painting and gilding of the interior are grandiose rather than grand; and although the collections, added to by many later bequests, contain many priceless and beautiful objects, the effect of the whole is a kind of mental and optical indigestion caused by the "fine confused feeding" afforded by the very mixed arrangement of these treasures,—a bad arrangement, like that of an overgrown private collection, and utterly unsuited for public and educational needs. You turn from a manuscript to a picture, from a picture to a case of china, from that to missals, and so all through the varied incarnations of art throughout the centuries.

Just beyond the Fitzwilliam Museum comes Peterhouse College, the oldest of all the colleges in the University. To understand something of the meaning of the colleges and their relation to the supreme teaching and governing body, it will be necessary to recount, as briefly as may be, the circumstances in which both University and Colleges had their origin.

The origin of Cambridge University, as of that of Oxford, is of unknown date, and the manner of its inception problematical. Who was the great teacher that first drew scholars to him at this place? We cannot tell. That he was a Churchman goes without saying, for the Church, in the dark ages when learning began to be, held letters and culture in fee-simple. Nor can we tell why Cambridge was thus honoured, for it was not the home, like Ely, Crowland, or Thorney, of a great monastic establishment, whence learning of sorts radiated. One of the untrustworthy early chroniclers of these things gives, indeed, a specific date to the beginnings of the University, and says that Joffrid, Abbot of Crowland, in 1110 sent monkish lecturers to the town; but the earliest record, beyond which we must not go into the regions of mere surmise, belongs to a hundred and twenty-one years later, when royal regulations respecting the students were issued. Already a Chancellor and a complete governing body appear to have been in existence. It is arguable that a century and more

TRUMPINGTON STREET, CAMBRIDGE.

must have been necessary for these to have been evolved from the earliest days of a teaching body; but these affairs are for pundits. Such special pleaders as John Caius and Thomas Key, who fought with great bitterness and amazing pertinacity in the sixteenth century on the question as to whether Oxford or Cambridge were the older of the two, had the hardihood to trace them back to astonishing lengths. According to Caius, arguing for Cambridge, it was one Cantaber, a Spanish prince, who founded the University here in the very remote days when Gurguntius was King of Britain. To this prince he traces the name of the town itself, and I think that fact alone serves to discredit anything else he has to say.

But no matter when and how the University originated. To those early teachers came so many to listen in the one room or hall, that probably constituted the original University, that the town did not suffice to accommodate them, and, both for the sake of convenience and discipline, the first college was founded, as primarily a lodgment or hostel for the scholars. As their numbers continually grew, and as benefactors began to look with increasing kindliness upon learning, so were more and more colleges added.

The first of all the colleges was, as already stated, this of Peterhouse, founded so far back as 1280 by Hugh de Balsham, Bishop of Ely. It was at first established in the Hospital of St. John the Evangelist, near by, but was removed, only six years later, to the present site, for convenient access to the Church of St. Peter. It is to the fact that the chancel of this church was used as its chapel that the college owes its official but rarely heard title of "St. Peter's." In 1352 St. Peter's Church was given a new consecration, and has ever since been known as St. Mary the Less. Meanwhile, in 1632, the college built a chapel of its own.

Peterhouse has points of interest other than being the first of the colleges. It has nurtured men not only of distinction, but of fame. Men so opposite in character as the worldly Cardinal Beaufort — the great Cardinal who figures in Shakespeare — and the pious Archbishop Whitgift were educated here; and in later times that great man of science, Lord Kelvin; but perhaps the most famous of all is Gray, the poet, whose "Elegy Wrote in a Country Churchyard" has done more to endear him to his country than the acts of any statesman or divine.

Peterhouse does not present a cheerful front to the street. It is heavy and gloomy, and its buildings, as a whole, do not help out the story of its age. The chapel, whose weather-vane bears the emblem of a key, an allusion to St. Peter, stands recessed behind the railings that give upon the street, and blocks the view into the first of the three quads. It is flanked on one side by the venerable brick building seen on the extreme left of the illustration representing Trumpington Street, and on the other by a great ugly three-storeyed block of stone, interesting only because the rooms overlooking the street on the topmost floor were those occupied by Gray. They are to be identified by iron railings across one of the windows. A story belongs to these rooms.

Gray, it seems, lived long in them as a Fellow of his College, and might have eked out his morbid life here, dining according to habit in Hall, and then, unsociable and morose, retiring to his elevated eyrie, reading the classics over a bottle of port. Gray had a very pretty taste in port, but it did not suffice to make him more clubbable. His solitary habits, perhaps, were responsible for a morbid fear of fire that grew upon him, and increased to such a degree that he caused the transverse bars, that still remain, to be placed outside his window overlooking the churchyard of Little St. Mary's, and kept in constant readiness a coil of rope to tie to them and so let himself down in case of an alarm. His precautions were matters of common knowledge, and at last his fears were taken advantage of by a band of skylarking students, who placed a bath full of water beneath his rooms one winter night and then, placing themselves in a favourable position for seeing the fun, raised cries of "Fire!"

Their best expectations were realised. The window was hurriedly flung up, and the frenzied poet, nightcapped and lightly clad, swiftly descended into the bath, amid yells of delight. These intimate facts seem to hint that Gray had not endeared himself to the scholars of Peterhouse. This practical joke severed his connection with the college, for he immediately removed across the street, to Pembroke.

Pembroke is prominent in this view down the long, quiet, grave street; and the quaint turret of its chapel, built by Sir Christopher Wren, is very noticeable. Gravity is, we have said, the note here, and so solid a quality is quite in order, for Trumpington Street and the road beyond have ever been the favourite walks of dons and professors, walking oblivious to their surroundings in what we are bound to consider academic meditation rather than that mere mental vacuity known as absent-mindedness. There is a story told of the late Professor Seeley exquisitely illustrating this mental detachment. It is a story that probably has been told of many earlier professors, to be re-incarnated to suit every succeeding age : a common enough thing with legends. It seems, however, that the late Professor of History was walking past the Conduit one fine day, speculating on who shall say what abstruse matters, when a mischievous boy switched a copious shower of water over him from the little stream in the gutter. The Professor's physical organism felt the descending drops, some lazy, unspeculative brain-cell gave him the idea of a shower of rain, and he immediately unfurled his umbrella, and so walked home.

Next the new buildings of Pembroke, over against Peterhouse, the Master of that college has his residence, behind the high brick walls of a seventeenth century garden. On the left hand are Little St. Mary's, a Congregational Church, and the church-like pinnacled square tower of the Pitt Press, all in succession. Beyond, but hid from this view-point by a gentle curve of the street, are " Cats," otherwise St. Catherine's, and Corpus ; and then we come to that continuation of Trumpington Street called " King's Parade," opposite King's College. Here we are at the centre of Cambridge, with Market Hill opening out on the right and the gigantic bulk of King's College Chapel on the left, neighboured by that fount of honour, or scene of disgraceful failure, the beautiful classic Senate House, where you take your degree or are ignominiously "plucked."

In midst of Market Hill stands the church of Great St. Mary's, the University Church. Town and University are at this point inextricably mixed. Shops and churches, colleges, divinity schools and Town Hall all jostle one another around this wide open space, void on most days, but on Saturday so crowded with the canopied stalls of the market that it presents one vast area of canvas. Few markets are so well supplied with flowers as this, for in summertime growing plants are greatly in demand by the undergrads to decorate the windows of their lodgings. This living outside the colleges is, and has always been, a marked feature of Cambridge, where college accommodation has never kept pace with requirements. It is a system that makes the town cheerful and lively in term, but at vacation times, when the "men" have all "gone down," its emptiness is correspondingly noticeable. To "go down" and to "come up" are, by the way, terms that require some little explanation beyond their obvious meaning of leaving or of arriving at the University. They had their origin in the old-standing dignity of Alma Mater, requiring that all other places should be considered below her—even the mighty Gog Magogs themselves. From Cambridge to London or elsewhere is therefore a καταβασις—a going downward.

The Cambridge system of lodging out does not

make for discipline, and creates a lamentable laxity in a man keeping his proper quota of chapels. To attend chapel at an early hour of the morning seems much more of an infliction when living in the freedom of lodgings than when in the cloistered shades of a college quad, and has led to many absences, summonses before the Dean, and mild lectures from that generally estimable and other-worldly personage. You, in the innocence of your heart and your first term, advance the excuse that late study makes it difficult to always keep chapels. Observe that it is *always* midnight study, never card-parties and the like, and never that very natural disinclination to turn out of bed in the morning that is answerable for these backslidings. All very specious and unoriginal, and that Dean has heard it all before, so many times, and years and years ago, from men now gone into the world and become middle-aged. Why, in his own youth *he* gave and attended parties, and missed chapels, and made these ancient blue-mouldy prevarications to the Dean of *his* college,—and so back and back to the infinities. Is he angry: does he personally care a little bit? Not at all. It is routine. "Don't you think, young man," he says, in his best pulpit-cum-grandfather style, "don't you think that if you were to *try* to study in the morning it would be much better for your health, much better in every way than reading at night? When I was *your* age *I* studied at night. It gave me headaches. Now try and keep chapel. It is *so* much better to become used to habits of discipline. They are of such value to us in after life"—and so forth.

## XXIII

CAMBRIDGE is often criticised because it is not Oxford. As well might one find fault with a lily because it is not a rose. Criticism of this kind starts with the belief that it is a worse Oxford, an inferior copy of the sister University. How false that is, and how entirely Cambridge is itself in outward appearance and in intellectual aims need not be insisted upon. It is true that Trumpington Street does not rival "the High" at Oxford, but it was not built with the object of imitating that famous academic street; and if indeed the Isis be a more noble stream than the Cam, Oxford at least has nothing to compare with the Cambridge "Backs."

"The Backs" are the peculiar glory of Cambridge, and he who has not seen them has missed much. They are the back parts of those of the colleges— Queens', King's, Clare, Trinity, and John's—whose courts and beautiful lawns extend from the main street back to the Cam, that much-abused and much idealised stream.

"The Cam," says a distinguished member of the University, with a horrid lack of enthusiasm for the surroundings of Alma Mater, "is scarcely a river at all; above the town it is a brook; below the town it is little better than a sewer." Can this, you wonder, be the same as that "Camus, reverend sire," of the poets; the stream that "went footing slow, His mantle hairy and his bonnet sedge."

That, undoubtedly, is too severe. Above the

town it is a brook that will at anyrate float such craft as Cambridge possesses, and has shady nooks like " Paradise " and Byron's Pool, where the canoe can be navigated and bathing of the best may be found; and now that Cambridge colleges no longer drain into the river, the stream below town does not deserve that reproach. Everything, it seems, depends upon your outlook. If you are writing academic odes, for example, like Gray's, you praise the Cam; if, like Gray again, writing on an unofficial occasion, you enlarge upon its sluggish pace and its mud. Gray, it will be observed, could be a dissembling poet. His "Installation Ode," as official in its way as the courtly lines of a Poet Laureate, pictures Cambridge delightfully, in the lines he places in the mouth of Milton—

> " Ye brown, o'er-arching groves,
>   That contemplation loves,
> Where willowy Camus lingers with delight!
>   Oft at the blush of dawn
>   I trod your level lawn—
> Oft wooed the gleam of Cynthia, silver bright,
> In cloisters dim, far from the haunts of Folly,
> With Freedom by my side, and soft-eyed Melancholy."

Few lines in the whole range of our poetry are so beautiful as these.

But Gray's own private and unofficial idea of the Cam was very different. When he took the gag off his Muse and allowed her to be frank, we hear of the " rushy Camus," whose

> " . . . Slowly-winding flood
> Perpetual draws his humid train of mud."

Yet " the Backs " give a picture of mingled

architecture, stately trees, emerald lawns, and placid stream not to be matched anywhere else: an ideal picture of what a poet's University should be. If, on entering the town from Trumpington Street, you turn to the left past the Leys School, down the lane called Coe Fen, you come first upon the Cam where it is divided into many little streams running and subdividing and joining together again in the oozy pasture of Sheep's Green, and then to a water-mill. Beyond that mill begin "the Backs," with Queens' College, whose ancient walls of red brick, like some building of romance, rise sheer from the water. From them springs a curious "mathematical" wooden bridge, spanning the river and leading from the college to the shady walks on the opposite side.

With so dreamy and beautiful a setting, it is not surprising that Cambridge, although the education she gave was long confined largely to the unimaginative science or art of mathematics, has been especially productive of poets. Dryden was an alumnus of Trinity; Milton sucked wisdom at Christ's; Wordsworth, of John's, wrote acres of verse as flat as the Cambridgeshire meads, and much more arid; Byron drank deep and roystered at King's; and Tennyson was a graduate of Trinity. Other poets owning allegiance to Cambridge are that sweet Elizabethan songster, Robert Herrick, Marlowe, Waller, Cowley, Prior, Coleridge, and Praed. Poetry, in short, is in the moist relaxing air of Cambridge, and in those

". . . . brown o'er-arching groves
That contemplation loves."

Cambridge would stand condemned were poets its only product. Fortunately, as some proof of the practical value of an University education, it can point to men like Cromwell, Pitt, and Macaulay, whose strenuous lives have in their several ways left a mark on the nation's history. Though one be not a champion of Cromwell's career, yet his savagery, his duplicity, his canting hypocrisy fade into the background and lose their significance beside the firmness of purpose, the iron determination and the wise policy that made England respected and feared abroad under the rule of the Protector. The beheading of a King weighs little in the scale against the upholding of the dignity of the State; and though a sour Puritanism ruled the land under the great Oliver, at least the guns of a foreign foe were never heard in our estuaries under the Commonwealth, as they were heard after the Restoration. Cambridge gives no sign that she is proud of Oliver, neither does Sidney Sussex, his old college. But if Cambridge be not outwardly proud of Old Noll, she abundantly glories in William Pitt. And rightly, too. None may calculate how the equation stands: how greatly his natural parts or to what extent his seven years of University education contributed to his brilliant career; but for one of her sons to have attained the dignity of Chancellor of the Exchequer at twenty-three years of age, to have been Prime Minister at twenty-five, the political dictator of Europe and the saviour of his country, is a triumph beyond anything they can show on the Isis. The Pitt Press, the Pitt Scholarship, the Pitt Club, all echo the fame of his astonishing genius.

## XXIV

THE impossibility of giving even a glimpse of the principal colleges of Cambridge in these pages of a book devoted to the road will be obvious. Thus, the great quads of Trinity, the many courts of John's, Milton's mulberry tree at Christ's, the Pepysian Library of Magdalen, and a hundred other things must be sought elsewhere. Turn we, then, to further talk of Thomas Hobson, the carrier and livery-stable keeper of "Hobson's Choice," who lies in an unmarked resting-place in the chancel of St. Benedict's Church, hard by the Market Hill. Born in 1544, he was not a native of Cambridge, but seems to have first seen the light at Buntingford, his father's native place. Already, in that father's time, the business had grown so profitable and important that we find Hobson senior a treasurer of the Cambridge Corporation; and when he died, in 1568, in a position to leave considerable landed and other property among his family. To Thomas, his more famous son, he bequeathed land at Grantchester and the waggon and horses that industrious son had been for some years past driving between Cambridge and London for him, with the surety and regularity of the solar system. "I bequeath," he wrote, "to my son Thomas the team-ware that he now goeth with, that is to say, the cart and eight horses, and all the harness and other things thereunto belonging, with the nag, to be delivered to him at such time and when as he shall attain and come to the age of twenty-five years; or £30 in money, for and in discharge thereof."

And thus he continued to go once a week, back and forth, for close upon sixty-three years, riding the nag and its successors beside the waggon that ploughed its ponderous way along the heavy roads. An ancient portrait of him, a large painting in oil, is now in the Cambridge Guildhall, and inscribed, "Mr. Hobson, 1620." This contemporary portrait has the curious information written on the back, "This picture was hung up at Ye Black Bull inn, Bishopsgate, London, upwards of one hundred years before it was given to J. Bûrleigh 1787."

Hobson scarce fitted the picture of the "jolly waggoner" drawn in the old song. Have you ever heard the song of the "Jolly Waggoner"? It is a song of lightly come and lightly go; of drinking with good fellows while the waggon and horses are standing long hours outside the wayside inn, and consignees are waiting with what patience they may for their goods. A song that bids dull care begone, and draws for you a lively sketch of the typical waggoner, who lived for the moment, whistled as he went in attempted rivalry with the hedgerow thrushes and blackbirds, spent his money as he earned it, and had a greeting, a ribbon, and a kiss for every lass along the familiar highway.

It is a song that goes to a reckless and flamboyant

HOBSON, THE CAMBRIDGE CARRIER.

"Laugh not to see so plain a man in print;
The Shadow's homely, yet ther's something in't.
Witness the Bagg he wears, (though seeming poore)
The fertile Mother of a hundred more;
He was a thriving man, through lawfull Gain,
And wealthy grew by warrantable paine,
    Then laugh at them that spend, not them that gather,
    Like thriveing Sonnes of such a thrifty Father."

tune, an almost Handelian melody that is sung with a devil-may-care toss of the head and much emphasis; a rare, sweet, homely old country ditty—

"When first I went a-waggoning, a-waggoning did go,
 I filled my parents' hearts with sorrow, trouble, grief, and woe;
 And many are the hardships, too, that since I have gone through.
   Sing wo! my lads, sing wo!
   Drive on, my lads, heigh-ho!
   For who can live the life that we jolly waggoners do?

It is a cold and stormy night: I'm wetted to the skin,
But I'll bear it with contentment till I get me to my inn,
And then I'll sit a-drinking with the landlord and his kin.
   Sing wo! my lads, etc.

Now summer is a-coming on—what pleasure we shall see!
The mavis and the blackbird singing sweet on every tree.
The finches and the starlings, too, will whistle merrily.
   Sing wo! my lads, etc.

Now Michaelmas is coming fast—what pleasure we shall find!
'Twill make the gold to fly, my lads, like chaff before the wind.
And every lad shall kiss his lass, so loving and so kind.
   Sing wo!" etc.

  And so forth.

  Hobson was not this kind of man. He had his horse-letting business in Cambridge, where, indeed, he had forty saddle-nags always ready, "fit for travelling, with boots, bridle, and whip, to furnish the gentlemen at once, without going from college to college to borrow"; but he continued throughout his long life to go personally with his waggon, and died January 1st, 1631, in his eighty-sixth year, of the irksome and unaccustomed inaction imposed upon him by the authorities, who forbade him to ply to London while one of the periodical outbreaks of plague was raging in the capital. Dependable in business as Hobson was, he prospered exceedingly, and amassed a very considerable fortune, "a much greater fortune," says one, "than a thousand men of genius and learning, educated at the University, ever acquired, or were capable of acquiring." This is not a little hard on the learned and the gifted, by whose favour and goodwill he prospered so amazingly. For, be it known, he was not merely and solely *a* carrier; but *the* carrier, especially licensed by the University, and thus a monopolist. Those were the days before a Government monopoly of the post was established, and one of Hobson's particular functions was the conveying of the mails. He was thus a very serious and responsible person.

You cannot conceive Hobson "carrying on" like the typical "jolly waggoner." Look at the portrait of him, taken from a fresco painted on a wall of his old house of call, the Bull, in Bishopsgate Street. A very grave and staid old man it shows us; looking out upon the world with cold and calculating eyes, deep-set beneath knitted brows, and with a long and money-loving, yet cautious, nose. His hand is unwillingly extracting a guinea from a well-filled money-bag, and you may clearly see from his expression of countenance how much rather he would be putting one in.

Yet in his last years he appeared in the guise of a benefactor to the town of Cambridge, for in 1628 he gave to town and University the land on which was built the so-called "Spinning House," or, more correctly, "Hobson's Workhouse," where poor people who had no trade might be taught some honest one, and all stubborn rogues and beggars be compelled to earn their livelihood. A bequest providing for the maintenance of the water-conduit in the Market Place kept his memory green for many a long year afterwards. It remained a prominent

HOBSON.
[*From a Painting in Cambridge Guildhall.*]

object in the centre of the town until 1856, when it was removed; but the little watercourses that of old used to run along the kennels of Cambridge streets still serve to keep the place clean and sweet.

It cannot be too strongly insisted upon that Hobson, although he fared the road personally, and attended to every petty detail of his carrying business, was both a very wealthy and a very important personage. The second condition is not necessarily a corollary of the first. But Hobson bulked large in the Cambridge of his time. Indeed, as much may be gathered from the mass of literature written around his name. In his lifetime even, some compiler of a Commercial Letter Writer, for instructing youths ignorant of affairs, could find no more apt and taking title than that of *Hobson's Horse Load of Letters, or Precedents for Epistles of Business*; and poets and verse-writers, from Milton downwards, wrote many epitaphs and eulogies on him. Milton, who had gone up to Christ's College in 1624, was twenty-three years of age when Hobson died, and wrote two humorous epitaphs on him, more akin to the manner of Tom Hood than the majestic periods usually associated in the mind with the style commonly called "Miltonic." "Quibbling epitaphs" an eighteenth century critic has called them. But you shall judge—

"On the University Carrier, who sickened in the time of the Vacancy, being forbid to go to London by reason of the Plague.

Here lies old Hobson : Death hath broke his girt,
And here, alas! hath laid him in the dirt;
Or else, the ways being foul, twenty to one
He's here stuck in a slough and overthrown.
'Twas such a shifter that, if truth were known,
Death was half glad when he had got him down;
For he had any time this ten years full
Dodged with him betwixt Cambridge and the Bull;
And, surely, Death could never have prevailed,
Had not his weekly course of carriage failed;
But, lately, finding him so long at home,
And thinking now his journey's end was come,

And that he had taken up his latest inn,
In the kind office of a Chamberlain
Showed him his room where he must lodge that night,
Pulled off his boots, and took away the light:
If any ask for him, it shall be said,
'Hobson hath supped, and's newly gone to bed.'"

The subject seems to have been an engrossing one to the youthful poet, for he harked back to it in the following variant:—

"Here lieth one who did most truly prove
That he could never die while he could move;
So hung his destiny, never to rot
While he might still jog on and keep his trot,
Made of sphere-metal, never to decay
Until his revolution was at stay!
Time numbers motion, yet (without a crime
'Gainst old truth) motion numbered out his time;
And, like an engine moved with wheel and weight,
His principles being ceased, he ended straight.
Rest, that gives all men life, gave him his death,
And too much breathing put him out of breath;
Nor were it contradiction to affirm
Too long *vacation* hastened on his *term*;
Merely to drive the time away he sickened,
Fainted and died, nor would with ale be quickened.
'Nay,' quoth he, on his swooning bed outstretched,
'If I may not carry, sure I'll ne'er be fetched;
But vow' (though the cross Doctors all stood hearers)
'For one *carrier* put down, to make six *bearers*.'
Ease was his chief disease, and, to judge right,
He died for heaviness that his cart went light;
His leisure told him that his time was come,
And lack of load made his life burdensome;
That even to his last breath, (there be that say't,)
As he were pressed to death, he cried 'More weight!'
But, had his doings lasted as they were,
He had been an immortal Carrier.
Obedient to the moon, he spent his date
In course reciprocal, and had his fate

Linked to the mutual flowing of the seas;
Yet, strange to think, his *wain* was his *increase*;
His letters are delivered all and gone;
Only remains this superscription."

The next example—an anonymous one—makes no bad third—

"Here Hobson lies among his many betters,
A man unlearned, yet a man of letters;
His carriage was well known, oft hath he gone
In Embassy 'twixt father and the son:
There's few in Cambridge, to his praise be't spoken,
But may remember him by some good Token.
From whence he rid to London day by day,
Till Death benighting him, he lost his way:
His Team was of the best, nor would he have
Been mired in any way but in the grave.
And there he stycks, indeed, styll like to stand,
Untill some Angell lend hys helpyng hand.
Nor is't a wonder that he thus is gone,
Since all men know, he long was drawing on.
Thus rest in peace thou everlasting Swain,
And Supream Waggoner, next Charles his wain."

The couplet printed below touches a pretty note of imagination, and is wholly free from that suspicion of affected scholarly superiority to a common carrier, with which all the others, especially Milton's, are super-saturated—

"Hobson's not dead, but Charles the Northerne swaine,
Hath sent for him, to draw his lightsome waine."

Charles's Wain, referred to in these two last examples, is, of course, that well-known constellation in the northern heavens usually known as the Great Bear, anciently "Charlemagne's Waggon," and more anciently still, the Greek Hamaxa, "the Waggon."

Coming, as might be expected, a considerable distance after Milton and the others in point of excellence, are the epitaphs printed in a little book of 1640, called the *Witt's Recreations, Selected from the Finest Fancies of the Modern Muses.* Some of them are a little gruesome, and affect the reader as unfavourably as though he saw the authors of these lines dancing a saraband on poor old Hobson's grave—

> "Hobson (what's out of sight is out of mind)
> Is gone, and left his letters here behind.
> He that with so much paper us'd to meet;
> Is now, alas! content to take one sheet.
>
> He that such carriage store was wont to have,
> Is carried now himselfe unto his grave:
> O strange! he that in life ne're made but one,
> Six Carriers makes, now he is dead and gone."

## XXV

The Market Hill is, as already hinted, the centre of Cambridge. The University church is there. There, too, the stalls of the Wednesday and Saturday markets still gather thickly, and on them the inquisitive stranger may yet discover butter being sold, as from time immemorial, by the yard. Here a yard of butter is the equivalent of a pound, and the standard gauge of such a yard—the obsolete symbol of a time when the University exercised jurisdiction over the markets as well as over the students—is to this day handed over to the Senior Proctor of the year on his taking office. It is a clumsy cylinder of sheet iron, a yard in length and an inch in diameter. A pound of butter rolled out to this measurement looks remarkably like a very yellow candle of inordinate length.

Hobson's Conduit, as already noted, once stood in the centre of this market-place. When his silent, hook-nosed Majesty, William the Third, visited

MARKET HILL, CAMBRIDGE.

Cambridge in 1689, the Conduit was made by the enthusiastic citizens to run wine. Not much wine, though, nor very good, we may surely suppose, for the tell-tale account-books record that it cost only thirty shillings!

Few of the old coach-offices or inns stood in this square, but were—and are now—to be found chiefly in the streets leading out of it. The Bull, anciently the Black Bull, still faces Trumpington

Street; the Lion flourishes in Petty Cury; the old Three Tuns, Peas Hill, is now the Central Temperance Hotel; and the Blue Boar, in whose archway an unfortunate clergyman, the Reverend Gavin Braithwaite, was killed in 1814 when seated on the roof of the Ipswich coach, still faces Trinity Street. The Sun, however, in Trinity Street, where

THE FALCON, CAMBRIDGE.

Byron and his cronies dined and caroused, is no more; and of late years the Woolpack and the Wrestlers, both very ancient buildings, have been demolished. Foster's Bank stands on the site of one and the new Post Office on that of the other. For a while the remains of the galleried, tumbledown

Falcon, stand in a court off Petty Cury; the inn in whose yard Cambridge students entertained and

INTERIOR OF ST. SEPULCHRE'S CHURCH.

shocked Queen Elizabeth with a blasphemous stage travesty of the Mass. In Bridge Street stands the

Hoop, notable in its day, and celebrated by Wordsworth—

> "Onward we drove beneath the Castle; caught,
> While crossing Magdalen Bridge, a glimpse of Cam;
> And at the Hoop alighted, famous inn."

Beyond the Hoop, the quaintly-named Pickerel Inn stands by Magdalen, or Great Bridge, just as it did in days when the carriers dumped down their loads here, to be transferred to the passage-boats for Ely and King's Lynn. In Benet Street the Eagle, once the Eagle and Child, still discloses a courtyard curiously galleried, and hard by is the old Bath Hotel. This list practically exhausts the old coaching inns, but of queer hostelries of other kinds there are many, with nodding gables and latticed windows, in every other lane and by-way. Churches, too, abound. Oldest among these is St. Sepulchre's, one of the four round churches in England; a dark Norman building that in the blackness of its interior accurately figures the grimness of the Norman mind.

## XXVI

CAMBRIDGE, now a town abounding in and surrounded by noble trees, was originally a British settlement, placed on that bold spur of high ground, rising from the surrounding treeless mires, on which in after years the Romans established their military post of Camboricum, and where in later ages William the Conqueror built his castle. The great artificial mound, which, like some ancient sepulchral tumulus, is all that remains to tell of William's fortress and to mark where Roman and Briton had originally seized upon this strategic point, crowns this natural bluff, overlooking the river Cam. Standing on it, with the whole of Cambridge town and a wide panorama of low-lying surrounding country disclosed, it is evident that this must have been the place of places for many miles on either hand where, in those remote

CAMBRIDGE CASTLE A HUNDRED YEARS AGO.

days, the river could be crossed. Everywhere else the wide-spreading swamps forbade a passage; and, consequently, those who held this position, and could keep it, could deny the whole country to the passage of a hostile force from either side. Whether one enemy sought to penetrate from London to Ely and Norfolk, or whether another would come out of Norfolk into South Cambridgeshire or Herts, he must first of necessity dispose of those who held the key of this situation. The Romans, before they could subdue the masters of this position, experienced, we may well believe, no little difficulty; and it is probable that the perplexity of antiquaries, confronted by the existence of a Roman camp or station here, and of another three miles higher up the Cam at Grantchester, may be smoothed out by the very reasonable explanation that Grantchester was the first Roman camp over against the British stronghold at Cambridge, and that, when the Romans had made themselves masters of Cambridge, that place remained their military post, while Grantchester became a civil and trading community and a place of residence.

Both place-names derive from this one river, masquerading now as the Granta and again as the Cam, but by what name the Romans knew Grantchester we do not know and never shall.

At Roman Camboricum those ancient roads, the Akeman Street and the Via Devana, crossed at right angles, meeting here on this very Castle hill: the Via Devana on its way from Colchester to the town of *Deva*, now Chester; the Akeman Street going from *Branodunum*, now Brancaster, on the coast of Norfolk, to *Aquæ Solis*, the Bath of our own day.

Cambridge Castle, built in 1068 by William the Conqueror to hold Hereward the Saxon and his East Anglian fellow-patriots in check, has entirely disappeared. It never accumulated any legends of sieges or surprises, and of military history it had none whatever. It was, therefore, a castle of the greatest possible success; for, consider, although the first impulse may be to think little of a fortress that can tell no warlike story, the very lack of anything of the kind is the best proof of its strength and fitness. It is not the purpose of a castle to invite attacks, but by its very menace to overawe and terrify. Torquilstone Castle and the story of its siege and downfall, in the pages of *Ivanhoe*, make romantic and exciting reading; but, inasmuch as it fell, it was a failure. That Cambridge Castle not only never fell, but was not even menaced, is the best proof of its power.

These great fortresses, with their stone keeps and spreading wards and baileys, dotted here and there over the land, rang the knell of English liberties. "New and strong and cruel in their strength—how the Englishman must have loathed the damp smell of the fresh mortar, and the sight of the heaps of rubble, and the chippings of the stone, and the blurring of the lime upon the greensward; and how hopeless he must have felt when the great gates opened and the wains were drawn in, heavily laden with the salted beeves and the sacks of corn and meal furnished by the royal demesnes, the manors which had belonged to Edward the Confessor, now the spoil of the stranger; and when he looked into the castle court, thronged by the soldiers in bright mail, and heard the carpenters working upon the ordnance—every blow and stroke, even of the hammer or mallet, speaking the language of defiance."

William himself occupied his castle of Cambridge on its completion in 1069, and from it he directed the long and weary military operations against Hereward across the fens toward the Isle of Ely, only twelve miles away. From his keep-tower he could see with his own eyes that Isle, rising from the flat, on the skyline, like some Promised Land, but two years were to pass before he and his soldiers were to enter there; admitted even then by treachery.

From the Castle Mound the Cam may be seen, winding away through the flats into the distant haze. Immediately below are Parker's Piece, and Midsummer and Stourbridge Commons; this last from time beyond knowledge the annual scene of Stourbridge Fair. "Sturbitch" Fair, as the country-folk call it, existed, like the University itself, before history came to take note of it. When King John reigned it was already an important mark, and so continued until, at the Dissolution of the Monasteries, its rights and privileges* were transferred to the Corporation of Cambridge.

Whether the story of its origin be well founded, or merely a picturesque invention, it cannot be said. It is a story telling how a Kendal clothier, at date unknown, journeying from Westmoreland to London, his pack-horses laden with bales of cloth, found the bridge over the Cam at this point broken down, and, trying to ford the river, fell in, goods and all. Struggling at last to the opposite bank, and fishing out his property, he spread his cloth to dry on Stourbridge Common, where so many of the townsfolk came to see it and to bid that in the end he sold nearly all his stock, and did much better than if he had gone on to London. The next year, therefore, he took care—not to fall into the Cam again—but to make Cambridge his mart. Other trades then became attracted to the place where he found business so brisk, and hence (according to the legend) the growth of a fair in its prime comparable only with that greatest of all fairs—the famous one of Nijni-Novgorod.

To criticise a legend of this kind would be to take it too seriously, else, among many things that might be inquired into would be the appearance at Cambridge of a traveller from Westmoreland bound for London. He must have missed his way very widely indeed!

The Fair still lasts three weeks, from 18th September to 10th October, but it is the merest shadow of its former self. The Horse Fair, on the 25th September, is practically all that remains of serious business. In old times its annual opening was attended with much ceremony. In those days, before the computation of time was altered, and Old Style became changed for New, the dates of opening and closing were 7th and 29th September. On Saint Bartholomew's Day the Mayor and Corporation rode out from the town to set out the ground, then cultivated. By that day all crops had to be cleared, or the stall-holders, ready to set up their stalls and booths, were at liberty to trample them down. On the other hand, they were under obligation to remove everything by St. Michael's Day, or the ploughmen, ready by this time to break ground for ploughing, had the right to carry off any remaining goods. Stourbridge Fair was then a town of booths. In the centre was the Duddery, the street where the mercers, drapers and clothiers sold their wares; and running in different directions were Ironmongers' Row, Cooks' Row, Garlick Row, Booksellers' Row, and many another busy street. In those times the three weeks' turnover of the various trades was calculated at not less than a quarter of a million sterling. The railways that destroyed the position of Lynn, Ely, and Cambridge as distributing places along the Cam and Ouse, have wrought havoc with this old-time Fair.

## XXVII

THROUGH Chesterton, overlooked by the Castle and deriving its name from it, the road leaves Cambridge for Ely, passing through the village of Milton, where the Fenland begins, or what is more by usage than true description so-called now the Fens are drained and the land once sodden with water and covered with beds of dense reeds and rushes made to bear corn and to afford rich pasture for cattle. This is the true district of the "Cambridgeshire Camels," as the folk of the shire are proverbially called. The term, a very old one, doubtless took its origin in the methods of traversing the Fens formerly adopted by the rustic folk. They used stilts, or "stetches," as they preferred to call them, and no doubt afforded an amusing spectacle to strangers, as they straddled high above the reeds and stalked from one grassy tussock to another in the quaking bogs.

There is a choice of routes at Milton, the road running in a loop for two miles. The left-hand branch, through Landbeach, selected by the Post Office as the route of its telegraph-poles, might on that account be considered the main road, but the right-hand route has decidedly the better surface. Midway of this course, where the Slap Up Inn stands, is the lane leading to Waterbeach, a scattered village near the Cam, much troubled by the floods from that stream in days gone by.

Something of what Waterbeach was like in the eighteenth century may be gathered from the correspondence of the Rev. William Cole, curate there from 1767 to 1770. Twenty guineas a year was the modest sum he received, but that, fortunately for him, was not the full measure of his resources, for he possessed an estate in the neighbourhood. The value of his land could not have been great, and may be guessed from his letters. Writing in 1769, he says: "A great part of my estate has been drowned these two years: all this part of the country is now covered with water and the poor people of this parish utterly ruined." And again in 1770: "This is the third time within six years that my estate has been drowned, and now worse than ever." Shortly after writing that letter he removed. "Not being a water-rat," he says, "I left Waterbeach," and went to the higher and drier village of Milton, two miles away.

Waterbeach long retained its old-world manners and customs. May Day was its greatest holiday, and was ushered in with elaborate preparations. The young women collected materials for a garland, consisting of ribbons, flowers, and silver spoons, with a silver tankard to suspend in the centre; while the young men, early in the morning, or late at night, went forth into the fields to collect emblems of their esteem or disapproval of the young women aforesaid. "Then," says the old historian of these things, "woe betide the girl of loose habits, the slattern and the scold; for while the young woman who had been foremost in the dance, or whose amiable manners entitled her to esteem, had a large branch or tree of whitethorn planted by her cottage door, the girl of loose manners had a blackthorn at hers." The slattern's emblem was an elder tree, and the scold's a bunch of nettles tied to the latch of the door.

After having thus (under cover of darkness, be it said) left their testimonials to the qualities or defects of the village beauties, the young men, just before the rising of the sun, went for the garland and suspended it in the centre of the street by a rope tied to opposite chimneys. This done, sunrise was ushered in by ringing the village bells. Domestic affairs were attended to until after midday, and then the village gave itself up to merrymaking. Dancing on the village green, sports of every kind, and kiss-in-the-ring were for the virtuous and the industrious; while the recipients of the elders, the blackthorns, and the nettles sat in the cold shade of neglect, wished they had never been born, and made up their minds to be more objectionable than ever. Such was Waterbeach about 1820.

Some thirty years later the village acquired an

enduring title to fame as the first charge given to that bright genius among homely preachers, Charles Haddon Spurgeon. It was in 1851, while yet only in his seventeenth year, that Spurgeon was made pastor of the Baptist Chapel here. Already his native eloquence had made him famed in Colchester, where, two years before, he had first spoken in public. The old thatched chapel where the youthful preacher ministered, on a stipend of twenty pounds a year, almost identical with that enjoyed by the Reverend William Cole, curate in the parish church eighty years before, has long since disappeared, destroyed by fire in 1861; and on its site stands a large and very ugly "Spurgeon Memorial Chapel" in yellow brick with red facings. Scarce two years and a half passed before the fame of Spurgeon's eloquence spread to London, and he was offered, and accepted, the pastorate of New Park Street Chapel, Southwark, there to fill that conventicle to overflowing, and presently draw all London to Exeter Hall. Even at this early stage of his wonderful career there were those who dilated upon the marvel of "this heretical Calvinist and Baptist" drawing a congregation of ten thousand souls while St. Paul's and Westminster Abbey resounded with the echoing footsteps of infrequent worshippers; but Spurgeon preached shortly afterwards to a congregation numbering twenty-four thousand, and maintained his hold until the day of his death, nearly forty years after. Where shall that curate, vicar, rector, dean, bishop, or archbishop of the Church of England be found who can command such numbers?

That his memory is held in great reverence at Waterbeach need scarce be said. There are still those who tell how the "boy-preacher," when announced to hold a night service in some remote village, not only braved the worst that storms and floods could do, but how, finding the chapel empty and the expected congregation snugly housed at home, out of the howling wind and drenching rain, he explored the place with a borrowed stable-lantern in his hand, and secured a congregation by dint of house-to-house visits!


## XXVIII

THE left-hand loop, through Landbeach, if an inferior road, has more wayside interest. Landbeach is in Domesday Book called "Utbech," that is to say Outbeach, or Beach out (of the water). "Beach" in this and other Fenland instances means "bank"; Waterbeach being thus "water bank." Wisbeach, away up in the extreme north of the county, is a more obscure name, but on inquiry is found to mean Ousebank, that town standing on the Ouse in days before the course of that river was changed. Landbeach Church stands by the wayside, and has its interest for the ecclesiologist, as conceivably also for those curious people interested in the stale and futile controversy as to who wrote Shakespeare's plays; for within the building lies the Reverend William Rawley, sometime chaplain to Bacon, and not only so, but the author of a life of him and the publisher of his varied acknowledged works. He, if anyone, would have known it if Bacon had been that self-effacing playwright, so we must needs think it a pity there is so little in spiritualism save idiotic manifestations of horseplay and showers of rappings in the dark; otherwise the obvious thing would be to summon Rawley's shade and discreetly pump it.

Beyond Landbeach, close by the fifty-sixth mile-

LANDBEACH.

stone from London, the modern road falls into the Roman Akeman Street, running from Brancaster (the Roman "Branodunum") on the Norfolk coast, through Ely, to Cambridge, to Dunstable, and eventually, after many leagues, to Bath. Those who will may attempt the tracing of it back between this point and Cambridge, a difficult enough matter, for it has mostly sunk into the spongy ground, but here, where it exists for a length of five miles, plain to see, it is still a causeway raised in places considerably above the levels, and occasionally showing stretches of imposing appearance. It remains thus a striking monument to the surveying and engineering skill of that great people, confronted here in far-off times with a wilderness of reeking bogs. The object in view—to reach the coast in as straight a line as possible—meant wrestling with the difficulties of road-making in the mixed and unstable elements of mud and water, but they faced the problem and worked it out with such completeness that a solid way arose that only fell into decay when the civilisation they had planted here, on the rim and uttermost verge of the known world, was blotted out. Onwards as far as Lynn a succession of fens stretched for sixty-five miles, but so judiciously did the Romans choose their route that only some ten miles of roadway were actually constructed in the ooze. It picked a careful itinerary, advancing from isle to isle amid the swamps, and, for all its picking and choosing of a way, went fairly direct. It was here that it took the first plunge into the sloughs and made direct, as a raised bank, through them for the Ouse, where Stretham Bridge now marks the entrance to the Isle of Ely. How that river, then one of great size and volume, was crossed we do not know. Beyond it, after some three miles of floundering through the slime, the causeway came to firm ground again where the village of Stretham (its very name suggestive of solid roadway) stands on a rise that was once an island. Arrived at that point, the road took its way for ten miles through the solid foothold of the Isle of Ely, leaving it at Littleport and coming, after struggling through six miles of fen, to the Isle of Southery. Crossing that islet in little more than a mile, it dipped into fens again at the point now known as Modney Bridge, whence it made for the eyot of Hilgay. Only one difficulty then remained: to cross the channel of the Wissey River into Fordham. Thenceforward the way was plain.

We have already made many passing references to the Fens, and now the district covered in old times by them is reached, it is necessary, in order to make this odd country thoroughly understood, to explain them. What are the Fens like? The Fens, expectant reader, are gone, like the age of miracles, like the dodo, the pterodactyl, the iguanodon, and the fancy zoological creatures of remote antiquity. Ages uncountable have been endeavouring to abolish the Fens. When the Romans came, they found the native tribes engaged upon the task, and carried it on themselves, in succession. Since then every age has been at it, and at length, some seventy or eighty years ago, when steam-pumps were brought to aid the old draining machinery, the thing was done. There is only one little specimen of natural fen now left, and that is preserved as a curiosity. But although the actual morasses are gone, the flat drained fields of Fenland are here, and we shall presently see in these pages that although the sloughs are in existence no longer, it is no light thing in these districts to venture far from the main roads.

No one has more eloquently or more truly described the present appearance of the Fen country than Cobbett. "The whole country," he says, "is as level as the table on which I am now writing. The horizon like the sea in a dead calm: you see the morning sun come up, just as at sea; and see it go down over the rim, in just the same way as at sea in a calm. The land covered with beautiful grass, with sheep lying about upon it, as fat as hogs stretched out sleeping in a stye. Everything grows well here: earth without a stone so big as a pin's head; grass as thick as it can grow on the ground."

The Fenland has, in fact, the wild beauty that comes of boundless expanse. Only the range of human vision limits the view. Above is the summer sky, blue and vast and empty to the sight, but filled to the ear with the song of the soaring skylark, trilling as he mounts higher and higher; the sound of his song diminishing as he rises, until it becomes like the "still small voice of Conscience," and at last fades out of hearing, like the whisper of that conscience overwrought and stricken dumb.

These levels have a peculiar beauty at sunset, and Cambridgeshire sunsets are as famous in their way as Cambridge sausages. They (the sunsets, not the sausages) have an unearthly glory that only a Turner in his most inspired moments could so much as hint at. The vastness of the Fenland sky and the humid Fenland atmosphere conspire to give these effects.

The Fenland is a land of romance for those who know its history and have the wit to assimilate its story from the days of fantastic legend to these of clear-cut matter-of-fact. If you have no reading, or even if you have that reading and do not bring to it the aid of imagination, the Fens are apt to spell dulness. If so, the dulness is in yourself. Leave these interminable levels, and in the name of God go elsewhere, for the flatness of the Great Level added to the flatness of your own mind will in combination produce a horrible monotony. On the other hand, if some good fairy at your cradle gave you the gift of seeing with a vision not merely physical, why, then, the Fenland is fairyland; for though to the optic nerve there is but a level stretching to the uttermost horizon, criss-crossed with dykes and lodes and leams of a severe straightness, there is visible to the mind's eye, Horatio, an ancient order of things infinitely strange and uncanny. Antiquaries have written much of the Fens, but they do not commonly present a very convincing picture of them. They tell of Iceni, of Romans, fierce Norsemen marauders, Saxons, Danes, and the conquering Normans, but they cannot, or do not, breathe the breath of life into those ancient peoples, and make them live and love and hate, fight and vanquish or be vanquished. The geologists, too, can speculate learnedly upon the origin of the Fens, and can prove, to their own satisfaction at least, that this low-lying, once flooded country was produced by some natural convulsion that suddenly lowered it to the level of the sea; but no one has with any approach to intimacy with the subject taken us back to the uncountable æons when the protoplasm first began to move in the steaming slime, and so conducted us by easy stages through the crucial and hazardous period when the jelly-fish was acquiring the rudiments of a backbone (if that was the order of the progress) to the exciting era when the crocodile played the very devil with aboriginal man, and the rhinoceros and the hippopotamus wallowed in the mud. The Iceni are very modern, compared with these very ancient inhabitants, and have done what those inarticulate protoplasms, neolithic men and others, could not do; that is, they gave their names to many places in these East Anglian shires, and a title that still survives to a great road. Look on any map of East Anglia and the surrounding counties and you shall see many place-names beginning with "Ick": Ickborough, Ickworth, Ickleton, Icklington, Ickleford, and Ickwell.

These are the surviving names of Icenian settlements. There is a "Hickling" on the Broads, in Norfolk, which ought by rights to be "Ickling"; but the world has ever been at odds on the subject of aspirate or no aspirate, certainly since the classic days of the Greeks and the Romans. Does not Catullus speak of a certain Arrius who horrified the Romans by talking of the "Hionian Sea"? and is not Tom Hood's "Ben Battle" familiar? "Don't let 'em put 'Hicks jacet' there," he said, "for that is not my name."

When the Romans came and found the Iceni here, the last stone-age man and the ultimate crocodile (the former inside the latter) had for ages past been buried in the peat of the Fens, resolving into a fossil state. The Iceni probably, the purposeful Romans certainly, endeavoured to drain the Fens, or at least to prevent their being worse flooded by the sea; and the Roman embankment between Wisbeach and King's Lynn, built to keep out the furious wind-driven rollers of the Wash, gave a name to the villages of Walsoken, Walton, and Walpole (once Wall-pool). When the Romano-British civilisation decayed, the defences against the sea decayed with it, and the level lay worse flooded than before. Far and wide, from Lynn, on the seacoast in the north, to Fen Ditton, in the south, almost at the gates of Cambridge; from Mildenhall in the east, to St. Ives and Peterborough in the west, a vast expanse of still and shallow water covered an area of, roughly, seventy miles in length and thirty in breadth: about 2100 square miles. Out of this dismal swamp rose many islands, formed of knobs of the stiff clay or gault that had not been washed away with the surrounding soil. It was on these isles that prehistoric man lived, and where his wretched wattle-huts were built beside the water. He had his dug-out canoe and his little landing-stage, and sometimes, when his islet was very diminutive and subject to floods, he built his dwelling on stakes driven into the mud. In peaceful and plenteous times he sat on his staging overhanging the water, and tore and gnawed at the birds and animals that had fallen to his arrow or his spear. Primitive man was essentially selfish. He first satisfied his own hunger and then tossed the remainder to his squaw and the brats, and when they had picked the bones clean, and saved those that might be useful for fashioning into arrow-heads, they threw the remains into the water, whence they sent up in the fulness of time an evil smell which did not trouble him and his in the least, primitive as they were in every objectionable sense of the word.

Relics of him and his domestic odds and ends are often found, ten feet or so beneath the present surface of the land. His canoe is struck by the spade of the gaulter, his primitive weapons unearthed, his dustbin and refuse-heap turned over and examined by curious antiquaries and naturalists, who can tell you exactly what his *menu* was. Sometimes they find primitive man himself, lying among the ruins of his dwelling, overwhelmed in the long ago by some cataclysm of nature, or perhaps killed by a neighbouring primitive.

To these isles in after centuries, when the Romans had gone and the Saxons had settled down and become Christians, came hermits and monks like Guthlac, who reared upon them abbeys and churches, and began in their several ways to cultivate the land and to dig dykes and start draining operations. For the early clergy earned their living, and were not merely the parasites they have since become. These islands, now that the Fens are drained, are just hillocks in the great plain. They are still the only villages in the district, and on those occasions when an embankment breaks and the Fens are flooded, they become the islands they were a thousand years ago. The very names of these hillocks and villages are fen-eloquent, ending as they do with "ey" and "ea," corruptions of the Anglo-Saxon words "ig," an island, and "ea," a river. Ely, the largest of them, is said by Bede to have obtained its name from the abundance of eels, and thus to be the "Eel Island." There are others who derive it from "helig," a willow, and certainly both eels and willows were abundant here; but the name, in an ancient elision of that awkward letter "h," is more likely to come from another "helig," meaning holy, and Ely to really be the "holy island."

Other islands, most of them now with villages of the same name, were Coveney, Hilgay, Southery, Horningsea, Swavesey, Welney, Stuntney, and Thorney. There was, too, an Anglesey, the Isle of the Angles, a Saxon settlement, near Horningsea. A farm built over the site of Anglesey Abbey now stands there.

But many Fenland place-names are even more eloquent. There are Frog's Abbey, Alderford, Littleport, Dry Drayton and Fenny Drayton, Landbeach and Waterbeach. Littleport, really at one time a port to which the ships of other ages came, is a port no longer; Fenny Drayton is now as dry as its fellow-village; and Landbeach and Waterbeach are, as we have already seen, not so greatly the opposites of one another as they were.

# XXIX

A GREAT part of the Fens seems to have been drained and cultivated at so early a time as the reigns of Stephen and Henry the Second, for William of

Malmesbury describes this as then "the paradise of England," with luxuriant crops and flourishing gardens; but this picture of prosperity was suddenly blotted out by the great gale that arose on the morrow of St. Martin 1236, and continued for eight days and nights. The sea surged over the embankments and flowed inwards past Wisbeach, and the rivers, instead of flowing away, were forced back and so drowned the levels. Some attempts to reclaim the land were made, but a similar disaster happened seventeen years later, and the fen-folk seem to have given up all efforts at keeping out the waters, for in 1505 we find the district described as "one of the most brute and beastly of the whole realm; a land of marshy ague and unwholesome swamps." But already the idea of reclamation was in the air, for Bishop Morton, in the time of Henry the Seventh,— a most worshipful Bishop of Ely, Lord Chancellor too, churchman, statesman, and engineer,—had a notion for making the stagnant Nene to flow forth into the sea, instead of doubling upon itself and seething in unimaginable bogs as it had done for hundreds of years past. He cut the drain that runs from Stanground, away up in the north near Peterborough, to Wisbeach, still known as Morton's Leam, and thus began a new era. But though he benefited the land to the north-west of Ely, the way between his Cathedral city and Cambridge was not affected, and remained in his time as bad as it had been for centuries; and he, like many a Bishop before him and others to come after, commonly journeyed between Ely and Cambridge by boat. Our road, indeed, did not witness the full activity of the good Bishop and his successors. Their doings only attained to great proportions in the so-called Great Level of the Fens, the Bedford Level, as it is alternatively called, that stretches over a district beginning eight miles away and continuing for sixteen or twenty miles, by Thorney, Crowland, and Peterborough.

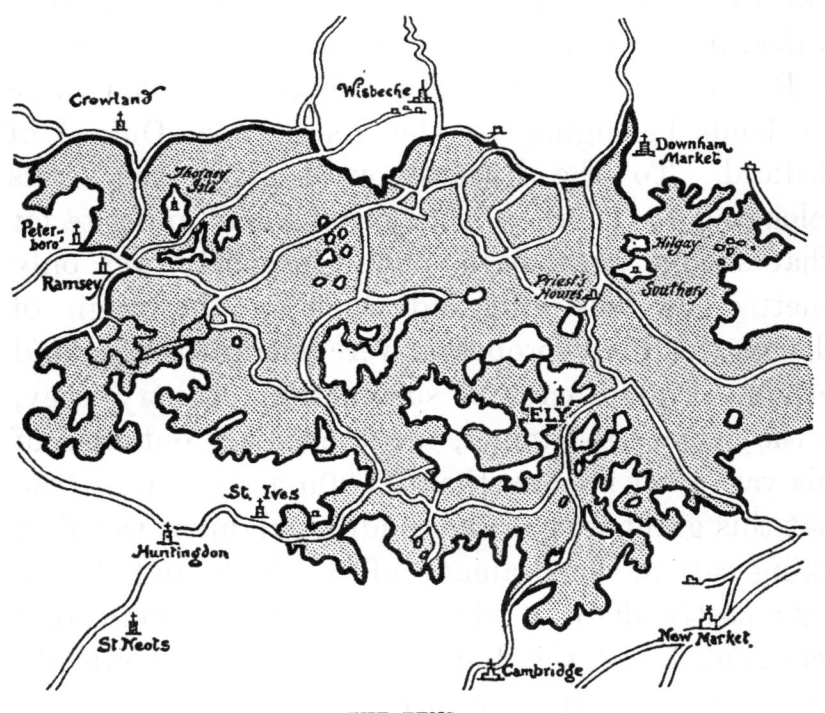

THE FENS.
[*After Dugdale.*]

This map, from Dugdale's work, showing the Fens as they lay drowned, and the islands in them, will give the best notion of this curious district. You will perceive how like an inland sea was this waste of mud and water, not full fathom five, it is true, but less readily navigable than the sea itself. Here you see the road from Cambridge to Ely and on to Downham Market pictured, with no great accuracy, you may be sworn, and doubtless with as much margin of error as it is customary to allow in the somewhat speculative charts of Arctic continents and regions of similarly difficult access. In this map, then, it will be perceived how remote the Bedford Level lies from our route. Why "Bedford Level," which, in point of fact, is in Cambridgeshire and not in Bedfordshire at all? For this reason: that these are lands belonging to the Earls (now Dukes) of Bedford. To the Russells were given the lands belonging to Thorney Abbey, but their appetite for what should have been public property was only whetted by this gift, and when in the reign of Charles the First proposals were made to drain and reclaim 310,000 acres of surrounding country, they, in the person of Francis, the then Earl, obtained of this vast tract no less than 95,000 acres. It is true that this grant was made conditional upon the Earl taking part in the drainage of the land, and that it was a costly affair in which the smaller adventurers were ruined and the Earl's own resources strained; but in the result a princely heritage fell to the Bedfords.

The great engineering figure at this period of reclamation was the Dutchman, Cornelius Vermuyden, who began his dyking and draining under royal sanction and with Bedfordian aid in 1629. Vermuyden's is a great figure historically considered, but his works are looked upon coldly in these times, and it is even said that one of the principal labours of modern engineers has been to rectify his errors. That view probably originated with Rennie, who in 1810 was employed to drain and reclaim the extensive marshland between Wisbeach and Lynn, and was bound, in the usual professional manner, to speak evil things of one of the same craft. There was little need, though, to be jealous of Vermuyden, who had died obscurely, in poverty and in the cold shade of neglect, some hundred and fifty years before. Vermuyden, as a matter of course, employed Flamands and Hollanders in his works, for they were not merely his own countrymen, but naturally skilled in labour of this technical kind. These strangers aroused the enmity of the Fenmen, not for their strangeness alone, but for the sake of the work they were engaged upon, for the drainage of the Fens was then a highly unpopular proceeding. The Fenmen loved their watery wastes, and little wonder that they did so, for they knew none other, and they were a highly specialised race of amphibions creatures, skilled in all the arts of the wildfowler and the fisherman, by which they lived. Farming was not within their ken. They trapped and subsisted upon the innumerable fish and birds that shared the wastes with them; birds of the duck tribe, the teal, widgeon, and mallard; and greater fowl, like the wild goose and his kind. For fish they speared and snared the eel, the pike, and the lamprey—pre-eminently fish of the fens; for houses they contrived huts of mud and stakes, thatched with the reeds that grew densely, to a height of ten or twelve feet, everywhere; and as for firing, peat was dug and stacked and burnt. Consider. The Fenman was a product of the centuries. His father, his grandfather, his uttermost ancestors, had squatted and fished and hunted where they would, and none could say them nay. They paid no rent or tithe to anyone, for the Fens were common, or waste. And now the only life the Fenman knew was like to be taken from him. What could such an one do on dry land? A farmer put aboard ship and set to navigate it could not be more helpless than the dweller in those old marshes, dependent only upon his marsh lore, when the water was drained off and the fishes gone, reed-beds cut down, the land cultivated, and the wild-fowl dispersed. The fears of this people were quaintly expressed in the popular verses then current, entitled "The Powte's Complaint." "Powte," it should be said, was the Fen name for the lamprey—

"Come, brethren of the water, and let us all assemble
To treat upon this matter, which makes us quake and tremble;
For we shall rue, if it be true the fens be undertaken,
And where we feed in fen and reed they'll feed both beef an bacon.

They'll sow both beans and oats where never man yet thought it;
Where men did row in boats ere undertakers bought it;
But, Ceres, thou behold us now, let wild oats be their venture,
And let the frogs and miry bogs destroy where they do enter.

Behold the great design, which they do now determine,
Will make our bodies pine, a prey to crows and vermine;
For they do mean all fens to drain and waters overmaster,
All will be dry, and we must die, 'cause Essex Calves want pasture.

Away with boats and rudders, farewell both boots and skatches,
No need of one nor t'other; men now make better matches;
Stilt-makers all and tanners shall complain of this disaster,
For they will make each muddy lake for Essex Calves a pasture.

The feather'd fowls have wings, to fly to other nations,
But we have no such things to help our transportations;
We must give place, O grievous case! to horned beasts and cattle,
Except that we can all agree to drive them out by battle."

Other verses follow, where winds, waves, and moon are invoked in aid, but enough has been quoted to show exactly how affairs stood at this juncture. But the Fenmen were not without their defender. He was found in a certain young Huntingdonshire squire and brewer, one Oliver Cromwell, Member of Parliament for Huntingdon, reclaimed from his early evil courses, and now, a Puritan and a brand plucked timeously from the burning, posing as champion of the people. Seven years past this draining business had been going forward, and now that trouble was brewing between King and people, and King wanted money, and people would withhold it, the popular idea arose that the Fens were being drained to provide funds for royal needs. Cromwell was at this time resident in Ely, and seized upon the local grievances and exploited them to his own end, with the result that the works were stopped and himself raised to the extreme height of local popularity. But when the monarchy was upset and Cromwell had become Lord Protector, he not only authorised the drainage being resumed, but gave extreme aid and countenance to William, Earl of Bedford, sending him a thousand Scots prisoners from Dunbar, as pressed men, practically slaves, to work in his trenches. Appeal from Philip drunk to Philip sober is a famous remedy, but appeal to Oliver, besotted with power, must have seemed helpless to our poor Fen-slodgers, for they do not seem to have made resistance, and the work progressed to its end.

## XXX

IF most of those who have described Fenland have lacked imagination, certainly the charge cannot be brought against that eighth-century saint, Saint Guthlac, who fled into this great dismal swamp and founded Crowland Abbey on its north-easterly extremity. Crowland has nothing to do with the Ely and King's Lynn Road, but in describing what he calls the "develen and luther gostes" that made his life a misery, Guthlac refers to the evil inhabitants of the Fens in general. Precisely what a "luther" ghost may be, does not appear. A Protestant spook, perhaps, it might be surmised, except that Lutheran schisms did not arise for many centuries later.

Saints were made of strange materials in ancient times, and Guthlac was of the strangest. Truth was not his strong point, and he could and did tell tales that would bring a blush to the hardy cheek of a Sir John Mandeville, or arouse the bitter envy of a Munchausen. But Guthlac's character shall not be taken away without good cause shown. He begins reasonably enough, with an excellent descriptive passage, picturing the "hideous fen of huge bigness which extends in a very long track even to the sea, ofttimes clouded with mist and dark vapours, having within it divers islands and woods, as also crooked and winding rivers"; but after this mild prelude goes on to make very large demands upon our credulity.

He had a wattle hut on an island, and to this poor habitation, he tells us, the "develen and luther gostes" came continually, dragged him out of bed and "tugged and led him out of his cot, and to the swart fen, and threw and sunk him in the muddy waters." Then they beat him with iron whips. He describes these devils in a very uncomplimentary fashion. They had "horrible countenances, great heads, long necks, lean visages, filthy and squalid beards, rough ears, fierce eyes, and foul mouths; teeth like horses' tusks, throats filled with flame, grating voices, crooked shanks, and knees big and great behind." It would have been scarce possible to mistake one of these for a respectable peasant.

After fifteen years of this treatment, Guthlac died, and it is to be hoped these hardy inventions of his are not remembered against him. No one else found the Fens peopled so extravagantly. Only the will-o'-wisps that danced fitfully and pallid at night over the treacherous bogs, and the poisonous miasma exhaled from the noxious beds of rotting sedge; only the myriad wild-fowl made the wilderness strange and eerie.

Guthlac was the prime romancist of the Fens,

but others nearly contemporary with him did not altogether lack imagination and inventive powers; as where one of the old monkish chroniclers gravely states that the Fen-folk were born with yellow bellies, like frogs, and were provided with webbed feet to fit them for their watery surroundings.

Asthma and ague were long the peculiar maladies of these districts. Why they should have been is sufficiently evident, but Dugdale, who has performed the difficult task of writing a dry book upon the Fens, uses language that puts the case very convincingly. He says, "There is no element good, the air being for the most part cloudy, gross, and full of rotten harrs; the water putrid and muddy, yea, full of loathsome vermin; the earth spungy and boggy." No wonder, then, that the terrible disease of ague seized upon the unfortunate inhabitants of this watery waste. Few called this miasmatic affection by that name: they knew it as the "Bailiff of Marshland," and to be arrested by the dread bailiff was a frequent experience of those who worked early or late in the marshes, when the poisonous vapours still lingered. To alleviate the miseries of ague the Fen-folk resorted to opium, and often became slaves to that drug. Another very much dreaded "Bailiff" was the "Bailiff of Bedford," as the Ouse, coming out of Bedfordshire, was called. He of the marshland took away your health, but the flooded Ouse, rising suddenly after rain or thaw, swept your very home away.

Still, in early morn, in Wicken Fen, precautions are taken by the autumn sedge-cutter against the dew and the exhalations from the earth, heavy with possibilities of marsh fever. He ties a handkerchief over his mouth for that purpose, while to protect himself against the sharp edges of the sedge he wears old stockings tied round his arms, leather gaiters on his legs, and a calfskin waistcoat.

The modern Fen-folk are less troubled with ague than their immediate ancestors, but the opium habit has not wholly left them. Whether they purchase the drug, or whether it is extracted from the white poppies that are a feature of almost every Fenland garden, they still have recourse to it, and "poppy tea" is commonly administered to the children to keep them quiet while their parents are at work afield. The Fenlanders are, by consequence, a solemn and grim race, shaking sometimes with ague, and at others "as nervous as a kitten," as they are apt to express it, as a result of drugging themselves. Another, and an entirely innocent, protection against ague is celery, and the celery-bed is a cherished part of a kitchen-garden in the Fens.

One of the disadvantages of these oozy flats is the lack of good drinking-water. The rivers, filled as they are with the drainings of the dykes and ditches, can only offer water unpleasant both to smell and taste, if not actually poisonous from the decaying matter and the myriad living organisms in it; and springs in the Fens are practically unknown. Under these circumstances the public-houses do a good trade in beer and spirits.

## XXXI

CAMBRIDGESHIRE is a singularly stoneless country, and in the Fens there is not so much as a pebble to be found. Thus it has become a common jest of the Cambridgeshire farmers to offer to swallow all the stones you can pick up in their fields. Farm horses for this reason are never shod, and it sounds not a little strange and uncanny to see one of the great waggon-horses plodding along a Fenland "drove," as the roads are named, and to hear nothing but the sound of his bells and the indistinct thudding of his shoeless feet in the dust or the mud, into whichever condition the weather has thrown the track.

A Fenland road is one thing among others peculiar to the Fens. It is a very good illustration of eternity, and goes on, flat and unbending, with a semi-stagnant ditch on either side, as far as eye can reach in the vast solitary expanse, empty save for an occasional ash-tree or group of Lombardy poplars, with perhaps a hillock rising in the distance crowned by a church and a village. No "metal" or ballast has ever been placed on the Fenland drove. In summer it is from six to eight inches deep in a black dust, that rises in choking clouds to the passage of a vehicle or on the uprising of a breeze; in winter it is a sea of mud, congealed on the approach of frost into ruts and ridges of the most appalling ruggedness. The Fen-folk have a home-made way with their execrable "droves." When they become uneven they just harrow them, as the farmer in other counties harrows his fields, and, when they are become especially hard, they plough them first and harrow them afterwards; a procedure that would have made Macadam faint with horror. The average-constituted small boy, who throws stones by nature, discovers something lacking in the scheme of creation as applied to these districts. Everywhere the soil is composed of the ancient alluvial silt brought down to these levels by those lazy streams, the Nene, the Lark, the Cam, and the Ouse, and of the dried peat of these sometime stagnant and festering morasses. Now that drainage has so thoroughly done its work, that in ardent summers the soil of this former inland sea gapes and cracks with dryness, it is no uncommon sight to see water pumped on to the baking fields from the leams and droves. The earth is of a light, dry black nature, consisting of fibrous vegetable matter, and possesses the well-known preservative properties of bog soil. Thus the trees of the primeval forest that formerly existed here, and were drowned in an early stage of the world's history, are often dug up whole. Their timber is black too, as black as coal, as may be seen by the wooden bridges that cross the drains and cuts, often made from these prehistoric trees.

Here is a typical dyke. Its surface is richly carpeted with water-weeds, and the water-lily spreads its flat leaves prodigally about it; the bright yellow blossoms reclining amid them like graceful naiads on fairy couches. But the Fenland children have a more prosaic fancy. They call them " Brandy-balls." The flowering rush, flushing a delicate carmine, and the aquatic sort of forget-me-not, sporting the Cambridge colours, are common inhabitants of the dykes; and in the more stagnant may be found the "water-soldier," a queer plant without any roots, living in the still slime at the bottom until the time comes for it to put forth its white blossoms, when it comes to "attention" in the light of day, displays its fleeting glory, and then sinks again, "at ease," to its fetid bed. There is a current in the dykes, but the water flows so imperceptibly that it does not deflect the upstanding spikes of the daintiest aquatic plant by so much as a hair's-breadth. Indeed, it would not flow at all, and would merely stagnate, were it not for the windmill-worked pumps that suck it along and, somewhere in the void distance, impel it up an inclined plane, and so discharge it into the longer and higher drain, whence it indolently flows into one of the canalised rivers, and so, through a sluice, eventually finds its way into the sea at ebb-tide.

The means by which the Fens are kept drained are not without their interest. A glance at a map of Cambridgeshire and its neighbouring counties will show the Great Level to be divided up into many patches of land by hard straight lines running in every direction. Some are thicker, longer, and straighter than others, but they all inter-communicate, and eventually reach one or other of the rivers. The longest, straightest, and broadest of these represents that great drain already mentioned, the Old Bedford River, seventy feet wide and twenty-one miles long; cut in the seventeenth century to shorten

A WET DAY IN THE FENS.

the course of the Ouse and to carry off the floods. Others are the New Bedford River, one hundred feet in width, cut only a few years later and running parallel with the first; Vermuyden's Eau, or the Forty Foot Drain, of the same period, feeding the Old Bedford River from the Nene, near Ramsey, with their tributaries and counter-drains. The North Level cuts belong principally to the early part of the nineteenth century, when Rennie drained the Wisbeach and Lynn districts.

The main drains are at a considerably higher level than the surrounding lands, the water in them only prevented from drowning the low-lying fields again by their great and solid banks, fourteen to sixteen feet high, and about ten feet in breadth at the top. These banks, indeed, form in many districts the principal roads. Perilous roads at night, even for those who know them well, and one thinks with a shudder of the dangers encountered of old by local medical men, called out in the darkness to attend some urgent case. Their custom was— perhaps it is in some places still observed—to mount their steady nags and to jog along with a lighted stable-lantern swinging from each stirrup, to throw a warning gleam on broken bank or frequent sunken fence.

At an interval of two miles along these banks is generally to be found a steam pumping-engine, busily and constantly occupied in raising water from the lodes and dykes in the lower levels and pouring it into the main channel. The same process is repeated in the case of raising the water from the field-drains into the smaller dykes by a windmill or "skeleton-pump," as it is often called. It is a work that is never done, but goes forward, year by year, and is paid for by assessments on the value of the lands affected by these operations. Commissioners, themselves local landowners and tenants, and elected by the same classes, look after the conduct and the efficiency of the work, and see that the main drains are scoured by the "scourers"; the banks duly repaired by the "bankers" and the "gaulters"; the moles, that might bring disaster by burrowing through them, caught by the "molers"; and the sluices kept in working order. The rate imposed for paying the cost of these works is often a heavy one, but the land is wonderfully rich and productive. Nor need the Fenland farmer go to extraordinary expense for artificial manure, or for marling his fields when at length he has cropped all the goodness out of the surface soil. The very best of restoratives lies from some five to twelve feet under his own land, in the black greasy clay formed from the decaying vegetable matter of the old forests that underlie the Fens. A series of pits is sunk on the land, the clay obtained from them is spread over it, and the fields again yield a bounteous harvest.

Harvest-work and farm-work in general in the Fens is in some ways peculiar to this part of the country, for farm-holdings are large and farmsteads far between. The practice, under these conditions, arose of the work being done by gangs; the hands assembling at break of day in the farmyard and being despatched in parties to their distant day's work in hoeing, weeding, or picking in the flat and almost boundless fields; returning only when the day's labour is ended. Men, women, and children gathered thus in the raw morning make a picture—and in some ways a pitiful picture—of farming and rustic life, worthy of a Millet. But our Millet has not yet come; and the gangs grow fewer. If he does not hasten, they will be quite gone, and something characteristic in Fenland-life quite lost. A Fenland farm-lass may wear petticoats, or she may not. Sometimes she acts as carter, and it is precisely in such cases that she sheds her feminine skirts and dons the odd costume that astonishes the inquisitive stranger new to these parts, who sees, with doubt as to whether he sees aright, a creature with the boots and trousers of a man, a nondescript garment, half bodice and half coat with skirts, considerably above the knees, and a sun-bonnet on her head, working in the rick-yards, or squashing heavily through the farmyard muck. Skirts are out of place in farmyards and in cattle-byres, and the milkmaid, too, of these parts is dressed in like guise. If you were to show a milkmaid in the Fens a picture illustrating "Where are you going to, my pretty maid?" in the conventional fashion, she would criticise very severely, as quite incorrect, the skirted figure of a poet's dream usually presented. She saves her skirts and her flower-trimmed hat for Sundays.

## XXXII

AND now we must come from the general to the especial; from Fens and Fen-folk in the mass to a bright particular star.

The greatest historical figure along the whole course of this road is that of Hereward the Wake, the "last of the English," as he has been called. "Hereward," it has been said, means "the guard of the army," while "the Wake" is almost self-explanatory, signifying literally the Wide Awake, or the Watchful. He is thought to have been the eldest son of Leofric, Earl of Mercia, and of the famous Godiva, and to have been banished by his father and outlawed. Like objects dimly glimpsed in a fog, the figure of Hereward looms gigantic and uncertain through the mists of history, and how much of him is real and how much legendary no one can say. When Hereward was born, in the mild reign of Edward the Confessor, the Anglo-Saxons who six hundred and fifty years before had conquered Britain, and, driving a poor remnant of the enervated race of Romanised Britons to the uttermost verge of the island, changed the very name of the country from Britain to England, had themselves degenerated. The Saxons were originally among the fiercest of savages, and derived their name from the "sæxe," or short sword, with which they came to close and murderous combat; but the growth of civilisation and the security in which they had long dwelt in the conquered island undermined their original combativeness, and for long before the invasion of England by William the Conqueror they had been hard put to it to hold their own against the even more savage Danes. Yet at the last, at Hastings under Harold, they made a gallant stand against the Normans, and if courage alone could have won the day, why then no Norman dynasty had ever occupied the English throne. The Battle of Hastings was only won by superior military dispositions on the part of William. His archers gained him the victory, and by their disconcerting arrow-flights broke the advance of the Saxons armed with sword and battle-axe.

That most decisive and momentous battle in the world's history was lost and won on the 14th day of October 1066. It was followed by a thorough-going policy of plunder and confiscation. Everywhere the Saxon landowners were dispossessed of their property, and Normans replaced them. Even the Saxon bishops were roughly deprived of their sees, and alien prelates from over sea took their place. The Saxon race was utterly degraded and crushed, and to be an Englishman became a reproach; so that the Godrics, Godbalds, and Godgifus, the Ediths, the Alfreds, and other characteristic Saxon names, began to be replaced by trembling parents with Roberts, and Williams, and Henrys, and other names of common Norman use.

Now, in dramatic fashion, Hereward comes upon the scene. Two years of this crushing tyranny had passed when, one calm summer's evening in 1068, a stranger, accompanied by only one attendant, entered the village of Brunne, in Lincolnshire, the place now identified with Bourne; Bourne and its Teutonic original form of Brunne meaning a stream. It was one of his father's manors. Seeking, unrecognised, shelter for the night, he was met by lamentations, and was told that Leofric, the great Earl, was dead; that his heir, the Lord Hereward, was away in foreign parts; and that his younger brother, now become heir, had only the day before been foully murdered by the Normans, who had in derision fixed his head over the doorway. Moreover, the Normans had seized the house and the manor. "Alas!" wailed the unhappy Saxon dependants, "we have no power to revenge these things. Would that Hereward were here! Before to-morrow's sunrise they would all taste of the bitter cup they have forced on us."

The stranger was sheltered and hospitably entertained by these unhappy folk. After the evening meal they retired to rest, but their guest lay sleepless. Suddenly the distant sounds of singing and applause burst on his ears. Springing from his couch, he roused a serving-man and inquired the meaning of this nocturnal merrymaking, when he was informed that the Norman intruders were celebrating the entry of their lord into the patrimony of the youth they had murdered. The stranger girded on his weapons, threw about him a long black cloak, and with his companion repaired to the scene of this boisterous revelry. There the first object that met his eyes was the head of the murdered boy. He took it down, kissed it, and wrapped it in a cloth. Then the two placed themselves in the dark shadow of a doorway whence they could command a view into the hall. The Normans were scattered about a blazing fire, most of them overcome with drunkenness and reclining on the bosoms of their women. In their midst was a jongleur, or minstrel, chanting songs of reproach against the Saxons and ridiculing their unpolished manners in coarse dances and ludicrous gestures. He was proceeding to utter indecent jests against the family of the youth they had slain, when he was interrupted by one of the women, a native of Flanders. "Forget not," she said, "that the boy has a brother, named Hereward, famed for his bravery throughout the country whence I come, ay, and even in Spain and Algiers. Were he here, things would wear a different aspect on the morrow."

The new lord of the house, indignant at this, raised his head and exclaimed, "I know the man well, and his wicked deeds that would have brought him ere this to the gallows, had he not sought safety in flight; nor dare he now make his appearance anywhere this side the Alps."

The minstrel, seizing on this theme, began to improvise a scurrilous song, when he was literally cut short in an unexpected manner—his head clove in two by the swift stroke of a Saxon sword. It was Hereward who had done this. Then he turned on the defenceless Normans, who fell, one after the other, beneath his furious blows; those who attempted to escape being intercepted by his companion at the door. His arm was not stayed until the last was slain, and the heads of the Norman lord and fourteen of his knights were raised over the doorway.

The historian of these things goes on to say that the Normans in the neighbourhood, hearing of Hereward's return and of this midnight exploit, fled. This proves their wisdom, at the expense of their courage. The Saxons rose on every side, but Hereward at first checked their zeal, selecting only a strong body of relations and adherents, and with them attacking and slaying those of the Normans who dared remain on his estates. Then he repaired to his friend Brand, the Saxon Abbot of Peterborough, from whom, in the Anglo-Saxon manner, he received the honour of knighthood. After suddenly attacking and killing a Norman baron sent against him, he dispersed his followers, and, promising to rejoin them in a year, sailed for Flanders. We next hear of Hereward in the spring of 1070, when he appears in company with the Danes whom William the Conqueror had allowed to winter on the east coast. Together they raised a revolt, first in the Humber and along the Yorkshire Ouse; and then they are found sacking and destroying Peterborough Abbey, by that time under the control of the Norman Abbot Turold. A hundred and sixty armed men were gathered by the Abbot to force them back to their lair at Ely, but they had already left. With the advent of spring Hereward's Danish allies sailed away, rich in plunder, and he and his outlaws were left to do as best they could. For a year he remained quiet in his island fastness, secured by the trackless bogs and fens from attack, while the discontented elements were being attracted to him. With him was that attendant who kept the door at Bourne: Martin of the Light Foot was his name. Others were Leofric "Prat," or the Cunning, skilful in spying out the dispositions of the enemy; Leofric the Mower, who obtained his distinctive name by mowing off the legs of a party of Normans with a scythe, the only weapon he could lay hands on in a hurry; Ulric the Heron, and Ulric the Black—all useful lieutenants in an exhausting irregular warfare. Greater companions were the Saxon Archbishop Stigand, Bishop Egelwin of Lincoln, and the Earls Morcar, Edwin, and Tosti. All these notables, with a large following, flocked into the Isle of Ely, as a Camp of Refuge, and quartered themselves on the monks of the Abbey of Ely. There they lay, and constituted a continual menace to the Norman power. Sometimes they made incursions into other districts, and burnt and slew; at others, when hard pressed, they had simply to retire into these fens to be unapproachable. None among the Norman conquerors of other parts of the land could cope with Hereward, and at last William, in the summer of 1071, found it necessary to take the field in person against this own brother to Will-o'-the-Wisp. His plan of campaign was to attempt the invasion of the Isle of Ely simultaneously from two different points; from Brandon on the north-east, and from Cottenham on the south-west. The Brandon attempt was by boat, and soon failed: the advance from Cottenham was a longer business. Why he did not advance by that old Roman road, the Akeman Street, cannot now be explained. That splendid example of a causeway built across the morasses must still have afforded the better way, even though the Romans who made it had been gone six hundred years. But the Conqueror chose to advance from Cambridge by way of Impington, Histon, and Cottenham. It is, of course, possible that the defenders of the Isle had destroyed a portion of the old road, or in some way rendered it impracticable. His line of march can be traced even to this day. Leaving the old coaching road here at Cottenham Corner, we make for that village, famed in these days for its cream cheeses and grown to the proportions of a small town.[1] It was here, at Cottenham and at Rampton, that William collected his invading force and amassed the great stores of materials necessary for overcoming the great difficulty of entering the Isle of Ely, then an isle in the most baulking and inconvenient sense to an invader. Before the Isle could be entered by an army, it was necessary to build a causeway across the two miles' breadth of marshes that spread out from the Ouse at Aldreth, and this work had to be carried out in the face of a vigorous opposition from Hereward and his allies. It was two years before this causeway could be completed. Who shall say what strenuous labour went to the making of this road across the reedy bogs; what vast accumulations of reeds and brush-

---

[1] Famous, too, in that Cambridgeshire byword, "a Cottenham jury," which arose (as the inhabitants of every other village will have you believe) from the verdict of a jury of Cottenham men, in the case of a man tried for the murder of his wife. The foreman, returning into Court, said, "They were unanimously of opinion that it sarved her right, for she were such a tarnation bad 'un as no man could live with."

wood, felled trees and earth? The place has an absorbing interest, but to explore it thoroughly requires no little determination, for the road that William made has every appearance of being left

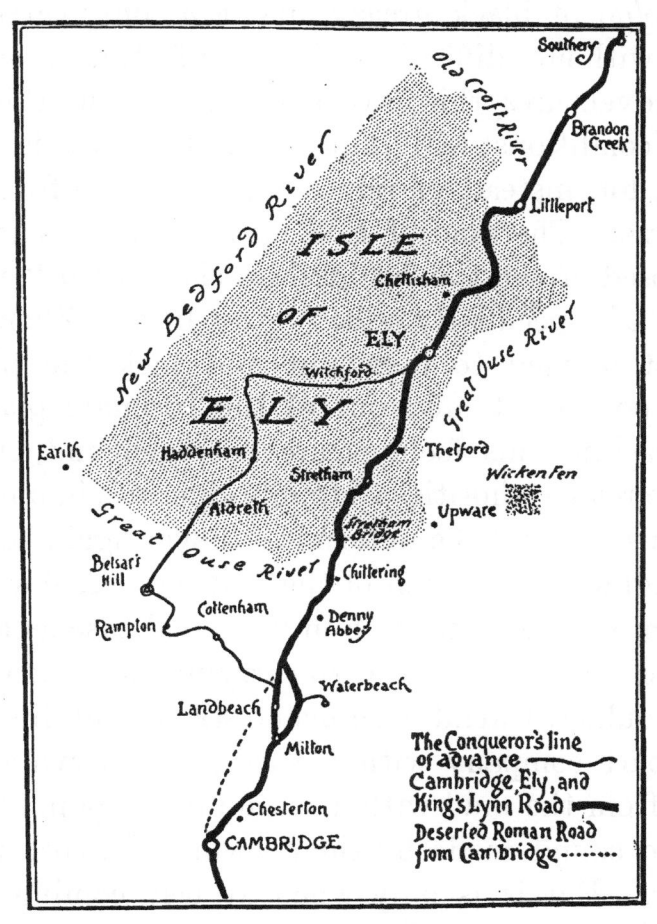

THE ISLE OF ELY AND DISTRICT.

just as it was when he had done with it, more than eight hundred years ago, and the way from Rampton, in its deep mud, unfathomable ruts and grassy hollows, soddened for lack of draining, is a terrible damper of curiosity. The explorer's troubles begin immediately he has left the village of Rampton. Turning to the right, he is instantly plunged into the fearful mud of a mile-long drove described on the large-scale Ordnance maps as "Cow Lane," a dismal *malebolge* of black greasy mud that only cattle can walk without difficulty. The unfortunate cyclist who adventures this way and pushes on, thinking these conditions will improve as he goes, is to be pitied, for, instead of improving, they go from bad to worse. The mud of this horrible lane is largely composed of the Cambridgeshire clay called "gault," and is of a peculiarly adhesive quality. When he is at last obliged to dismount and pick the pounds upon pounds of mud out of the intimate places of his machine, his feelings are outraged and, cursing all the road authorities of Cambridgeshire in one comprehensive curse, he determines never again to leave the highways in search of the historic. A few yards farther progress leaves him in as bad case as before, and he is at last reduced to carrying the machine on his shoulder, fearful with every stride that his shoes will part company with his feet, withdrawn at each step from the mud with a resounding "pop," similar to the sound made by the drawing of a cork from a bottle. But it is only when at last, coming to the end of Cow Lane and turning to the left into Iram Drove, he rests and clears away the mud and simultaneously finds seven punctures in one tyre and two in the other, that his stern indignation melts into tears. The wherefore of this havoc wrought upon the inoffensive wheelman is found in the cynical fact that although Cow Lane never receives the attentions of the road-repairer, its thorn-hedges are duly clipped and the clippings thrown into what, for the sake of convenience, may be called the road.

The geographical conditions here resemble those of Muckslush Heath in Colman's play, and although Iram Drove is paradise compared with what we have already come through, taken on its own merits it is not an ideal thoroughfare. One mile of it, past Long Swath Barn, brings us to the beginning of Aldreth Causeway, here a green lane, very bumpy and full of rises and hollows. Maps and guide-books vaguely mention Belsar's Hill near this point, and imaginative guides who have not explored these wilds talk in airy fashion of it "overlooking" the Causeway. As a matter of fact, the Causeway is driven squarely through it, and it is so little of a hill, and so incapable of overlooking anything, that you pass it and are none the wiser. The fact of the Causeway being thus driven through the hill and the ancient earthworks that ring around six acres of it, proves sufficiently that this fortress is much more ancient than William the Conqueror's time. It is, indeed, prehistoric. Who was Belsar? History does not tell us; but lack of certain knowledge has not forbidden guesswork, more or less wild, and there have been those who have found the name to be a corruption of Belisarius. We are not told, however, what that general — that unfortunate warrior whom tradition represents as begging in his old age an obolus in the streets of Constantinople— was doing here. But the real "Belsar" may perhaps have been that "Belasius, Præses Militum versus Elye," mentioned in the "Tabula Eliensis," one of William's captains in this long business, from whom descended the Belasyse family.

Two miles of green lane, solitary as though foot of man had not passed by for years, lead down to the Ouse. Fens spread out on either hand—Mow Fen, Willingham Fen, Smythy Fen, Great North Fen—fens everywhere. It is true they are now chiefly

ALDRETH CAUSEWAY AND THE ISLE OF ELY.

cultivated fields, remarkable for their fertility, but they are saved from being drowned only by the dykes and lodes cut and dug everywhere and drained by the steam pumping-station whose chimney-shaft, with its trail of smoke, is seen far off across the levels. In front rises the high ground of the Isle of Ely, a mile or more away across the river: high ground for Cambridgeshire, but likely, in any other part of England, to be called a low ridge. Here it is noticeable enough of itself, and made still more so by a windmill and a row of tall slender trees on the

ALDRETH CAUSEWAY.

skyline. A new bridge now building across the Ouse at this point is likely to bring Aldreth Causeway into use and repair again. On the other shore, at High Bridge Farm, the Causeway loses its grassy character, becoming a rutted and muddy road, inconceivably rugged, and so continuing until it ends at the foot of the rising ground of Aldreth. Drains and their protecting banks lie to the left of it; the banks used by the infrequent pedestrians in preference to the Causeway, low-lying and often flooded.

## XXXIII

THIS, then, was the way into that Isle of Refuge to which the Normans directed their best efforts. At the crossing of the Ouse, the fascines and hurdles, bags of earth and bundles of reeds, that had thus far afforded a foundation, were no longer of use, and a wooden bridge had of necessity to be constructed in the face of the enemy. Disaster attended it, for the unlucky timbering gave way while the advance was actually in progress, and hundreds were drowned. A second bridge was begun, and William, calling in supernatural aid, brought a "pythonissa"—a sorceress—to curse Hereward and his merry men and to weave spells while the work was going forward. William himself probably believed little in her unholy arts, but his soldiers and the vast army of helpers and camp-followers gathered together in this unhealthy hollow, dying of ague and marsh-sickness, and disheartened by failure and delay, fancied forces of more than earthly power arrayed against them. So the pythonissa was provided with a wooden tower whence she could overlook the work and exercise her spells while the second bridge was building. Fishermen from all the countryside were impressed to aid in the work. Among them, in disguise, came Hereward, so the legends tell, and when all was nearly done, he fired the maze of woodwork, so that the sorceress in her tower was sent, shrieking, in flames to Ahrimanes, and this, the second bridge, was utterly consumed. Kingsley, in his very much overrated romance of *Hereward the Wake*, makes him fire the reeds, but the Fenland reed does not burn and refuses to be fired outside the pages of fiction.

It was at last by fraud rather than by force that the Isle of Ely was entered. A rebel earl, a timorous noble, might surrender himself from time to time, and most of his allies thus fell away, but it was the false monks who at last led the invader in where he could not force his way. Those holy men, with the Saxon Abbot, Thurston, at their head, who prayed and meditated while the defenders of this natural fortress did the fighting, came as a result of their meditations to the belief that William, so dogged in his efforts, must in the end be successful. He had threatened—pious man though he was—to confiscate the property of the monastery when he should come to Ely, and so, putting this and that together, they conceived it to be the better plan to bring him in before he broke in; for in this way their revenues might yet be saved. It is Ingulphus, himself a monk, who chronicles this treachery. Certain of them, he says, sending privily to William, undertook to guide his troops by a secret path through the fens into the Isle. It was a chance too good to be thrown away, and was seized. The imagination can picture the mail-clad Normans winding single file along a secret path among the rushes, at the tail of some guide whose life was to be forfeit on the instant if he led them into ambush; and one may almost see and hear the swift onset and fierce cries when they set foot on firm land and fell suddenly upon the Saxon camp, killing and capturing many of the defenders.

But history shows the monks of Ely in an ill light, for it really seems that William's two years' siege of the Isle might have been indefinitely prolonged, and then been unsuccessful, had it not been for this treachery. Does anyone ever stop to consider how great a part treachery plays in history? It was the monks who betrayed the Isle, otherwise impregnable, and endless in its resources, as Hereward himself proved to a Norman knight whom he had captured. He conducted his prisoner over his water-and-morass-girdled domain, showed him most things within it, and then sent him back to the besieging camp to report what he had seen. This is the tale he told, as recorded in the *Liber Eliensis*:—

"In the Isle, men are not troubling themselves about the siege; the ploughman has not taken his hand from the plough, nor has the hunter cast aside his arrow, nor does the fowler desist from beguiling birds. If you care to hear what I have heard and seen with my own eyes, I will reveal all to you. The Isle is within itself plenteously endowed, it is supplied with various kinds of herbage, and in richness of soil surpasses the rest of England. Most delightful for charming fields and pastures, it is also remarkable for beasts of chase, and is, in no ordinary way, fertile in flocks and herds. Its woods and vineyards are not worthy of equal praise, but it is begirt by great meres and fens, as though by a strong wall. In this Isle there is an abundance of domestic cattle, and a multitude of wild animals; stags, roes, goats, and hares are found in its groves and by those fens. Moreover, there is a fair sufficiency of otters, weasels, and polecats; which in a hard winter are caught by traps, snares, or any other device. But what am I to say of the kinds of fishes and of fowls, both those that fly and those that swim? In the eddies at the sluices of these meres are netted innumerable eels, large water-wolves, with pickerels, perches, roaches, burbots, and lampreys, which we call water-snakes. It is, indeed, said by many that sometimes salmon are taken there, together with the royal fish, the sturgeon. As for the birds that abide there and thereabouts, if you are not tired of listening to me, I will tell you about them, as I have told you about the rest. There you will find geese, teal, coots, didappers, water-crows, herons, and ducks, more than man can number, especially in winter, or at moulting-time. I have seen a hundred—nay, even three hundred—taken at once; sometimes by bird-lime, sometimes in nets and snares." • The most eloquent auctioneer could not do better than this, and if this knight excelled in fighting as he did in description, he must have been a terrible fellow.

It is pleasant to think how the monks of Ely met with harder measures than they had expected. William was not so pleased with their belated submission as he was angered by their ever daring to question his right and power. Still, things might have gone better with them had they not by ill-luck been at meals in the refectory when the King unexpectedly appeared. None knew of his coming until he was seen to enter the church. Gilbert de Clare, himself a Norman knight, but well disposed towards the monks, burst in upon them: "Miserable fools that you are," he said, "can you do nothing better than eat and drink while the King is here?"

Forthwith they rushed pellmell into the church; fat brothers and lean, as quickly as they could, but the King, flinging a gold mark upon the altar, had already gone. He had done much in a short time. Evidently he was what Americans nowadays call a "hustler," for he had marked out the site for a castle within the monastic precincts, and had already given orders for its building by men pressed from the three shires of Cambridge, Hertford, and Bedford. Torn with anxiety, the whole establishment of the monastery hasted after him on his return to Aldreth, and overtook him at Witchford, where, by the intercession of Gilbert de Clare, they were admitted to an audience, and after some difficulty allowed to purchase the King's Peace by a fine of seven hundred marks of silver.

Unhappily, their troubles were not, even then, at an end, for when on the appointed day the money, raised by the sacrifice of many of the cherished ornaments of the church, was brought to the King's officers at Cambridge, the coins were found, through some fraud of the moneyers, to be of light weight. William was studiously and politically angry at what he affected to believe an attempt on the part of the monks to cheat him, and his forbearance was only purchased by a further fine of three hundred marks, raised by melting down the remainder of the holy ornaments. The quality of William's piety is easily to be tested by a comparison of the value of his single gold mark, worth in our money one hundred pounds, with that of the one thousand silver marks, the sum total of the fines he exacted. A sum equal to thirty thousand pounds was extracted from the monastery and church of Ely, and forty Norman knights were quartered upon the brethren; one knight to each monk, as the old "Tabula Eliensis" specifies in detail.

## XXXIV

WHAT in the meanwhile had become of Hereward? What was he doing when these shaven-pated traitors were betraying his stronghold? One would like to find that hero wreaking a terrible vengeance upon them, but we hear of nothing so pleasing and appropriate. The only vengeance was that taken by William upon the rank and file of the rebels, and that was merely cowardly and unworthy. It was not politic to anger the leaders of this last despairing stand of the Saxons, and so they obtained the King's Peace; but the churls and serfs felt the force of retribution in gouged eyes, hands struck off, ears lopped, and other ferocious pleasantries typical of the Norman mind. Hereward who, I am afraid, was not always so watchful as his name signifies, seems to have found pardon readily enough, and one set of legends tells how at last he died peacefully and of old age in his bed.

Others among the old monkish chroniclers give him an epic and more fitting end, in which, like Samson, he dies with his persecutors. They marry him to a rich Englishwoman, one Elfthryth, who had made her peace with the King, and afterwards obtained pardon for her lover. But the Normans still hated him, and one night, when his chaplain Ethelward, whose duty was to keep watch and ward within and without his house and to place guards, slumbered at his post, a band of assassins crept in and attacked Hereward as he lay. He armed himself in haste, and withstood their onslaught. His spear was broken, his sword too, and he was driven to use his shield as a weapon. Fifteen Frenchmen lay dead beneath his single arm when four of the party crept behind him and smote him with their swords in the back. This stroke brought him to his knees. A Breton knight, one Ralph of Dôl, then rushed on him, but Hereward, in a last effort, once more wielded his buckler, and the Englishman and the Breton fell dead together.

However, whenever, or wherever he came to his end, certainly the great Hereward was laid to rest in the nave of Crowland Abbey, but no man knows his grave. Just as the bones and the last resting-place of Harold at Waltham Abbey have disappeared, so the relics of " the Watchful," that " most strenuous man," that hardy fighter in a lost cause, are scattered to the winds.

There are alleged descendants of Hereward to this day, and a " Sir Herewald Wake " is at the head of them; but we know nothing of how they prove their descent. " Watch and pray " is their motto, and a very appropriate one, too; although it is possible that Hereward's praying was spelt with an " e," and himself not so prayerful as predatory.

Hereward, the old monkish chroniclers tell us, was " a man short in stature but of enormous strength." By that little fragment of personal description they do something to wreck an ideal. Convention demands that all heroes be far above the height of other men, just as all knights of old were conventionally gentle and chivalric and all ladies fair; though, if history do not lie and limners painted what they saw, the chivalry and gentleness of knighthood were as sadly to seek as the loving-kindness of the hyæna, and the fair ladies of old were most furiously ill-favoured. Hereward's figure, without that personal paragraph, is majestic. The feet of him squelch, it is true, through Fenland mud and slime, but his head is lost in the clouds until this very early piece of journalism disperses the mists and makes the hero something less of the demi-god than he had otherwise been.

The name of Hereward's stronghold offers a fine blue-mouldy bone of contention for rival antiquaries to gnaw at. In face of the clamour of disputants on this subject, it behoves us to take no side, but just to report the theories advanced. The most favoured view, then, is that "Aldreth" enshrines a corruption of St. Etheldreda's name,—that Etheldreda who was variously known as St. Ethelthryth and St. Audrey,—and that it was originally none other than St. Audrey's Hythe, or Landing, on this very stream of Ouse, now much shrunken and running in a narrow channel, instead of spreading over the country in foul swamps and unimaginable putrid bogs. "Aldreche"—the old reach of this Ouse—is another variant put forward; but it does not seem to occur to any of these disputants that, at anyrate, the termination of the place-name is identical with that in the names of Meldreth and Shepreth, where little streams, the mere shadows and wraiths of their former selves, still exist to hint that it was once necessary to ford them, and that, whatever the first syllable of Meldreth may mean, "reth" is perhaps the Celtic "rhyd," a ford, and Shepreth just the "sheep ford."

But whatever may have been the original form of Aldreth's name, the village nowadays has nothing to show of any connection with St. Etheldreda, save the site only of a well dedicated to her, situated halfway up the steeply rising street. It is a curious street, this of Aldreth, plunging down from the uplands of the Isle into the peat and ooze that William so laboriously crossed. Where it descends you may still see the stones with which he, or others at some later time, paved the way. For the rest, Aldreth is one long street of rustic cottages very scattered and much separated by gardens: over all a look of listlessness, as though this were the end of the known world, and nothing mattered very much. When a paling from a garden fence falls into the road, it lies there; when the plaster falls from a cottage wall, no one repairs the damage; when a window is broken, the hole is papered or stuffed with rags: economy of effort is studied at Aldreth.

The curious may still trace William's route through the Isle, to Ely city. It is not a straight course. Geographical conditions forbade it to be so, and I doubt not, that if the road were to make again, they would still forbid; for to rule a straight line across the map from Aldreth to Ely is to plunge into hollows where water still lies, though actual fens be of the past. His way lay along two sides of a square; due north for three miles and almost due east for a like distance, along the track pursued nowadays by the excellent road uphill to where the mile-long and populous village of Haddenham stands on a crest, and down again and turning to the right for Witchford, whence, along a gentle spur, you come presently into Ely.

## XXXV

RETURNING to the high road at Cottenham Corner, and passing the junction of the road from Waterbeach, we come presently, at a point six and a half miles from Cambridge, to a place marked "Dismal Hall" on large-scale Ordnance maps. Whatever this may have been in old days, it is now a small white-brick farmhouse, called by the occupier "The Brambles," and by the landlord "Brookside." The name perhaps derived originally from some ruined Roman villa whose walls rose, roofless and desolate, beside the ancient Akeman Street. It is a name belonging, in all probability, to the same order as the "Caldecotes" and "Coldharbours," met frequently beside, or in the neighbourhood of, Roman ways; places generally conceded to have been ruined houses belonging to that period. The modern representative of "Dismal Hall" stands beside a curiously small and oddly-shaped field, itself called "Dismal"; triangular in form and comprising only two acres.

Half a mile beyond this point, a pretty group of cottages marks where the way to Denny Abbey lies to the right across a cow-pasture. A field-gate whose posts are the battered fragments of some Perpendicular Gothic pillars from that ruined monastery, crowned incongruously with a pair of eighteenth-century stone urns, clearly identifies the spot. There has been a religious house of sorts on this spot since eight hundred years ago, and most of the remains are of the Norman period, when a settlement of

Black Monks from Ely settled here. In succession to them came the Knights Templars, who made it a preceptory, and when their Order was suppressed and ceased out of the land, in consequence of its corruption and viciousness, the nuns of St. Clare were given a home in these deserted halls. Close upon four hundred years have gone since they, too, were thrust forth, and it has for centuries past been a farmhouse. Indeed, if you regard Denny Abbey, as also many another, in anything else save a conventional light, you will see that it was really always a farm. What else than a farm was the great Abbey of Tintern, and what other than farmers those Cistercian monks who built it and cultivated those lands, the godless, growing fearful and in expiatory mood, had given them? So also with the Benedictines, the Templars, and the Clares who succeeded one another here. You may note the fact in their great barns, and in the fields they reclaimed. To-day, groups of buildings of uncertain age, as regards their outer walls, enclose littered rick-yards, but the dwelling-house, for all the uninteresting look of one side, shows, built into its inner face, the sturdy piers and arches of one of the aisles; and the otherwise commonplace hall and staircase of the interior are informed with a majestic dignity by two columns and a noble arch of the Norman church. A large and striking barn, approached and entered across a pig-haunted yard rich in straw and mud, proves, on entering, to be a beautiful building of the Decorated period, once the refectory.

Leaving Denny Abbey behind, we come to

Chittering, a place unknown to guide-books and chartographers. We need blame neither the one nor the other for this omission, for Chittering is remarkable for nothing but its insignificance and lack of anything that makes for interest. It consists, when you have counted everything in its constituent parts, of two lonely public-houses, the Traveller's Rest and the Plough and Horses, a grotesquely unbeautiful Baptist Chapel and a school, five or six scattered cottages, and one new house, entrenched as it were in a defensive manner behind a sedgy and duckweedy drain. It is here, at a right-hand turning, that the exploratory cyclist turns off for Wicken Fen, the last remaining vestige of the natural Fenland that once overspread the greater part of the county. In Wicken Fen, a square mile of peaty bog and quaking morass, where the reeds still grow tall, and strange aquatic plants flourish, the rarer Fenland lepidoptera find their last refuge. Dragon-flies, in glittering panoply of green-and-gold armour and rainbow-hued wings, flash like miniature lightnings over the decaying vegetation, and the sulphur-coloured, white-and-scarlet butterflies find a very paradise in the moist and steamy air. Wicken Fen is jealously preserved in its natural state, and is a place of pilgrimage, not only for the naturalist, with his butterfly-net and his collecting-box, but for all who would obtain some idea of what this country was like in former ages. At the same time it is a place difficult to find, and the route to it a toilsome one. The Fens express flatness to the last degree, it is true, but, even though they be drained, they are not easy to explore. Mountain-ranges are, indeed, not more weariful than these flats, where you can never make a straight course when once off the main roads, but are compelled by dykes and drains to make for any given point by questing hither and thither as though following the outlines of the squares on a chessboard. The distance to Wicken Fen, measured from Chittering in a direct line on the map, is not more than four miles. Actually, the route is nearly eight.

We have already seen what a Fenland drove is like. To such a complexion does this treacherous by-way descend in less than a quarter of a mile, bringing the adventurer into an apparently boundless field of corn. If the weather has recently been wet, he is brought to a despairing pause at this point, for the rugged drove here becomes a sea of a curious kind of black buttery mud, highly tenacious. The pedestrian is to be pitied in this pass, but the cyclist is in worse case, for his wheels refuse to revolve, and he finds, with horror, his brake and his forks clogged with the horrible mess, and his mud-guards become mud-accumulators instead. To shoulder his machine and carry it is the only course. If, on the other hand, the weather be dry, with a furious wind blowing, the mud becomes dust and fills the air with a very respectable imitation of a Soudan sandstorm. In those happy climatic conditions when it is neither wet nor too dry, and when the stormy winds have sunk to sleep, the way to Wicken Fen, though long and circuitous, loses these terrors. At such times the ditchers may be seen almost up to their knees in what looks like dry sand, hard at work clearing out the dykes and drains choked up by this flying dust, and it becomes of interest to examine the nature of this curious soil. A handful, gathered at haphazard, shows a kind of black sand, freely mixed with a fine snuff-coloured mixture of powder and minute fibrous shreds; pulverised peat from the vanished bogs and morasses that once stewed and festered where these fields now yield abundant harvests. This peaty soil it is that gives these fields their fertility, for, as Sir Humphry Davy once said, "A soil covered with peat is a soil covered with manure."

It is a curious commentary on the fame of Wicken Fen as an entomologist's paradise, and on its remoteness, that all the ditchers and farming-folk assume the stranger who inquires his way to it to be a butterfly-hunter.

At last, after crossing the railway to Ely, making hazardous passage over rickety plank-bridges across muddy dykes, and wending an uncertain way through farmyards inhabited by dogs keenly desirous of tearing the infrequent stranger limb from limb, the broad river Cam is approached, at Upware. Upware is just a riverside hamlet, remote from the world, and only in touch with its doings on those occasions when boating-parties from Ely or Cambridge come by on summer days.

On the opposite shore, across the reedy Cam, stands a queer building, partly ferry-house, partly inn, with the whimsical legend, "Five Miles from Anywhere. No Hurry," painted on its gable. The real sign of Upware Inn, as it is generally called, is the "Lord Nelson," but this knowledge is only acquired on particular inquiry, for signboard it has none.

The roystering old days at Upware are done. They came to an end when the railway between Cambridge, Ely, and King's Lynn was opened, and coals and heavy goods no longer went by barge along the Ouse and Cam. In that unregenerate epoch, before modern culture had reached Cambridge, and undergrads had not begun to decorate their rooms with blue china and to attempt to live up to it, the chief delight of Cambridge men was to walk or scull down to Upware and have it out with the bargees. Homeric battles were fought here by the riverside in those days of beef and beer, and it was not always the University man who got the worst of it in these sets-to with or without the gloves. In the last days of this Philistine era the railway navvy came as a foeman equally well worth the attention of young Cambridge; and thus, in a final orgie of bloody noses and black eyes, the fame of Upware culminated. When the navvy had completed his work and departed, the bargee went also, and peace has reigned ever since along the sluggish reaches of the Cam. There are, it is true, a few of the barging craft and mystery still left along this waterway, but, beyond a singular proficiency in swearing, they have nothing in common with their forebears, and drink tea and discuss social science.

In those old robustious days—famous once, but now forgot—flourished the Republic of Upware, a somewhat blackguardly society composed chiefly of muscular undergrads. Admission to the ranks of this precious association was denied to none who could hit hard and drink deep. In the riverside field that still keeps its name of "Upware Bustle," the Republic held many of its drunken, uproarious carouses, presided over by the singular character who called himself, not President, but "King of Upware." Richard Ramsay Fielder, this pot-house

UPWARE INN.

monarch, "flourished," as histories would say, *circa* 1860. He was an M.A. of Cambridge, a man of good family and of high abilities, but cursed with a gipsy nature, an incurable laziness, and an unquenchable thirst: the kind of man who is generally, for his sake and their own, packed off by his family to the Colonies. Fielder perhaps could not be induced to cross the seas; at anyrate, he enjoyed an allowance from his family, on the degrading condition that he kept himself at a distance. He earned the allowance loyally, and found the society that pleased him most at Upware and in the inns of the surrounding Fenland villages; so that on leaving the University he continued to cling to the neighbourhood for many years, becoming a hero to all the dissolute youngsters at Cambridge. He it was who originally painted the apt inscription, "Five Miles from Anywhere," on the gable-wall of this waterside inn, his favourite haunt, where he lounged and smoked and tippled with the bargees; himself apeing that class in his dress: coatless, with corduroy breeches and red waistcoat. A contemporary sketch of him tells of his thin flowing hair of inordinate length, of his long dirty finger-nails, and of the far from aromatic odour he gàve forth; and describes his boating expeditions. "He used to take about with him in his boat an enormous brown-ware jug, capable of holding six gallons or more, which he would at times have filled with punch, ladling it out profusely for his aquatic friends. This vast pitcher or 'gotch,' which was called 'His Majesty's pint' ('His Majesty' in allusion to his self-assumed title), had been made to his own order, and decorated before kilning with incised ornaments by his own hand. Amongst these figured prominently his initials 'R. R. F.' and his crest, actual or assumed, a pheon, or arrow-head." Alluding to his initials, he would often playfully describe himself as "more R. than F.," which means (is it necessary to explain?) "more rogue than fool." Eccentric in every way, he would change his quarters without notice and without reason, and would remain in bed, smoking and drinking, for weeks together.

This odd character lingered here for some years after the bargees had gone, and into the time when even the most rowdy of Cambridge undergraduates began to find it "bad form" to booze and be hail-fellow with the village rapscallions of Fenland. Then Fielder himself "forswore sack and lived cleanly"; or at anyrate deserted his old haunts. Report tells how he died at last at Folkestone, in comfortable circumstances and in a quite respectable and conventional manner.

## XXXVI

Upware Inn has lost a great deal of its old-time look. With something akin to melancholy the sentimental pilgrim sees a corrugated iron roof replacing the old thatch of reeds, characteristic of Fenland. The great poplar, too, has had its curious spreading limb amputated: that noble branch whereon the King of that Republic sat on summer evenings and held his disreputable Court. But not everything is modernised. The Cam is not yet bridged. You still are ferried across in an uncouth flat-bottomed craft, and they even yet burn peat in the domestic grates at Upware, so that links yet bind the present with the past. Peat is the traditional fuel of the Fens, largely supplanted nowadays by coal, but should coal become permanently dear, these Cambridgeshire villages would, for sake of its cheapness, go back to peat and endure its acrid smell and dull smouldering humour in place of the brightness of a coal fire. At Wicken Fen the peat is still forming: perhaps the only place in England where the process is going on. It is still three miles from Upware to this relic of the untamed wilderness, past Spinney Abbey, now a farmhouse with few or no relics of the old foundation to be seen. It was in this farmstead that Henry Cromwell, one of the Protector's sons, lived in retirement. He was visited here one September day in 1671 by Charles the Second, come over from Newmarket for the purpose. What Charles said to him and what Henry Cromwell replied we do not know, and imagination has therefore the freer rein. But we spy drama in it, a "situation" of the most thrilling kind. What would *you* say to the man who had murdered— judicially murdered, if you like it—your father? Charles, however, was a cynic of an easy-going type, and probably failed to act up to the theatrical requirements of the occasion. At anyrate, Henry Cromwell was not consigned to the nearest, or any, dungeon. Nothing at all was done to him, and he died, two years later, at peace with all men. He lies buried in the little church of Wicken, and was allowed to rest there.

Wicken Fen is just beyond this abbey farmstead. You turn to the right, along a green lane and across a field, and there you are, with the reeds and the sedge growing thick in the stagnant water, water-lilies opening their buds on the surface, and a lazy hum of insects droning in the still and sweltering air.

The painted lady, the swallow-tail, the peacock, the scarlet tiger, and many other gaily-hued butterflies float on silent wings; things crawl and creep in the viscous slime, and on warm summer days, after rain, the steam rises from the beds of peat and wild growths as from some natural cookshop. Old windmill pumps here and there dot the banks of the fen, and in the distance are low hills that form, as it

WICKEN FEN.

were, the rim of the basin in which this relic is set.

Away in one direction rises the tall majestic tower of Soham Church, deceiving the stranger into the belief that he is looking at Ely Cathedral, and overlooking what are now the pastures of Soham Fen; in the days of King Canute that inland sea—that *mare de Soham*—which stretched ten miles wide between Mildenhall and Ely. It was across Soham

Mere that Canute came voyaging by Ely, rowed by knights in his galley, when he heard, while yet a long way off, the sound of melody. Bidding his knights draw nearer to the Isle, he found the music to be the monks in the church singing vespers. The story is more than a legend, and is alluded to in the only surviving stanza of an ancient song—

"Merie sungen the Muneches binnen Ely
Tha Cnut Ching rew therby.
Roweth cnites noer the lant,
And here we thes Muneches saeng."

It is a story that well pictures the reality—the actual isolation—of the Isle, just as does that other, telling how that same Canute, coming again to Ely for Christmas, found the waters that encompassed it frost-bound, but so slightly that crossing the ice was perilous in the extreme. He was thus of necessity halted on the shores of the frozen mere, and until they found one Brithmer, a Saxon cheorl of the Fen, skilled in Fen-lore and able to guide the King and his train across the shallow places where the ice lay thick and strong, it seemed as though he and his retinue would be unable to keep the Feast of the Nativity in Ely. Brithmer was a man of prodigious bulk, nicknamed "Budde," or "the Fat," and where he led the way in safety men of ordinary weight could follow without fear. So Canute followed in his sledge, with his Court, and kept Christmas on the Isle. As for Brithmer, who had performed this service, he was enlarged from serfdom to be a free man, and loaded with honours. Indeed, he was probably only known as "the Fat" before this time, and was doubtless called Brithmer, which means "bright mere," after this exploit.

## XXXVII

RETURNING to the old coach road from this expedition, and coming to it again with a thankful heart, we presently come to Stretham Bridge, a narrow old hunch-backed brick structure spanning the Great Ouse, or Old West River, and giving entrance to this Isle of Ely, of which already we have heard so much, and will now hear more. The sketch-map that has already shown the Conqueror's line of march indicates also the size and shape of the Isle: the physical Isle. For there are really two, the physical and the political. The last-named comprises the whole of the northern part of Cambridgeshire, from this point along the Ouse to Upware, and thence, following the Cambridgeshire border, round to Littleport and Tydd St. Giles in the north, by the neighbourhood of Crowland and Peterborough, and so down to the Ouse again at Earith, Aldreth, and Stretham Bridge. It is still a political division, and has its own government, under the style of the County Council of the Isle of Ely. The real geographical Isle—the one sketched in the map—is much smaller; only one-third the size of the other; measuring in its greatest length and breadth but some twelve and eight miles, and bounded by the Great Ouse from Earith to Upware, by Cam and Little

Ouse to Littleport, and thence by the Old Croft River to the New Bedford River, returning along that cut to Earith.

As you approach Stretham Bridge along this old causeway the Isle is plain to see in front, its gentle hills glimpsed between the fringe of willows and poplars that now begin to line the way. No one has bettered the description Carlyle wrote of the Fen-country seen from this causeway that was once the Akeman Street; and no one *can* better it. " It has a clammy look," he says, clayey and boggy; the produce of it, whether bushes and trees or grass and crops, gives you the notion of something lazy, dropsical, gross. From the "circumfluent mud," willows, "Nature's signals of distress," spring up by every still slime-covered drain : willows generally polled and, with that process long continued, now presenting a very odd and weird appearance. The polled crown of an ancient willow bears a singularly close resemblance to a knuckly fist, and these, like so many gnarled giant arms of bogged and smothered Goliaths thrust upwards in despair, with clenched and imprecatory hands, give this road the likeness of a highway into fairyland whose ogres, under the spell of some Prince Charming, have been done to death in their own sloughs. Pollards, anathema to Cobbett, are in plenty in these lowlands, but it must not be thought that because of them, or even because Carlyle's description of the country is so apt, it is anything but beautiful. Only, to see its beauties and appreciate them, it is necessary here, more than elsewhere, to have fine weather.

A FENLAND ROAD: THE AKEMAN STREET NEAR STRETHAM BRIDGE.

Stretham Bridge, that makes so great a business of crossing the Ouse, seems an instance of much ado about nothing, for that river, "Great Ouse" though it be named, is very much to seek in summer, trickling away as it does between tussocks of rough grass. The Great Ouse is not of the bigness it once boasted, in days before the Old and New Bedford Rivers were cut, two hundred and sixty years ago, to carry its sluggish waters away by a direct route to the sea, and the fair-weather pilgrim marvels at the bridge and at the great banks he sees stretching away along its course to protect the surrounding lands from being flooded. That they are needed is evident enough from the care taken to repair them, and from a sight of the men digging hard by in the greasy gault to obtain the repairing materials. These are the "gaulters" and the "bankers" of Fenland life. It was one of these who, as a witness in some cause at the Cambridge Assizes, appearing in his working clothes, was asked his occupation. "I am a banker, my Lord," he replied. "We cannot have any absurdity," said Baron Alderson testily; to which the man answered as before, "I am a banker"; and things were at cross-purposes until the meaning of the term was explained to the Court.

The local occupations all have curious names, and the inhabitants of the Fens in general were long known as "Fen-slodgers," a title that, if indeed unlovely, is at least as expressive of mudlarking as it is possible for a word to be. You picture a slodger as a half-amphibious creature, something between a water-sprite and a sewer-man, muddy from head to foot and pulling his feet out of the ooze as he goes with resounding "plops," like the noise made in drawing the cork of a bottle. But if the Fenman did not quite fill all the details thus conjured up, he was, and is still, a watery kind of creature; half-farmer, half-fisherman and wild-fowler. He is sometimes a "gozard," that is to say, a goose-ward or goose-keeper. This occupation does not seem to have given an abiding surname, as many others have done, and you may search in many directories for it without avail, although the Haywards, the Cartwrights, and the Cowards are prominent enough. The Fenman digs his land with a becket or a hodden spade. The design of the first-named goes back to Roman times, and is seen figured on columns and triumphal arches in the Imperial City, just as it is fashioned to-day. It is this form of spade that is alluded to in such wayside tavern-signs as the Plough and Becket, apt to be puzzling to the uninitiated. When the Fenland rustic, weary of the daily routine, wants a little sport or seeks to grace his table with fish, he goes "dagging for eels" along the rivers and the drains, "leams," "lodes," or "eaus" (which he calls "ees") with a "gleve," which, translated into ordinary English, means an eel-spear, shaped very like Neptune's trident.

HODDEN SPADE AND BECKET.

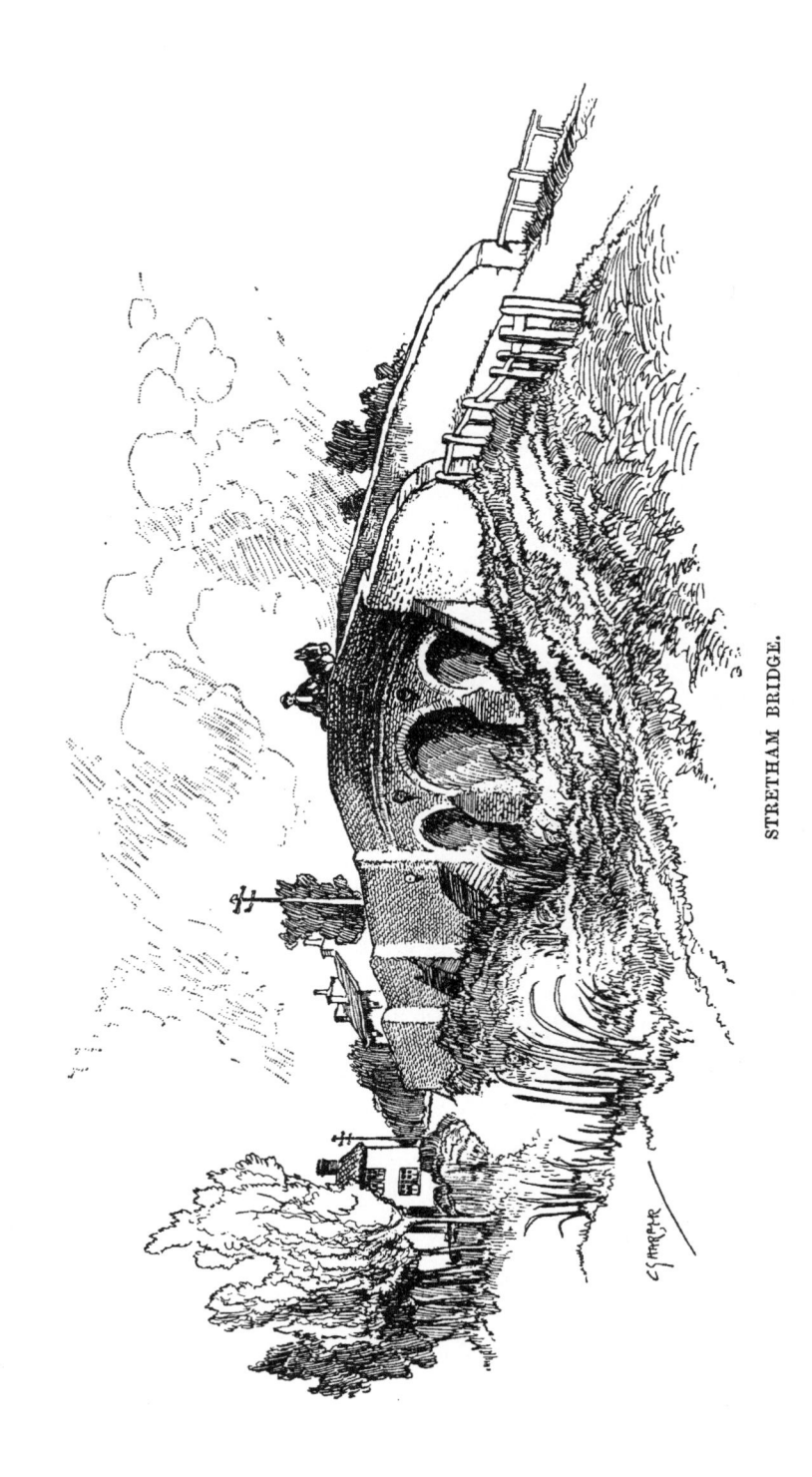

STRETHAM BRIDGE.

## XXXVIII

CROSSING Stretham Bridge, with Stretham Common on the right and Stretham village two miles ahead, the Akeman Street appears to be soon lost, for the way is crooked, and much more like a mediæval than a classic road. Indeed, the entrance to Stretham is by two striking right-angle turns and a curve past a low-lying tract called Beggars' Bush Field.

"Beggars' Bush" is so frequent a name in rural England[1] that it arouses curiosity. Sometimes these spots bear the unbeautiful name of "Lousy Bush," as an apt alternative. They were probably the lurking-places of mediæval tramps. The tramp we have always had with us. He, his uncleanliness and his dislike of work are by no means new features. Only, with the increase of population, there is naturally a proportional increase in the born-tired and the professional unemployed. That is all. So long ago as Queen Elizabeth's time legislation was found necessary to suppress the tramp. The Elizabethan statute did not call him by that name: they were not clever enough in those times to invent so descriptive a term, and merely called him a "sturdy rogue and vagrant." Of course he was not

[1] There was once a Beggars' Bush on the Old North Road, fifty-five miles from London and two and a half from Huntingdon. King James the First seems to have heard of it, when on his progress to London from Scotland, for he said, on the road, in a metaphorical sense to Bacon, who had entertained him with a lavish and ruinous hospitality, "Sir Francis, you will soon come to Beggars' Bush, and I may e'en go along with you too, if we be both so bountiful."

suppressed by the hardness, the whips and scorpions, of the Elizabethans, but endured them and the branded "R" and "V," and sporting them as his trade-marks, went tramping to the end of his earthly pilgrimage. These are the "strangers" whom you will find mentioned in the burial registers of many a wayside parish church; the "strangers" found dead on the road, or under the "Beggars' Bushes," and buried by the parish.

It was the indiscriminate almsgiving of the religious houses—the Abbeys and the Priories of old—that fostered this race of vagrom men and women, the ancestors of the tramps of to-day. Like the Salvation Army in our times,—either better or worse, whichever way you regard it,—they fed, and sometimes sheltered, the outcast and the hungry. Only the hungry are not fed for nothing, nor without payment sheltered by the Salvationists. They purchase food and lodging off the Army for a trifle in coin or by a job of work: the monks exacted nothing in return for the dole or the straw pallet that any hungry wretch was welcome to. Thus, throughout the land a great army of the lazy, the unfortunate, and the afflicted were in mediæval times continually tramping from one Abbey to another. Sometimes they stole, oftener they begged, and they found the many pilgrims who were always making pilgrimage from one shrine to another handy to prey upon. Ill fared the straggler from the pilgrim train that wound its length along the ancient ways; for there were those among the vagrom gang who would not scruple to rob or murder him, and that is one among many reasons why pilgrimage was made in company.

Stretham village, it is scarce necessary in these parts to say, is set on a hill, or what in the Fens is by courtesy so-called. No village here has any other site than some prehistoric knob of clay that by strange chance raised itself above the ooze. The site of Stretham, being in the Isle of Ely, was an isle within an isle. Still one goes up to and down from it. Still you see ancient houses there with flights of steps up to the front doors, so hard put to it were the old inhabitants to keep out of the way of the water; and even yet, when you are come to the levels again, the houses cease and no more are seen until the next rise is reached, insignificant enough to the eye, but to the mind stored with the old lore of the Fens significant of much. Stretham is a large village. It does not run to length, as do places in other parts of the country situated, like it, on a great road. *They* commonly consist of one long street: Stretham, built on the crown of a hill, has odd turns and twists, and streets unexpectedly opening on either hand as the explorer advances, and is, so to speak, built round and round itself. In its midst, where the road broadens into as wide a space as a village squeezed on to the crown of an island hill-top could anciently afford, stands a market cross.

You may seek far and wide for information about this cross, but you will not find. All we know is that, by its look, it belongs to the fifteenth century, and we may shrewdly suspect that the nondescript plinth it stands upon replaces a broad approach of steps. When the steps were taken away is a matter as unknown as the history of the cross itself; but if we do not know the when, we at least, in the light of Stretham's circumstances, know the why. The street was inconveniently narrowed by them.

STRETHAM.

The fine church stands to the left of the road by the cross, and is adjoined by an ancient vicarage. At the top of the main street, where the village ends, the traveller obtains his first glimpse of Ely Cathedral, four miles away. It must have been here, or close by, that Jack Goodwin, guard on the Lynn "Rover," about 1831, met Calcraft the hangman, for he tells how the executioner got up as an outside passenger "about four miles on the London side of Ely," to which city he had been paying a professional visit, to turn off an unhappy agricultural labourer sentenced to death for incendiarism, then a capital offence. Calcraft had been at considerable pains to avoid recognition, and had appeared in the procession to the scaffold on Ely Common as one of the Sheriff's javelin-men. Probably he feared to be the object of popular execration.

When he mounted the coach, he was dressed like a Cambridgeshire farmer, and thought himself quite unknown. Goodwin took charge of his baggage, comprising a blue bag, half a dozen red cabbages, *and a piece of rope*—the identical rope that had put an end to the unhappy wretch of the day before. He then offered him a cigar (guards were fine fellows in their way) and addressed Calcraft by name.

The hangman replied that he was mistaken. "No, no," said Goodwin, "I am not; I saw you perform on three criminals at the Old Bailey a few weeks ago."

That, of course, was conclusive, and they chatted more or less pleasantly; although, to be sure, the conversation chiefly turned on Mr. Calcraft's professional experiences. He told Goodwin, when he left, that "if ever he had the pleasure of doing the job for him, he would soap the rope to make it as comfortable as possible."

## XXXIX

THERE is little or nothing to say of the way into Ely, and only the little village of Thetford, and that to one side of the road, intervenes. Nothing distracts the attention from the giant bulk of the Cathedral.

How shall we come into Ely? As archæologists, as pilgrims spiritually inclined and chanting a *sursum corda* as we go, or shall we be gross and earthly, scenting lamb and green peas, spring duckling and asparagus from afar, for all the world like our hearty grandfathers of the coaching age, to whom the great whitefaced Lamb Inn, that is still the principal hostelry of this city, appealed with much more force than that great grey religious pile? We will to the Lamb, which is not a difficult house to find, and in fact presents itself squarely and boldly as you enter. "Come," it seems to say, "you are expected. The cloth is laid, you shall dine royally on Ely delicacies. This is in no traditional way the capital of the Fens. Our ducklings are the tenderest, our asparagus the most succulent, there never were such eels as those of Ouse; and you shall conclude with the cream-cheese of Cottenham." Is an invitation so alluring to be despised?

It is strange to read how Thomas Cross in his *Autobiography of a Stage Coachman* devotes pages to an elaborate depreciation of the Lamb in coaching times. From a "slip of a bar," with a netful of mouldy lemons hanging from the ceiling, to the catering and the appointments of the hostelry, he finds nothing good. But who shall say he was not justified? Lounging one day in this apology for a bar, there entered one who was a stranger to him, who asked the landlady what he could have for dinner. "Spitchcocked eels and mutton chops," replied the hostess, naming what were then, and are still, the staple commodities. The stranger was indignant. Turning to Cross, he said, "I have used this house for five-and-twenty years and never had any other answer."

Presently they both sat down to this canonical dinner in a sparsely-furnished room. The stranger cleaned his knife and fork (brought into the room in a dirty condition) by thrusting them through the soiled and ragged tablecloth. The sherry was fiery, if the port was good; and for gooseberry tart they had a something in a shallow dish, with twenty bottled gooseberries under the crust. The good cheer of the Lamb was then, it seems quite evident, a matter of conventional belief rather than of actual existence.

It has been already said that nothing distracts the attention of the traveller on approaching the city. Ely, indeed, is nearly all Cathedral, and very little of that which is not can claim any interest. It is true that six thousand five hundred people live in Ely, but the figures are surprising. Where do these thousands hide themselves? The streets are not so many, and even at that are all emptiness, slumber, and yawns. The shopkeepers (who surely keep shop for fun) come to their doors and yawn, and regard the stray customer with severity; the Divinity students yawn, and the Dean and the Cathedral staff yawn horribly at the service they have gone through so many times and know by heart. The only place where they don't yawn is the railway station, down below by the Ouse, by whose banks you get quite the finest near view of the Cathedral. Ely, in short, lives chiefly by and on the Cathedral. If there had never been a cathedral here, it would have been a village the size of Stretham. Perhaps to that size it will even yet decline.

"Ely," wrote Cobbett eighty years ago, "is what one may call a miserable little town; very prettily situated, but poor and mean. Everything seems to be on the decline, as, indeed, is the case everywhere where the clergy are masters." True enough, enterprise and industry are deadened in all such places; but this bull-headed old prevaricator, in proceeding to account for the decay, furiously assaults the Protestant religion, and pretends to find it responsible. It is true that the cleric is everywhere a brake on the wheels of progress, but what religion plunges its adherents in so abject a condition of superstitious dependence as the Roman Catholic creed? Cobbett on Ely is, in short, a monument of blundering clap-trap.

"Arrived at Ely," he says, "I first walked round the beautiful cathedral, that honour to our Catholic forefathers and that standing disgrace to our Protestant selves. It is impossible to look at that magnificent pile without feeling that we are a fallen race of men. You have only to open your eyes to be convinced that England must have been a far greater and more wealthy country in those days than it is in these days. The hundreds of thousands of loads of stone of which this cathedral and the monasteries in the neighbourhood were built must all have been brought by sea from distant parts of the kingdom.[1] These foundations were laid more than a thousand years ago; and yet there are vagabonds who have the impudence to say that it is the Protestant religion that has made England a great country."

Here we have Cobbett, who ought to have known better, and *did* actually know, repeating the shambling fallacy that the architectural art of the Middle Ages was so artistic because it was inspired by religion, and that its artistry decayed by consequence of the Reformation. Such an argument loses sight of the circumstance that edifices dedicated to religious use were not the only large or beautiful buildings erected in those ages, and that those who wrought upon secular castle or manor-house wrought as well and as truly as those who reared the soaring minster or noble abbey. And whence came the means wherewith to build cathedrals like this of Ely? Did they not derive from the lands settled upon monasteries by those anxious only to save their own souls, and by others who sought thus to compound for their deeds of blood or infamy? And is it possible to think without aversion of a Church that, accepting such gifts, absolved the givers in consideration of them?

Life is endeavour; not all cloistered prayer. He prays best whose prayers are an interlude of toil; and so, when we read Cobbett's long account of the wretched condition of Ely Cathedral, of its "disgraceful irrepair and disfigurement," and of the two

[1] The stone really came from Barnack, in Northamptonshire, thirty-five miles distant.

old men who on a week-day afternoon formed the whole of the congregation, coupled with his regretful surmise that in Catholic times five thousand people would have been assembled here, we are apt to think that sparse congregation a very healthy sign, and that even those two old men would have been better employed out in the workaday world. He would be a Goth who should fail to perceive the beauty of Ely Cathedral and of its like, but those noble aisles, those soaring towers tell a tale of an enslaved land, of fettered souls, of a priestcraft that sought to rule the State, as well as to hold the keys of Heaven and of Hell. No man, whether he be Pope, Archbishop, or merely the Boanerges of some hideous Bethel, has the right to enslave another's soul. Let even the lovely cathedrals of our land be levelled in one common ruin if the sight of them harks us back to Popery, for in that harking back England would be utterly undone.

But since the saving common-sense of the Englishman can never again permit him to deliver up his soul into another's keeping, and since it follows naturally from this that the Romanising tendencies of our clergy must of necessity lead nowhere and bear no fruit, it becomes possible to look with a dispassionate eye upon these architectural relics of discredited beliefs.

Why was the Cathedral built here? That is a long story. It originated in the monastery founded on this spot in A.D. 673 by Etheldreda, daughter of Auna, King of the East Angles. Etheldreda has long since been canonised, and it behoves us to deal as gently as may be with a saint; but she was, if the chroniclers tell truth, an eccentric and original creature, twice wed by her own consent, and yet vowed to a life-long chastity. Her first husband was one Tondbert, a kinglet of the Gyrvians or Fen-folk, a monarch of the mudlarks, ruling over many miles of reed and sedge, in whose wastes Ely was centred. He gave his Queen this Isle, and died. For five years she remained a widow and then married again; this time a sturdier and less manageable man, King Egfrid of Northumbria. He respected her vows for twelve years, but when at last she took the veil in the north of England and fled from her Northumbrian home he took the only way open in the seventh century of asserting conjugal rights, and pursued her with an armed force. When, however, he arrived at the monastery of Coldingham she was gone, and I do not think Egfrid ever saw her again, or wanted to, for that matter. We will not follow Etheldreda in her long and adventurous journey to Ely, whither she had fled, nor recount the many miracles that helped her on the way. Miracles were cheap at that period, and for at least four hundred years to come were freely invented and elaborated by monkish chroniclers, who were the earliest novelists and writers of fairy tales, in the scriptorium of many a monastery.

## XL

In the year 673, then, behold the ecstatic Etheldreda come out of many perils to Ely. Here, where she thought the Isle lifted its crest highest above the waters, she founded a mixed monastery for monks and nuns. At this point the ground is one hundred and nine feet above sea-level: at Haddenham, the crowning crest is but thirteen feet higher. Here she ruled as Abbess for six years, when she died, and was succeeded by her sister, the sainted Sexburga. It was Sexburga who, sixteen years from this time, determined to honour Etheldreda to the best of her ability, bethought her of translating the body from the humble graveyard of the monastery to the church itself. She sent forth a number of the brethren on a roving commission to find a block of stone for a coffin, and as stone of any kind is the least likely thing to find for many miles around Ely, theirs looked to be a long and difficult quest. They had, indeed, wandered as far as the ruins of Roman Cambridge before they discovered anything, but there they found a magnificent sarcophagus of white marble, which they joyfully brought back, and in it the remains of Etheldreda, entire and incorrupt, were laid.

In 870, the time of the fourth Abbess, St. Withburga, a great disaster befell the monastery of Ely. For years past the terror of the heathen Vikings, the ruthless Danes and Jutes from over sea, had been growing. Wild-eyed fugitives, survivors of some pitiless massacre of the coastwise settlements by these pirates, had flung themselves, exhausted, upon the Isle, and now the peril was drawing near to this sanctuary. A special intercession, "Deliver us, O Lord, from the Northmen," distinguished morning and evening office, but the prayer was unanswered. Presently along the creeks came the beaked prows of the ruthless sea-rovers, and the monastery was sacked and burnt and all upon the Isle slain. That is history. To it the old chronicler must needs put a clinching touch of miraculous vengeance, and tells how a bloodstained pirate, thinking the marble shrine of St. Etheldreda to be a treasure-chest, burst it open. "When he had done this there was no delay of Divine vengeance, for immediately his eyes started miraculously from his head, and he ended there and then his sacrilegious life."

Before many years had passed, a new monastery was founded upon the blackened and bloodstained ruins of the old. This was a College of Secular Clergy, patronised by King Alfred. It was succeeded by a new foundation, instituted by Ethelwold, Bishop of Winchester, who made it a Benedictine House; but even of that we have no trace left, and the church under whose roof Canute worshipped and Edward the Confessor was educated was swept away in the great scheme of rebuilding, entered upon by Simeon, the first Norman Abbot, in 1080. Twenty-six years later the relics of St. Etheldreda were translated to the choir just completed. The translation took place on October

17th, a day ever afterwards, while the Roman Catholic religion prevailed, celebrated by a religious festival and a secular fair. Pilgrims flocked throughout the year to St. Audrey's shrine, but many thousands assembled on her feast-day, and, that no doubt should rest upon their pilgrimage, purchased such favours and tokens as "St. Audrey's chains," and images of her. The chains were lengths of coloured silks and laces, and were, like most articles sold at the stalls, cheap and common. From them, their vulgar showiness, and their association with the Saint, comes the word "tawdry."

Two years after this translation of St. Audrey, the Abbey Church was made the Cathedral of the new diocese of Ely, carved out of the vast See of Lincoln. Of the work wrought by Abbot Simeon and his successor, Richard, the great north and south transepts alone remain. The choir they built was replaced in the thirteenth century by that lovely Early English work we now see; the nave they had not reached. This is a work of some sixty years later than their time, and is one of the finest examples of late Norman architecture in the country. The Norman style went out with a blaze of architectural splendour at Ely, where the great west front shows it blending almost imperceptibly into Early English. It is a singular architectural composition, this western entrance and forefront of Ely Cathedral; the piling up to a dizzy height of a great tower, intended to be flanked on either side by two western transepts each ending in a smaller tower. The north-western transept fell in ruins at some unknown period and has never been rebuilt, so that a view of this front presents a curiously unbalanced look, very distressing to all those good folk whose sensibilities would be harrowed if in their domestic establishment they lacked a *pendant* to everything. To the

THE WEST FRONT, ELY CATHEDRAL.

housewife to whom a fender where the poker is not duly and canonically neighboured by the tongs looks a debauched and sinful object; to the citizen who would grieve if the bronze or cut-glass lustre on one side of his mantel-shelf were not matched on the other, this is a sight of the most dolorous sort. It must have been to soothe the feelings of all such that a sum of £25,000 was appealed for when Sir Gilbert Scott was restoring the Cathedral, many years ago, and its rebuilding was proposed. The money was not forthcoming, the work was not done, and so Scott did not obtain the £2500 commission. Scott's loss is our gain, for we are spared one more example of his way with old cathedrals.

The ruins of the missing transept are plain to see, and a huge and ugly buttress props up the tower from this side; but, were that building restored, we should only have again, in its completeness, a curiously childish design. For that is the note of this west front and of this great tower, rising in stage upon stage of masonry until the great blocks of stone, dwarfed by distance, look like so many courses of grey brick. So does a child build up towers and castles of wooden blocks.

We must, however, not accuse the original designers of the tower of this mere striving after enormous height. The uppermost stage, where the square building takes an octagonal form, is an addition of nearly two hundred years later, when the nice perceptions and exquisite taste of an earlier period were lost, and size was the goal of effort, rather than beauty. Those who built at that later time would have gone higher had they dared, but if they lacked something as artists, they must at least be credited with engineering knowledge. They knew that the mere crushing weight of stone upon stone would, if further added to, grind the lower stages into powder and so wreck the whole fabric. So, at a height of two hundred and fifteen feet, they stayed their hands; but, in earnest of what they would have done, had not prudence forbade, they crowned the topmost battlements with a tall light wooden spire, removed a century ago in one of the restorations. It was from the roof of this tower, in 1845, that Basevi, an architect interested in a restoration then in progress, fell and was killed.

The octagonal upper stage of this great western tower was added in the Decorated period, about 1350, when the great central octagon, the most outstanding and peculiar feature of the Cathedral, was built. Any distant view of this vast building that commands its full length shows, in addition to the western tower, a light and fairylike lantern, like some graceful coronet, midway of the long roof-ridge, where choir and nave meet. This was built to replace the tall central tower that suddenly fell in ruins in 1332 and destroyed much of the choir. To an architect inspired far above his fellows fell the task of rebuilding. There are two works among the whole range of ancient Gothic art in these islands that stand out above and beyond the rest and proclaim the hand and brain of genius. They are the west front of Peterborough Cathedral and the octagonal lantern of Ely. We do not know who designed Peterborough's daring arcaded front, but the name of that resourceful man who built *the* great feature of Ely has been preserved. He was Alan of Walsingham, the sacrist and sub-prior of the monastery. He did not build it in that conventional and deceitful sense we are accustomed to when we read that this or that mediæval Abbot or Bishop built one thing or another, the real meaning of the phrase being that they provided the money and were anything and everything but the architects. No: he imagined it; the idea sprang from his brain, his hands drew the plans, he made it grow and watched it to its completion.

No man dared rebuild the tower that had fallen; not even Alan, or perhaps he did not want to, being possessed, as we may well believe, by this Idea. What it was you shall hear, although, to be sure, no words have any power to picture to those who have not seen it what this great and original work is like. The fallen tower had been reared, as is the manner of such central towers, upon four great pillars where nave and choir and transepts met. Alan cleared the ruins of them away, and built in their stead a circle of eight stone columns that not only took in the width of nave and the central alleys and transepts and choir that had been enclosed by the fallen pillars, but spread out beyond it to the whole width of nave aisles and the side aisles of choir and transepts. This group of columns carries arches and a masonry wall rising in octagonal form above the roofs, and crowned by the timber structure of the lantern itself. The interior view of this lantern shows a number of vaulting ribs of timber spreading inwards from these columns, and supporting a whole maze of open timber-work pierced with great traceried windows and fretted and carved to wonderment. The effect is as that of a dome, "the only Gothic dome in the world" as it has been said. How truly it is a "lantern" may be seen when the sun shines through the windows and lights up the central space in the great church below. Puritan fury did much to injure this beautiful work, and its niches and tabernacles, once filled with Gothic statuary, are now supplied with modern sculptures, good in intention but a poor substitute. The modern stained-glass, too, is atrocious.

To fully describe Ely Cathedral in any but an architectural work would be alike impossible and unprofitable, and it shall not be attempted here: this giant among English minsters is not easily disposed of. For it *is* a giant. Winchester, the longest, measuring from west front to east wall of its Lady Chapel five hundred and fifty-five feet, is but eighteen feet longer. Even in that particular, Ely would have excelled but for the Lady Chapel here being built to one side, instead of at the end, owing to the necessity that existed for keeping a road open at the east end of the building.

Like the greater number of English minsters, Ely stands in a grassy space. A triangular green spreads out in front, with the inevitable captured Russian gun in the foreground, and the Bishop's Palace on the right. By turning to the south and passing through an ancient gateway, once the entrance to the monastery, the so-called "Park" is entered, the hilly and magnificently wooded southern side of what would in other cathedral cities be named the "Close," here technically "the College," and preserving in that title the memory of the ancient College of Secular Clergy which ruled sometime in that hundred years between A.D. 870 and 970.

It was from this point of view, near the ancient mound of "Cherry Hill," the site of William the Conqueror's Castle, that Turner painted his picture. Many remains of the monastic establishment are to be seen, built into charming and comfortable old houses, residences of the Cathedral dignitaries. Here are the time-worn Norman pillars and arches of the Infirmary, and close by is the Deanery, fashioned out of the ancient thirteenth-century Guesten Hall. Quiet dignity and repose mark the place; every house has its old garden, and everyone is very well satisfied with himself. It is a pleasant world for sleepy shepherds, if a sorry one for the sheep.

## XLI

LET them sleep, for their activity, on any lines that may be predicated from past conduct, bodes no one good. Times have been when these shepherds themselves masqueraded as wolves, acting the part with every convincing circumstance of ferocity. The last of these occasions was in 1816. I will set forth in detail the doings of that time, because they are intimately bound up with the story of this road between Ely and Downham Market.

It was not until after Waterloo had been fought and Bonaparte at last imprisoned, like some bottle-

ELY CATHEDRAL.

imp, at St. Helena, that the full strain of the past years of war began to be felt in its full severity. It is true that for years past the distress had been great, and that to relieve it, and to pay for Imperial needs, the rates and taxes levied on property had in many places risen to forty and even forty-eight shillings in the pound, but when military glory had faded and peace reigned, internal affairs grew more threatening. Trade was bad, harvests were bad, wheat rose to the unexampled figure of one hundred and three shillings a quarter, and any save paper money was scarce. A golden guinea was handled by many with that curiosity with which one regards some rare and strange object. Everywhere was the one-pound note, issued for the purposes of restricting cash payments and restoring credit; but so many banks issuing one-pound notes failed to meet their obligations that this medium of exchange was regarded with a very just suspicion, still echoed in the old song that says—

"I'd rather have a guinea than a one-pound note."

Everyone at this period of national exhaustion was "hard up," but worse off than any were the unfortunate rural folk—the farm-labourers and their like.

The agricultural labourer is now an object of solicitude, especially at election times. There are, in these happy days, always elections; elections to Parliament, elections to parish and other councils, always someone to be elected to something, and as our friend Hodge has oftentimes a vote to give his best friend, his welfare is greatly desired. But at this unhappy time of which we have been speaking, Hodge had no vote and, by consequence, no friends. His wages, when he could get any work, ranged from seven to nine shillings a week, and the quartern loaf cost one shilling and sixpence. Tea was eight shillings a pound, sugar one shilling, and other necessaries at famine prices. How, then, did Hodge live? It is a difficult question to answer. In many cases the parish made him an allowance in augmentation of wages, but it need scarce be added that this extraordinary system did not help him much. Indeed, the odd idea of financially relieving a man in work tended directly to injure him, for it induced the farmers to screw him down by a corresponding number of shillings. This difficulty of answering the question of how Hodge managed to exist was felt by himself, in the words of a doleful ballad then current—

> "Eighteen pence for a quartern loaf,
> And a poor man works for a shilling:
> 'Tis not enough to find him bread,
> How can they call it living?"

Observe: Hodge did not ask for anything more than to be allowed to live. It is not a great thing to ask. His demand was for his pay to be raised to the equivalent of a stone of flour a day; eleven shillings a week. He desired nothing to put by; only enough to fill the hungry belly. No one paid the least heed to his modest wants. Rather did events grind him and his kind deeper into the dust. Many rustics in those days, when half the land was common fields, kept geese. Some, a little better off, had a cow. Fine pasturage was found on these commons. But towards the end of the eighteenth century, and well on into the nineteenth, there began, and grew to enormous proportions, a movement for enclosing the commons. Most of them are gone now. Very early in this movement Hodge began to feel the pinch, and, when his free grazing was ended, was provided with a grievance the more bitter because entirely new and unusual.

All over the country there were ugly disturbanecs, and at last the stolid rustics of the Fens began to seethe and ferment. Still no one cared. If Hodge threatened, why, a troop or so of Yeomanry could overawe him, and were generally glad of the opportunity, for those yeomen were drawn from the squirearchy and the farming classes, who regarded him as their natural slave and chattel. To no one occurred the idea of relieving or removing these grievances.

At last the starving peasantry of these districts broke into revolt. The village of Southery seems to have been the origin of the particular disturbance with which we are concerned. One May day the farm-labourers assembled there to the number of some eight hundred, and marched to Downham Market, nearly seven miles distant, calling at the farms on the way and bringing out the men engaged on them. Arrived at Downham,. they numbered fifteen hundred; a very turbulent and unruly mob, ready for any mischief. The first to feel their resentment were the millers and the bakers, who had put up the price of flour and bread. Their mills and shops were sacked and the contents flung into the roadway, so that the streets of the little town were ankle-deep in flour, and loaves were kicked about like footballs. The butchers suffered next, and by degrees the whole shopkeeping fraternity. It is not to be supposed that the inns were let alone. Determined men stormed them and brought out the beer in pails. At one inn—the Crown—the local magistrates were holding their weekly sitting, and with some difficulty escaped from an attack made upon them. Their escape enraged the rioters, who redoubled their energies in wrecking the shops, and were still engaged upon this pastime when the magistrates returned, either at the head, or perhaps (counsels of prudence prevailing) in the rear, of a troop of Yeomanry. The Riot Act was read while the air was thick with stones and brickbats, and then the Yeomanry fell upon the crowds and belaboured them with the flat of their swords. The net results of the day were streets of pillaged shops, and ten men and four women arrested by the special constables who had hastily been sworn in. A renewal of the riot was threatened the next morning, and only stopped by the release of these prisoners and an agreement among employers to advance the rate of wages.

This first outbreak was no sooner suppressed than another and much more serious one took place at Littleport. Gathering at the Globe Inn one morning to the number of a hundred and fifty, armed with cleavers, pitchforks, and clubs, the

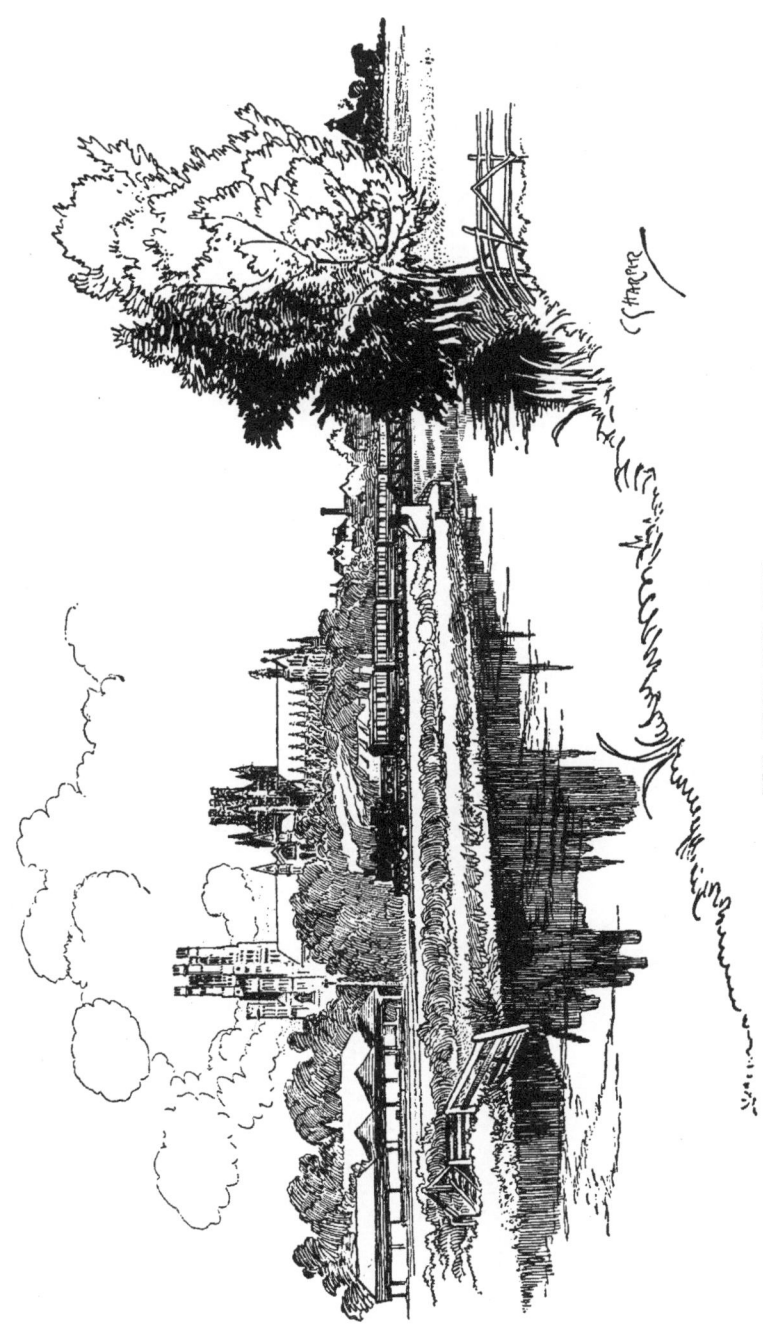

ELY, FROM THE OUSE.

desperate labourers set out to plunder the village. At their head marched a man bearing a pole with a printed statement of their grievances flying from it. The first object to feel their rage was a shop kept by one Martin, shopkeeper and farmer. Martin attempted to buy them off with the offer of a five-pound note, but they took that and burst into the shop as well, smashing everything and carrying off tea and sugar. An amusing side to these incidents is seen in an account telling how one plunderer staggered away with a whole sugarloaf, and how a dozen of Martin's shirts, "worth a guinea apiece," as he dolefully said afterwards, disappeared in the twinkling of an eye.

Then they visited a retired farmer and demolished his furniture. He had a snug hoard of a hundred guineas tucked away in an old bureau. Alas! when these men of wrath had gone, the guineas were found to have gone with them. And so forth, throughout the long day.

## XLII

NIGHT at last shuts down on Littleport. The village is in deshabille: furniture lying broken in the streets, the household gods defiled, the beer-barrels of all the public-houses run dry. Every oppressor of the poor has been handsomely served out, and, incidentally, a good many unoffending people too: for a mob maddened with the sense of wrongs long endured is not discriminating. One there is, however, not yet punished. This is the vicar, conspicuous earlier in the day, alternately threatening and cajoling, but, many hours since, prudently retired to his vicarage. With a savage growl, they invest the house and batter at the door, demanding money. The vicar offers two one-pound notes; scornfully rejected, and ten pounds at the very least is demanded. He refuses, and to his refusal he adds the folly of presenting a pistol at the heads of these furious men; a pistol instantly snatched from his hands and like to be used against him. From this very patent danger and the sudden dread of murder he runs; runs upstairs to his wife and daughters, and presently they are out somewhere at the back door, all flying together,—the women, as I gather, in their night-gowns,—making for Ely, where they arrive at midnight.

Meanwhile, all this night, Littleport is trembling: the shopkeepers, the farmers, anyone who has anything to lose, with fear: those who have nothing to lose, something even to gain, with certain wild hopes and exaltations. Not without fear, they, either; for it is a brutal Government with which, in the end, they must reckon. So far, these wild despairing folk have had no leader, but now they turn to one well-known to sympathise with them: one John Dennis, an innkeeper and small farmer, and by consequence of the hated class of oppressors. By conviction, however, he sides with them: a very Saul among the prophets. To him, late at night, they come. He is abed and asleep, but they rouse him. Will he lead them to Ely on the morrow, to urge their needs and their desperate case upon the authorities?

He will not: it is useless, he says. Nay, but you must, you shall, say they, else we will shoot you, as one forsworn.

So poor Dennis, whose fate is sealed from this hour, leaves his bed and dresses himself, while the excited peasantry loot all Littleport of its gunpowder, bullets, and small shot, used in wild-fowling. Some sixty muskets and fowling-pieces they have found, and eight of those curious engines of destruction called "punt-guns" or "duck-guns." A gun of this kind is still used in duck-shooting. It has a barrel eight feet long, with two inches bore, and is loaded with three-quarters of a pound of shot and about an ounce of gunpowder. It is mounted on a swivel, generally at the end of a punt.

Guns of this calibre they have mounted in a farm-waggon, drawn by two horses, and at the back of the waggon they have placed a number of women and children: with some idea of moving hearts, if not by fear of their quaint artillery, at least in pity for their starving families. It is daybreak when at last they set out on the five miles to Ely, a band of two hundred, armed with muskets, fowling-pieces, scythes, pitchforks, clubs, and reaping-hooks. Ely has heard something of this projected advance, and sends forth three clerical magistrates and the chief constable to parley and ask the meaning of this unlawful assembly. The meaning, it seems, is to demand wages to be fixed at not less than two shillings a day, and that flour shall be sold at not more than two shillings and sixpence a stone. Meanwhile, the duck-guns look these envoys in the eyes perhaps a little more sternly than we are disposed nowadays to credit. At anyrate, the magistrates temporise and promise to inquire into these things. They retire to the Cathedral precincts to consult, and—ah! yes, will these demonstrators please go home?

No; they will not do anything of the kind. Instead, they advance into the Market Square, where their battery is wheeled, pointing up the High Street, much to the consternation of the citizens, firmly persuaded that this is the end of all things and now busily engaged in secreting their little hoards, their silver spoons and precious things, in unlikely places. The rioters, conscious of having easily overawed the place, now determine to put it under contribution, beginning with those who have ground the faces of the poor—the millers and their kind. Dennis, armed with a gun, and at the head of a threatening crowd, appears before the house of one Rickwood, miller. "They must have fifty pounds," he says, "or down come house and mill." Little doubt that they mean it: in earnest thereof, observe, windows are already smashed. Bring out those fifty sovereigns, miserable ones, before we pull the house about your ears!

They send off to the bank accordingly; Mrs. Rickwood going in haste. On the way she meets the Bank Manager, a person who combines that post with the civil overlordship of Ely. He is, in point of fact, the chief constable. Something grotesquely appropriate, if you think of it, in these two posts being in the hands of one man. "They shall not have a penny," he stoutly declares, assisting Mrs. Rickwood from the crowds that beset her; but certain blows upon head and body determine him to be more diplomatic, and after some parley he agrees to pay the fifty pounds in cash to those who constitute themselves leaders of three divisions of rioters. These three men alone, representing Ely, Littleport, and Downham, shall be admitted to the bank, and each shall—and does actually—receive one-third of that sum, signing for it. Resourceful manager! They are paid the coin, and sign: they might as well have signed their death-warrants, for those signatures are evidence of the very best against them when proceedings shall subsequently be taken.

Other houses are visited and people terrified, and then they are at a loss for what next. You cannot make a revolution out of your head as you go on: what is needed is a programme, some definite scheme, and of such a thing these poor wretches have no idea. So, gradually, as afternoon comes on, they disperse and fall back upon discontented Littleport, just before the arrival of a troop of the 18th Dragoons and a detachment of the Royston Volunteer Cavalry, sent for to Bury St. Edmunds and Royston by the magistrates who had in the early morning parleyed with the rioters. Ely is saved!

We—we the authorities—have now the upper hand, and mean to be revenged. On the morrow, then, behold the military, with the Prebendary of

Ely, Sir Bate Dudley, and many gentlemen and persons of consideration, invading Littleport and wilfully stirring up again the excitement that had spent itself. Rumours of this advance have been spread, and on entering the village they find the men of the place hidden behind doors and windows, whence they fire with some effect, wounding a few. The soldiers return the fire, and one man is killed and another pitifully mangled. The rest flee, soldiers and magistracy after them, hunting for some days in fen and dyke, and taking at last seventy-three; all marched into Ely and clapped in gaol, there to await the coming of the Judge presiding over the Special Assize appointed to try them.

The proceedings lasted six days, opened in state by a service in the Cathedral: an exultant service of thanksgiving to God for this sorry triumph. To it the Judge and his javelin-men went in procession, behind the Bishop, and escorted by fifty of the principal inhabitants carrying white wands. The Bishop himself, the last to wield the old dual palatine authority of Church and State, was preceded by his butler, bearing the Sword of State that symbolised the temporal power; and as he entered the Cathedral the organ burst forth in the joyful strains of Handel's anthem: "Why do the heathen rage and the people imagine a vain thing?" with its triumphant chorus, "Let us break their bands asunder!"

Nothing else so well portrays the unchristian savagery of the time as the doings of this prelate—let us record his name, Bishop Bowyer Edward

Sparke, that it may be execrated—a veritable Hew-Agag-in-pieces-before-the-Lord, who preached earthly vengeance and spiritual damnation to the three-score and thirteen in prison close by. Truly, a wolf sent to shepherd the flock.

Those were times when to steal to the value of forty shillings, and to steal to the value of a shilling, accompanied by violence, were capital offences. Five of the prisoners, convicted on these counts, were sentenced to be hanged, and five were transported for life. To the others were dealt out various terms of imprisonment. Chief among the ill-fated five was John Dennis, the leader, somewhat against his own judgment, of the outbreak. His, we must allow, is a figure tragical above the rest, touched with something like the dignity of martyrdom. They hanged him and the four others, in due course, on Ely Common, on a day of high holiday, when three hundred wand-bearers and bodies of troops assembled to protect the authorities and to see execution done. It may be read, in old records, how the whole of the city was searched for a cart to take the condemned men to the scaffold, and how at last five pounds was paid for the use of one; so there was evidently a public opinion opposed to this policy of bloodshed. Let us not seek to discover who was that man who took those five pounds, and with the taking of them sold his immortal soul.

The victims of the combined fear and rage of the authorities were buried in one common grave in the churchyard of St. Mary's, hard by the great Cathedral's western front, and on the wall of that church-tower was placed the tablet that may still be seen, recording that—

"Here lye in one grave the bodies of William Beamiss, George Crow, John Dennis, Isaac Harley, and Thomas South, who were all executed at Ely on the 28th day of June 1816, having been convicted at the Special Assizes holden there of divers robberies during the riots at Ely and Littleport in the month of May in that year. May their awful fate be a warning to others!"

There is no place more sacred to me in the whole of Ely than this humble and neglected spot, where these men, victims of this pitiful tragedy in corduroy and hobnailed boots, martyrs to affrighted and revengeful authority, lie. It is a spot made additionally sad because the sacrifice was sterile. Nothing resulted from it, so far as our human vision can reach. Bishop Sparke and Prebendary Sir Bate Dudley and the host of Cathedral dignitaries continued to feast royally, to clothe themselves in fine raiment, and to drink that old port always so specially comforting to the denizens of cathedral precincts; and every night the watchman went his rounds, as even now, in our time, he continues to do, calling the hours with their attendant weather, and ending his cry with the conventional "All's Well!"

To the soldiers employed in the unwelcome task of suppressing these disturbances and of shooting down their fellow-countrymen, no blame belongs: they did but obey orders. Yet they felt it a disgrace. The 18th Dragoons had fought at Waterloo the year before, and one of the troopers who had come through that day unscathed received in this affair a wound that cost him his arm. He thought it hard that fate should serve him so scurvy a trick. But among the soldiery employed was a Hanoverian regiment, whose record is stained deeply and foully with the doings of one German officer. Patrolling Ely in those tempestuous days, his company were passing by the old Sextry Barn, near the Cathedral, when he heard a thatcher employed on the roof call to his assistant in the technical language of thatchers "Bunch! bunch!" He was merely asking for another bundle of reeds, but the foreign officer, not properly understanding English, interpreted this as an insult to himself, and ordered his men to fire. They did so, and the unfortunate thatcher fell upon the open doors of the barn, his body pierced by a dozen bullets. There it hung, dropping blood, for three days, the officer swearing he would serve in the same way anyone who dared remove it.

## XLIII

THOSE days are far behind. When Bishop Sparke died in 1836, the temporal power was taken away from the See, and his Sword of State was buried with him: a fitting piece of symbolism. These memories alone are left, found only after much diligent and patient search; but with their aid the grey stones and the soaring towers of Ely, the quiet streets, and the road on to Littleport, take on a more living interest to the thoughtful man, to whom archæology, keenly interesting though it be, does not furnish forth the full banquet of life.

Save for these memories, and for the backward glance at the Cathedral, looming dark on the skyline, much of the way to Littleport might almost be called dull. A modern suburb called "Little London" has thrown out some few houses in this direction during the last century, but why or how this has been possible with a dwindling population let others explain, if they can do so. At anyrate, when the Reverend James Bentham, the historian, was Canon here, from 1737 to 1794, no dwellings lined the way, for he planted a mile-long avenue of oaks where these uninteresting houses now stand. A few only of his trees remain, near the first milestone; a clump of spindly oaks, more resembling elms in their growth, and in midst of them a stone obelisk with a Latin inscription stating how Canon James Bentham, Canon of the Cathedral Church of Ely, planted them in 1787, his seventieth year, not that he himself might see them, but for the benefit of future ages. The Latin so thoroughly succeeds in obscuring this advertisement of himself from the understanding of the country-folk that the obelisk is generally said to mark the grave of a favourite racehorse!

The descent from the high ground of the Isle begins in another half mile from this point. Past Chettisham Station and its level crossing, standing solitary on the road, we come down Pyper's Hill, at whose foot is the field called, on the large Ordnance maps, "Gilgal." Why so-called, who shall say?

Did some old landowner, struck perhaps by its situation near the verge of this ancient Fen-island, name this water-logged meadow after that biblical Gilgal where the Israelites made their first encampment across the Jordan, and where they kept their first Passover in the Land of Canaan? It may be, for we have already seen how that Norman knight, shown the riches of the Isle of Ely by Hereward,

ELY CATHEDRAL, FROM THE LITTLEPORT ROAD.

described it even as another Canaan, a land figuratively flowing with milk and honey.

An old toll-house still stands here by the wayside and heralds the approach to Littleport, whose name, preparing the stranger for some sleepy, old-world decayed creek-side village, with rotting wharves and a general air of picturesque decrepidness, ill fits the busy, ugly place it is. Littleport is more populous than Ely. It stands at the confluence of the Great Ouse and the Old Croft rivers, and at the lower end of its long, long gritty streets, lined with whitey-grey brick houses, the road is bordered by yet another stream—the "Holmes River." Indeed, speaking of its situation in the Fens and by these waters, Carter, the eighteenth-century historian of Cambridgeshire, tells us that in his time it was "as rare to see a coach there as a ship at Newmarket." Much of its recent prosperity derives from the factories of the prominent London firm of hosiers and clothiers, "Hope Brothers," established here. The church and the adjoining vicarage, where the rioters of 1816 so terrified the clergyman and his family, stand on an elevated site behind the main street. There was, until recent years, when it was built up, a passage through the tower, said to have been a short cut to the Fenland. If this was its real purpose, it vividly shows how little solid ground there was here in old days. The tower top, too, has its story, for it burnt a nightly beacon in those times; a light in beneficent competition with the marshland Jacks-o'-Lantern, to guide the wanderer to the haven where he would be.

It must not be forgotten that Littleport is a place famed in the annals of a certain sport. It is not a sport often to be practised, for a succession of open winters will render the enjoyment of it impossible, and its devotees stale and out of form. It is the healthful and invigorating sport and pastime of skating. Nowhere else in all England is there such a neighbourhood as this for skating and sliding, for when the flooded fields of winter are covered with a thin coating of ice you may skate pretty well all the way to Lynn on the one hand and to Peterborough on the other. The country is then a vast frozen lake. Indeed, years before skating was a sport it had been a necessity; the only way by which a Fenman could travel from place to place in a hard winter. That is why Fenland skaters became such marvellous proficients, rivalling even the Dutchmen. Who that knows anything of skating and skating-matches has not heard of those champions of the Fens,

LITTLEPORT.

"Turkey" Smart and "Fish" Smart? And Littleport even yet takes the keenest of interest in skating carnivals, as the traveller along the roads in midsummer may see, in the belated bills and placards relating to them that still hang, tattered and discoloured, on the walls of roadside barn and outhouse. Reading them, he feels a gentle coolness steal over him, even on a torrid afternoon of the dog-days.

One leaves Littleport by a bridge, a single-span iron bridge of great width, that crosses the Great Ouse. As you cross it, the way to Mildenhall lies straight and flat, as far as eye can see, ahead. When that picturesque tourist, William Gilpin, visited Mildenhall a century ago, he found little to say in its praise, and of the scenery all he can find to record is that the roads were lined with willows whose branches were hung with slime.

Our way is not along the Mildenhall road, but by the left-hand track following the loops and windings of the Ouse; flat, like that other way, but by no means straight. It is a road of the most peculiar kind, somewhat below the level of that river and protected from it by great grassy banks, in some places from twelve to fourteen feet high. Windmills are perched picturesquely on the opposite shore, patient horses drag heavy barges along the stream, and the sodden fields stretch away on the right to infinity. Houses and cottages are few and far between; built below the river banks, with their chimney-pots rarely looking over them.

The reclaimed Fens being themselves things of recent history, there are few houses in the Fenland, except on the islands, and these few are comparatively modern. A cottage or a farmstead in these levels may be a weather-boarded affair, or it may be of brick, but it is always built on timber piles, for there is no other way of obtaining a sure foundation; and a frequent evidence of this is the sight of one of the older of these buildings, perched up at an absurd height through the gradual shrinkage of the land in consequence of the draining away of the water and the wasting of the peat. This subsidence averages six feet over the whole extent of the Fens, and in some places is as much as eight or nine feet. As a result of this, a man's front door, once on a level with the ground, is often approached by a quite imposing flight of steps, and instances are not

THE RIVER ROAD, LITTLEPORT.

unknown where a room has been added underneath the original ground floor, and a two-floored cottage promoted by force of circumstances to the dignity of a three-storeyed residence.

A brick building in these districts is apt to be exceedingly ugly. For one thing, it has been built within the severely utilitarian period, and is just a square box with a lid for roof and holes for doors and windows. For another, the brick, made of the local gault, is of the kind called by courtesy "white," but really of a dirty dough-like hue: distressing to an artist's eye.

## XLIV

BRANDON CREEK bridge, where the Great Ouse and the Little Ouse and Crooked Dyke pour their waters into one common fund, and send it crawling lazily down to Lynn, marks the boundaries of Cambridgeshire and Norfolk. On the hither side you are in the territory of the Cambridgeshire Camels, and on the thither are come into the land of the Norfolk Dumplings.

It is here, at this meeting of the waters, that "Rebeck, or Priests' Houses," is marked on the maps of Speed and Dugdale, and attributed to the thirteenth century, but what this place was, no man knoweth. It has clean vanished from sight or knowledge, and the houses of Brandon Creek hamlet afford no clue, being wholly secular and commonplace, from the inn that stands at the meeting of the rivers to the humble cottages of the bankers and the gaulters.

Southery Ferry is but a little distance ahead, to be recognised by the inn that stands on the river bank. It is a lonely ferry, and little wonder that it should be, considering the emptiness of the country on the other side,—all fens at the Back of Beyond, to whose wastes cometh the stranger never, where the bull-frogs croak, the slodger slodges among the dykes, and the mists linger longest.

Away ahead sits Southery village, enthroned upon its hillock, once an island in the surrounding fen, and still, in its prominence against the skyline, telling its story plain for all to learn. Even if it were not thus evident from Southery Ferry how the village of old sat with its feet in the mud and its

THE OUSE.

head on the dry land, at least the pilgrim's wheels presently advise him in unmistakable fashion that he is on an ascent. There is little in the village itself to interest the stranger. The spire so picturesquely crowning the hill in the distant view is found on close acquaintance to be that of a modern church, filled with the Papistical abominations commonly found in these days of the forsworn clergy of the Church of England. The old church of St. Mary, disused forty years ago, and now in ruins, stands at a little distance, in a bend of the road, overlooking many miles of what was once fen. There it stands in its heaped-up graveyard, a shattered and roofless shell of red-brick and rubble walls, thickly overgrown with ivy, and neighboured by an old windmill as battered and neglected as itself. From a field-gate overlooking the levels you see, in the distance, the high ground about Thetford, and, near at hand, an outlying part of Southery called Little London. An old inhabitant

SOUTHERY FERRY.

shares the field-gate and the outlook with the present writer, and surveys the many miles with a jaundiced eye. He remembers those lands below, when he was a boy, all swimming with water. Now they are drained, and worth ever so much an acre, "'cause they'll, as you might say, grow anything. But a man can't earn mor'n fourteen shillun a week here. No chance for nobody."

No local patriot he. He was born here, married in the old church forty years ago, and went away to live in Sheffield. "Ah! that *is* a place," says he.

That is a phrase capable of more than one interpretation, and we feelingly remark, having been there, that indeed a place it *is*. His regretful admiration of Sheffield is so mournful that we wonder why he ever left.

The road between Southery and Hilgay dips but slightly and only for a short distance, proving the accuracy, at this point at least, of Dugdale's map showing the Fen-islands of Hilgay and Southery conjoined. They are divided by the long, straight, and narrow cut called "Sam's Cut Drain," crossed here at Modney Bridge. Here the true Fenland begins only to be skirted, and hedgerows once more line the way, a sign that of itself most certainly proclaims fields enclosed and cultivated in the long ago. The ditches, too, are dry, and not the brimming water-courses they have been these last twenty-five miles. Moreover, here is hedgerow timber: ancient elms and oaks taking the place of the willows and poplars that have been our only companions throughout a whole county. They have not consciously been missed, but now they are come again, how fresh and dear and welcome they are, and how notable the change they produce!

Between Hilgay and that old farmhouse called "Snore Hall," from an absurd tradition that King Charles once slept there, we cross the river Wissey and the Catchwater Drain. The road between is still known as "the Causeway," and, with the succeeding village of Fordham, teaches in its name a lesson in old-time local geography.

In 1809, when that old tourist, William Gilpin,

passed this way, Hilgay Fen extended to one thousand acres. According to the picturesque story told him, the district was periodically visited, every six or seven years, by an innumerable host of field-mice, which began to destroy all vegetation and would have laid everything bare but for a great flight of white horned-owls that, as if by instinct, always arrived at such times from Norway and, immediately attacking the mice, destroyed them all, when they disappeared as suddenly as they had come.

## XLV

Ryston Station, between Ryston Park and Fordham, marks the neighbourhood of a very interesting spot, for Ryston, though a place of the smallest size and really but a woodland hamlet, is of some historic note, with "Kett's Oak," or the Oak of Reformation, standing in the Park, as a visible point of contact with stirring deeds and ancient times. It is a gigantic tree with hollow trunk and limbs carefully chained and bound together, and marks one of the encampments of the Norfolk peasantry in Kett's Rebellion of 1549. This was a popular outbreak caused by the lawless action of the Norfolk gentry of that time in enclosing wastes and common lands. "The peasant whose pigs and cow and poultry had been sold, or had died because the commons where they had once fed were gone; the yeoman dispossessed of his farm; the farm-servant out of employ because where once ten ploughs had turned the soil, one shepherd watched the grazing of the flocks; the artisan smarting under the famine prices the change of culture had brought—all these were united in suffering, while the gentlemen were doubling, trebling, quadrupling their incomes, and adorning their persons and their houses with splendour hitherto unknown."

The outbreak began at Attleborough in June 1549, and a fortnight later there was fighting at Wymondham, where the country-folk, led by Robert Kett, a tanner, of that place, destroyed many illegal fences. Thence, headed by Kett and his brother William, an army of sixteen thousand peasants marched to Mousehold Heath, overlooking Norwich, where their greatest camp was pitched. Under some venerable tree in these camps Robert Kett was wont to sit and administer justice, and Conyers, chaplain to the rebel host, preached beneath their shade while the rising of that memorable summer lasted. Never were the demands of rebellion more reasonable than those put forward on this occasion. They were, that all bondsmen should be made free, "for God made all free with His precious blood-shedding"; that all rivers should be made free and common to all men for fishing and passage; that the clergy should be resident, instead of benefices being held by absentees; and, in the interest of tenants' crops, that no one under a certain degree should keep rabbits unless they were paled in, and that no new dove-houses should be allowed. That last stipulation sounds mysterious, but it referred to a very cruel grievance of olden times, when only the Lord of the Manor might keep pigeons and doves, and did so at the expense of his tenants. The manorial pigeon-houses often seen adjoining ancient Hall or old-world Grange are, in fact, relics of that time when the feudal landowner's pigeons fattened on the peasants' crops.

The story of how the people's petition was dis-

KETT'S OAK.

regarded, and how the city of Norwich was taken and retaken with much bloodshed, does not belong here. The rebellion was suppressed, and Robert and William Kett hanged, but the memory of these things still lingers in the rural districts, and everyone in the neighbourhood of Ryston knows "Ked's Oak," as they name it. There were Pratts of Ryston

Hall then, as now, and old legends still tell how Robert Kett seized some of the Squire's sheep to feed his followers, leaving this rhymed note in acknowledgment—

> "Mr. Prat, your shepe are verry fat,
> And wee thank you for that.
> Wee have left you the skinnes
> To buy your ladye pinnes
> And you may thank us for that."

Some of the insurgents were hanged from this

DENVER HALL.

very tree, as the rhyme tells us—

> "Surely the tree that nine men did twist on
> Must be the old oak now at Ryston."

The present Squire has recorded these things on a stone placed against the trunk of this venerable relic.

Denver, which presently succeeds Fordham and Ryston, is remarkable for many things. Firstly, for that beautiful old Tudor mansion, Denver Hall, by the wayside, on entering the village; secondly, for the semicircular sweep of the high road around the church; and, thirdly, for the great "Denver Sluice" on the river Ouse, a mile away. This is the massive lock that at high tide shuts out the tidal waters from flooding the reclaimed Fens, and at the ebb is opened to let out the accumulated waters of the Ouse and the innumerable drains of the Great Level.

THE CROWN, DOWNHAM MARKET.

The failure of Denver Sluice would spell disaster and ruin to many, and it has for that reason been specially protected by troops on several occasions when Irish political agitators have entered upon "physical force" campaigns, and have been credited with a desire to blow up this main protection of two thousand square miles of land slowly and painfully won back from bog and waste.

Denver gives its name to a town in America—Denver, Colorado—and has had several distinguished natives; but, despite all these many and varied attributes of greatness, it is a very small and very modest place, quite overshadowed by the little town of Downham Market, a mile onward. Downham, as Camden informs us, obtains its name from "Dun"

THE CASTLE, DOWNHAM MARKET.

and "ham," signifying the home on the hill; and the ancient parish church, which may be taken as standing on the site of the original settlement, does indeed rise from a knoll that, although of no intrinsic height, commands a vast and impressive view over illimitable miles of marshland. It is not a church of great interest, nor does the little town offer many attractions, although by no means unpleasing.

They still point out the house where Nelson once went to school; and two old inns remain, very much as they were in coaching days. In the Crown yard you may still look up at the windows of the room where the magistrates were sitting on that day in 1816 when the rioters made them fly.

Villages on these last twelve miles between Downham and Lynn are plentiful. No sooner is the little town left behind than the church of Wimbotsham comes in sight, with that of Stow Bardolph plainly visible ahead. Both are interesting old buildings, with something of almost every period of architecture to show the curious. Beyond its church, and a farmstead or two, Wimbotsham has nothing along the road, but Stow Bardolph is a village complete in every story-book particular. Here is the church, and here, beneath a spreading chestnut (or other) tree the village smithy stands; while opposite are the gates of the Park and the shady avenue leading up to the Hall where, not Bardolphs nowadays, but Hares, reside in dignified ease; as may be guessed from the village inn, the Hare Arms, with its armorial sign and motto, *Non videre, sed esse*—"not to seem, but to be," the proud boast or noble aspiration of the family. Almshouses, cottages with pretty gardens, and a very wealth of noble trees complete the picture of "Stow," as the country-folk solely know it, turning a bewildered and stupid gaze upon the stranger who uses the longer title.

The pilgrim through many miles of fen revels in this wooded mile from Stow Bardolph village to

Hogge's Bridge, where the road makes a sharp bend to the left amid densely overarching trees, commanding a distant view of Stow Bardolph Hall at the farther end of a long green drive. South Runcton Church, standing lonely by the road beyond this pretty scene, is an example of how not to restore a

HOGGE'S BRIDGE, STOW BARDOLPH.

pure Norman building. It still keeps a very beautiful Norman chancel arch, but the exterior, plastered to resemble stone, is distressing.

At Setchey, originally situated on a navigable creek of the river Nar and then named Sedge-hithe, or Seech-hithe—meaning a sedge and weed-choked harbour—we are come well within the old Dutch circle of influence over local building design. There are still some characteristic old Dutch houses at Downham; and Lynn, of course, being of old a port in closest touch with Holland, is full of queer gables and quaint architectural details brought over from the Low Countries. Here at Setchey, too, stands a very Dutch-like old inn—the Lynn Arms.

THE LYNN ARMS, SETCHEY.

Commons — "Whin Commons" in the local phrase—and the scattered houses of West Winch, lead on to Hardwick Bridge, where, crossing over the railway, the broad road bends to the right. There, facing you, is an ancient Gothic battlemented gatehouse, and beyond it the long broad street of a populous town: the town of King's Lynn.

## XLVI

THERE is a tintinnabulary, jingling sound in the name of Lynn that predisposes one to like the place, whether it be actually likeable or not. Has anyone ever stopped to consider how nearly like the name of this old seaport is to that of London? Possibly the conjunction of London and Lynn has not occurred to any who have visited the town, but to those who have arrived at it by the pages of this book, the similarity will be interesting. The names of both London and Lynn, then, derive from the geographical peculiarities of their sites, in many respects singularly alike. Both stand beside the lower reaches of a river, presently to empty itself into the sea, and the ground on which they stand has always been marshy. At one period, indeed, those were not merely marshes where Lynn and London now stand, but wide-spreading lakes—fed by the lazy overflowings of Ouse and Thames. The Celtic British, who originally settled by these lakes, called them *llyns*, and this ancient seaport has preserved that prehistoric title in its original purity, only dropping the superfluous "l"; but London's present name somewhat disguises its first style of *Llyn dun*, or the "hill by the lake"; some inconsiderable, but fortified, hillock rising above the shallow waters.

When the Saxons came, Lynn was here, and when the Norman conquerors reached the Norfolk coast they found it a busy port. To that early Norman prelate, Herbert de Losinga, a tireless builder of churches throughout East Anglia, the manor fell, and the town consequently became known for four hundred and thirty years as Lynn Episcopi. It was only when the general confiscation of religious property took place under Henry the Eighth that it became the "King's Lynn" it has ever since remained.

To the "average man," Lynn is well known.

THE SOUTH GATES, LYNN.

Although he has never journeyed to it, he knows this ancient seaport well; not as a port or as a town at all, but only as a name. The name of Lynn, in short, is rooted in his memory ever since he read Hood's poem, the "Dream of Eugene Aram."

Aram was no mere creation of a poet's brain, but a very real person. His story is a tragic one, and appealed not only to Hood, but to Bulwer Lytton, who weaved much romance out of his career. Aram was born in 1704, in Yorkshire, and adopted the profession of a schoolmaster. It was at Knaresborough, in 1745, that the events happened that made him a wanderer, and finally brought him to the scaffold.

How a scholar, a cultured man of Aram's remarkable attainments (for he was a philologist and student of the Celtic and Aryan languages) could have stooped to commit a vulgar murder is not easily to be explained, and it has not been definitely ascertained how far the motive of revenge, or in what degree that of robbery, prompted him to join with his accomplice, Houseman, in slaying Daniel Clarke. The unfortunate Clarke had been too intimate a friend of Aram's wife, and this may explain his share in the murder, although it does not account for Houseman's part in it. Clarke was not certainly known to have been murdered when he suddenly disappeared in 1745, and when Aram himself left Knaresborough, although there may have been suspicions, he was not followed up. It was only when some human bones were found in 1758 at Knaresborough that Houseman himself was suspected. His peculiar manner when they were found, and his assertions that they "could not be Dan Clarke's" because Dan Clarke's were somewhere else, of course led to his arrest. And, as a matter of fact, they were *not* Clarke's, as Houseman's confession under arrest sufficiently proved.

Whose they were does not appear. He told how he and Aram had killed that long-missing man and had buried his body in St. Robert's Cave; and, on the floor of that place being dug up, a skeleton was in due course discovered.

Aram was traced to King's Lynn and arrested. Tried at York, he defended himself with extraordinary ability, but in vain, and was sentenced to death. Before his execution at York he confessed his part, and so to this sombre story we are at least spared the addition of a mystery and doubt of the justice of his sentence.

Hood's poem makes Aram, conscience-struck, declare his crime to one of his Lynn pupils, in the form of a horrible dream. How does it begin, that ghastly poem? Pleasantly enough—

> "'Twas in the prime of summer time,
> An evening calm and cool;
> And four-and-twenty happy boys
> Came bounding out of school."

The Grammar School of those young bounders was pulled down and rebuilt many years ago, and so much of association lost.

> "Pleasantly shone the setting sun
> Over the town of Lynn,"

but Eugene Aram, the Usher, on this particular evening,

> "Sat remote from all,
> A melancholy man."

Presently, Hood tells us, he espied, apart from the romping boys, one who sat and "pored upon a book." This morbid youngster was reading the "Death of Abel," and Aram improved the occasion, and "talked

JOSEPH BEETON IN THE CONDEMNED CELL.

with him of Cain." With such facilities for entering intimately into Cain's feelings of blood-guiltiness, he conjured up so many terrors that, if we read the trend of Hood's verses correctly, the boy thought there was more in this than the recital of some particularly vivid nightmare, and informed the authorities, with the well-known result—

> "Two stern-faced men set out from Lynn,
> Through the cold and heavy mist,
> And Eugene Aram walked between,
> With gyves upon his wrist."

Twenty-five years later, Lynn turned off a local criminal on its own account, Joseph Beeton being executed, February 22, 1783, on the spot where a few weeks previously he had robbed the North Mail, on what is called the "Saddlebow Road." This spot, now commonplace enough, was long marked by a clump of trees known as "Beeton's Bush." An old engraving shows poor Joseph in the condemned hold, and represents him of an elegant slimness, heavily shackled and wearing what, under the circumstances, must be described as an extraordinarily cheerful expression of countenance. A contemporary account of his execution makes interesting, if gruesome, reading—

"The culprit was conveyed from Lynn Gaol in a mourning coach to the place of execution near the South Gates, and within a few yards of the spot where the robbery took place, attended by two clergymen :—the Rev. Mr. Horsfall and the Rev. Mr. Merrist. After praying some time with great fervency, and a hymn being sung by the singers from St. Margaret's Church, the rope was fixed about his neck, which was no sooner done than he instantly threw himself off and died amidst the pitying tears of upwards of 5000 spectators. His behaviour was

THE GUILDHALL, LYNN.

devout and excellent. This unfortunate youth had just attained his 20th year, and is said to have been a martyr to the villainy of a man whom he looked upon as his sincere friend. Indeed, so sensible were the gentlemen of Lynn that he was betrayed into the commission of the atrocious crime for which he suffered by the villainy of this supposed friend, that a subscription was entered into and money collected to employ counsel to plead for him at his trial."

The barbarous method of execution in those days placed the condemned in the dreadful alternative of slow strangulation, or what was practically suicide. To save themselves from the lingering agonies of strangulation, those who were possessed of the slightest spirit flung themselves from the ladder and so ended, swiftly and mercifully.

The old account of Beeton's execution ends curiously like a depraved kind of humour: "The spirit of the prisoner, the constancy of his friends, and the church-parade made bright episodes in a dreadful scene."

## XLVII

It is a long, long way from the entrance through the South Gates, on the London road, into the midst of the town, where, by the Ouse side, along the wharves of the harbour, and in the maze of narrow streets between the Tuesday and the Saturday market-places, old Lynn chiefly lies. In the Tuesday market-place, Losinga's great church of St. Margaret stands; that church whose twin towers are prominent in all views of the town. Many of the old merchants and tradesmen lie there, but many more in the vast church of St. Nicholas, less well known to the casual visitor. On the floor of that noble nave, looked down upon by the beautiful aisle and clerestory windows, and by the winged angels that support the open timber roof, you may read the epitaphs of many an oversea trader and merchant prince, as well as those of humbler standing. Crusos are there, and among others a certain Simon Duport " Marchand, Né en l'Isle de Ré en France," whose epitaph is presented bi-lingually, in French and English, for the benefit of those not learned in both. That of " Mr. Thomas Hollingworth, an Eminent Bookseller," is worth quoting. He, it appears, was " a Man of the Strictest Integrity In His Dealings and much esteemed by Gentlemen of Taste For the neatness and Elegance of his Binding."

The merchants of Lynn are an extinct race, and most of their old mansions are gone. Yet in the old days, when Lynn supplied seven counties with coals, timber, and wine from the North of England, from the Baltic, and from many a port in Holland, France, Italy, and Spain, to be a Lynn merchant was no mean or inconsiderable thing. They lived, these princely traders, in mansions of the most noble architectural character, furnished with the best that money could buy and hung with tapestry and stamped leather from the most artistic looms and workshops of France and Spain. It never occurred to them that trade was a thing despicable and to be disowned. Instead of disconnecting themselves from their business, they lived with it; their residences and their warehouses in one range of buildings.

A typical mansion of this old period is Clifton's House. The Cliftons and their old business are alike gone, and many of the beautiful fittings of their mansion have been torn out and sold, but the

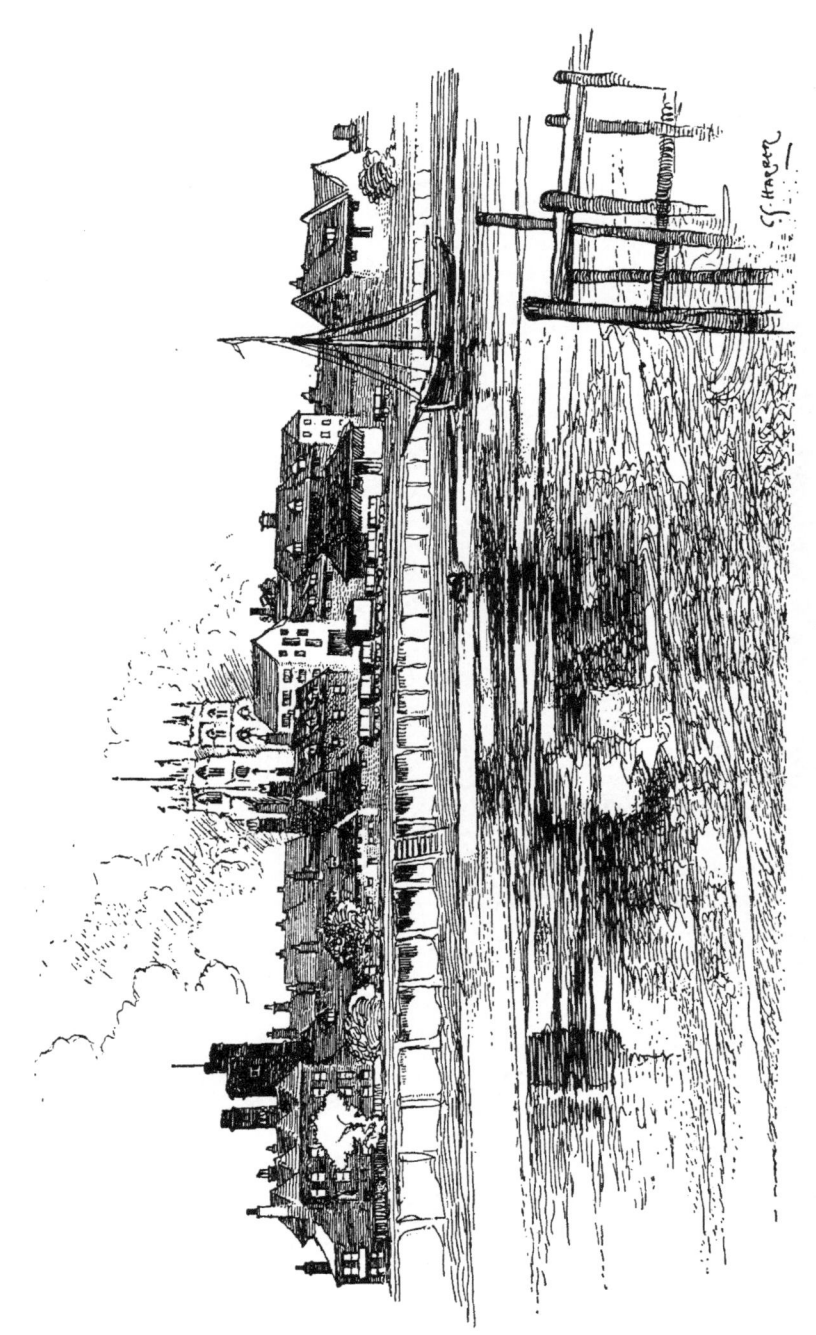

THE TOWN AND HARBOUR OF LYNN, FROM WEST LYNN.

house itself stands, a grand memorial of their importance and of the patronage they and their kind extended to art. It faces Queen Street, at the corner of King's Staith Lane, and its courts and warehouses extend back to those quays where Clifton's ships, richly laden, once came to port from many a foreign clime. How anxiously those vessels were awaited may perhaps be judged from the tall red-brick tower rising in many storeys from the first courtyard, and commanding panoramic views down the river, out to the Wash, and away to the open sea at Lynn Deeps; so that from the roof-top the coming of Clifton's argosies might early be made known.

This house owes its fine Renaissance design to a Lynn architect whose name deserves to be remembered. Henry Bell, who built it in 1707, and whose works still enrich the town in many directions, flourished between 1655 and 1717. To him is due the beautiful Custom House overlooking the river and harbour, a work of art that in its Dutch-like character seems to have been brought bodily from some old Netherlands town and set down here by the quay. It was built as an Exchange, in the time of Charles the Second, whose statue still occupies an alcove; but very shortly afterwards was taken over by the Customs.

The great Tuesday market-place was once graced by a Renaissance market-cross from Bell's designs, but it was swept away in 1831. The Duke's Head Hotel, so originally named in honour of James, Duke of York, is another of Bell's works, not

"CLIFTON'S HOUSE."

improved of late by the plaster that has been spread entirely over the old red-brick front.

The Duke's Head was in coaching days one of those highly superior houses that refused to entertain anyone who did not arrive in a carriage, or, at the very least of it, in a post-chaise. The principal inns for those plebeian persons who travelled by coach were the Globe and the Crown. It was to the Crown that old Thomas Cross and his "Lynn Union"

THE DUKE'S HEAD, LYNN.

came. It is still standing, in Church Street, over against the east end of St. Margaret's Church, but in a pitifully neglected and out-at-elbows condition, as a Temperance House, its white plastered front, contemporary with the coaching age, even now proclaiming it to be a "Commercial and Family Hotel."

The coaching age ended, so far as Lynn was concerned, in 1847, when the East Anglian Railway, from Ely to Lynn, with branches to Dereham,

Wisbeach, and Huntingdon, was opened. It was an unfortunate line, an amalgamation of three separate undertakings: the Lynn and Dereham, the Ely and Huntingdon, and the Lynn and Ely Railways. By its junction with the Eastern Counties, now the Great Eastern, at Ely, a through journey to London was first rendered possible. Three trains each way, instead of the twenty now running, were then considered sufficient for all needs. They were not, at that early date, either swift or dignified journeys, for engine-power was often insufficient, and it was a common thing for a train to be stopped for hours while engine-driver and stoker effected necessary repairs. It was then, and on those not infrequent occasions when trains ran by favour of the sheriff, accompanied by a "man in possession" and plastered with ignominious labels announcing the fact, that passengers lamented the coaches. The East Anglian Railway, indeed, like the Great Eastern, which swallowed it, had a very troubled early career.

Lynn in those early years of innovation still retained many of its old-world ways. It was a sleepy time, as Mr. Thew, who has written his reminiscences of it, testifies. For police the town possessed one old watchman, who bore the old East Anglian name of Blanchflower, and patrolled the streets "with one arm and a lantern." The posting of letters was then a serious business, calling for much patience, for you did not in those days drop them into a letter-box, but handed them through a window at which you knocked. When the clerk in

THE CUSTOM-HOUSE, LYNN.

charge, one John Cooper, had satisfied his official dignity and kept you waiting long enough, he was graciously pleased to open the window and receive the letters. The successor to this upholder of official traditions, was one Charles Rix, addicted to declaiming Shakespeare from his window.

The postmaster of Lynn at this easy-going time was Mr. Robinson Cruso, who also filled the miscellaneous occupations of auctioneer and estate agent, and wine and spirit merchant, and was a member of the Town Council. He was a descendant of an old Lynn family, many of whose representatives lie in the church of St. Nicholas. This Cruso (they spelled their name without the "e") was an upholsterer, and born ten years after Defoe's famous book was published; hence the "Robinson." There are still a number of the name in Norfolk and Suffolk.

## XLVIII

WE must now make an end. Of Lynn's long municipal history, of the treasures stored in its ancient Guildhall, of King John's disastrous journey from the town across the Wash; of many another stirring scene or historic pile this is not the place to speak. The Story of the Road is told, and, that being done, the task is completed; but it is not without regret that a place like Lynn, so rich in picturesque incident, is thus left. Many a narrow, cobbled lane, lined with quaint houses, calls aloud to be sketched; there, too, are the ancient Red Mount Chapel, in the lovely park-like "walks" that extend into the very heart of the town, and the ancient Greyfriars Tower to be noted; but Lynn has been, and will be again, the subject of a book entirely devoted to itself.

One pilgrimage, however, must be made ere these pages close: to Islington, four miles away on the Wisbeach road, for it is to that secluded place the sweet old ballad of the "Bailiff's Daughter of Islington" refers, and not to the better known "merry Islington" now swallowed up in London.

The ballad of the "Bailiff's Daughter" is of unknown origin. It is certainly three hundred years old, and probably much older; and has survived through all those centuries because of that sentiment of true love, triumphant over long years and distance and hard-hearted guardians, which has ever appealed to the popular imagination. Who was that Marshland bailiff and who the squire's son we do not know. It is sufficient to be told, in the lines of the sweet old song, that

> "There was a youth, and a well belovèd youth,
> And he was a Squire's son;
> He loved the Bailiff's daughter dear
> That lived at Islington."

She was coy and reluctant and rejected his advances; so that, in common with many another, before and since, love-sickness claimed him for its own. Then, for seven long years, he was sent away, bound apprentice in London. Others in those

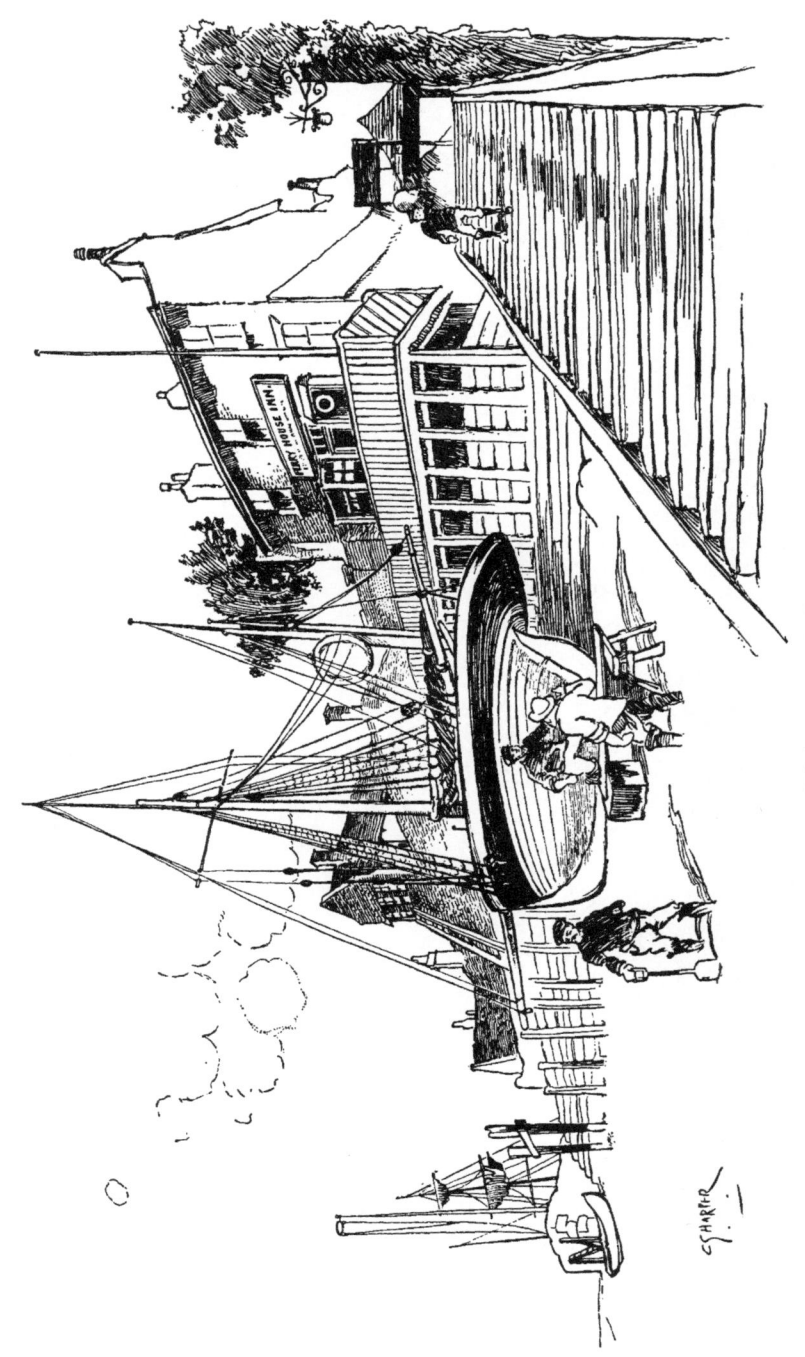

THE FERRY INN, LYNN.

circumstances would have forgotten the fair maid of Islington, but our noble youth was constancy itself, and, when his seven years had passed, came riding down the road, eager to see her face again. With what qualities of face and head and heart that maid must have been endowed!

Meanwhile, if we read the ballad aright, no one

ISLINGTON.

else came a-courting. Seven years mean much in such circumstances, and our maid grew desperate—

> "She pulled off her gown of green,
>   And put on ragged attire,
> And to fair London she would go,
>   Her true love to enquire.
>
> And as she went along the high road
>   The weather being hot and dry,
> She sat her down upon a green bank,
>   And her true love came riding by.

> She started up, with a colour so red,
>   Caught hold of his bridle rein;
> 'One penny, one penny, kind sir,' she said,
>   'Will ease me of much pain.'
>
> 'Before I give you a penny, sweetheart,
>   Pray tell me where you were born.'
> 'At Islington, kind sir,' said she,
>   'Where I have had many a scorn.'
>
> 'Prythee, sweetheart, then tell to me,
>   Oh, tell me whether you know
> The Bailiff's Daughter of Islington?'
>   'She is dead, sir, long ago.'
>
> 'If she be dead, then take my horse,
>   My saddle and bridle also;
> For I will into some far countrye
>   Where no man shall me know.'
>
> 'Oh, stay, oh stay, thou goodly youth,
>   She is standing by thy side;
> She is here alive, she is not dead,
>   But ready to be thy bride.'"

I cannot read those old lines, crabbed and uncouth though they be, without something suspiciously like a mist before the eyes and a certain difficulty in the throat. "God forbid I should grieve any young hearts," says Miss Matty, in *Cranford*. Sentiment will have its way, deny it though you will.

Islington itself is, for these reasons, a place for pious pilgrimage. And a place difficult enough to find, for it is but an ancient church, a Park and Hall, and two cottages, approached through a farmyard. That is all of Islington, the sweet savour of whose ancient story of true love has gone forth to all the world, and to my mind hallows these miles more than footsteps of saints and pilgrims.

THE END

# INDEX

Akeman Street, 5, 172, 181–183, 213, 231, 244 251.
Aldreth, 214, 225, 229, 243.
—— Causeway, 217–221.
Alfred the Great, 88–91, 263.
Amwell, Great, 86.
Aram, Eugene, 308–313.
Arnim, Count, 108–110.
Arrington Bridge, 4.

Balloon Stone, 100.
Barkway, 102–104.
Barley, 102, 107–110, 123.
Beggars' Bush, 251.
Bishopsgate Street, 8–10, 32.
Brandon Creek, 294.
Braughing, 81, 102.
Bread Riots, 273–287.
Broxbourne, 35, 81.
Bruce Grove, 40.
Buckland, 120.
Buntingford, 81, 110, 117–119, 157.

Cam, The, 153–155, 171, 172, 174, 177, 201, 235, 236, 239, 243.
Cambridge, 4, 14, 134–176, 226, 262.
—— Castle, 170–174.
Caxton, 4.
—— Gibbet, 127.
Chaucer, Geoffrey, 135.
Cheshunt, 35, 67, 69, 72, 75–80.
—— Great House, 7, 77–80.
—— Wash, 75–79.
Chesterton, 176.
Chettisham, 288.
Chipping, 120.
Chittering, 233.
Clarkson, Thos., 98–100.

Coaches—
  Bee Hive, 21, 32.
  Cambridge Auxiliary Mail, 19.
  —— Lynn, and Wells Mail, 20.
  —— Mail, 15, 19, 21.
  —— Stage, 14.
  —— and Ely Stage, 19.
  —— Telegraph, 16, 19, 21, 82, 103.
  —— Union, 19.
  Day (Cambridge and Wisbeach), 21.
  Defiance (Cambridge and Wisbeach), 21.
  Diligence (Cambridge), 13, 15.
  Fly (Cambridge), 14, 15, 19.
  Hobson's Stage (Cambridge), 15.
  Lord Nelson (Lynn), 20.
  Lynn and Fakenham Post Coach, 20.
  —— Post Coach, 20.
  —— Union, 20, 26, 29, 31, 107, 321.
  Night Post Coach (Cambridge), 16.
  Norfolk Hero (Lynn and Wells), 21.
  Prior's Stage (Cambridge), 15.
  Rapid (Cambridge and Wisbeach), 21.
  Red Rover (Lynn), 21, 254.
  Rocket (Cambridge), 21, 32.
  Royal Regulator (Cambridge), 19, 21.
  Safety (Cambridge, Lynn, and Wells), 19, 31.
  Star of Cambridge (Cambridge), 16–19, 21, 31.
  Tally Ho (Cambridge), 19.

# INDEX

Coaches—*continued*.
  Telegraph (Cambridge), 16, 19, 21, 82, 103.
  Times (Cambridge), 21.
  York Mail, 69.
Coaching, 12–32, 69, 133.
  Notabilities—
    Briggs, —, 32.
    Clark, William, 32.
    Cross, John, 22–25.
    Cross, Thomas, 22–31, 107, 256, 321.
    Elliott, George, 30.
    Goodwin, Jack, 254.
    Pryor, —, 31.
    "Quaker Will," 30.
    Reynolds, James, 31.
    Vaughan, Richard, 30.
    Walton, Jo, 31.

Denny Abbey, 231.
Denver, 301–303.
—— Sluice, 14, 302.
Dismal Hall, 231.
Downham Market, 192, 270, 275, 283, 303, 306.

Edmonton, Lower, 5, 34, 35, 36, 46–52.
——, Upper, 6, 34, 36, 43–46.
Eleanor, Queen, 56–68.
Ely, 4, 190, 195, 225, 230, 241, 258, 270, 281–288, 321, 322.
—— Cathedral, 254, 256–270.
——, Isle of, 3, 182, 189, 212–226, 230, 243, 289.
Enfield Highway, 54.
—— Wash, 54.
Ermine Street, 3, 4–7, 75, 122.
Etheldreda, Saint, 229, 260–264.

Fens, The, 176, 182–208, 214–223, 233–235, 239–248, 253, 275, 291–298.
Fielder, Richard Ramsay, 237–239.
Fordham, 183, 298, 301.
Fowlmere, 110, 112–115.
Foxton, 132.
Freezywater, 54.

Gog Magog Hills, 140–142, 151.
Granta, The, 133, 172.
Grantchester, 135, 172.

Gray, Thomas, 148, 154.
Great Amwell, 86.
—— Eastern Railway, 31–34, 120, 132, 236, 322.
—— Northern Railway, 120, 132.
—— Shelford, 133, 140.
Guthlac, Saint, 196–198.

Haddenham, 230, 262.
Hardwick Bridge, 306.
Hare Street, 102.
Harston, 117, 133.
Hauxton, 133.
Hereward the Wake, 172, 208–214, 221–223, 226–229.
High Cross, 100.
Highwaymen (in general), 54.
Highwaymen—
  Beeton, Joseph, 313–315.
  Gatward, —, 125–127.
  King, Tom, 55.
  Shelton, Dr. Wm., 80.
  Turpin, Dick, 55.
Hilgay, 297.
Hobson, Thomas, 10–12, 32, 140, 157–166.
Hobson's Conduit, 140, 167.
Hoddesdon, 7, 37, 82–86.
Hogge's Bridge, 305.

Iceni, The, 185.
Inns (mentioned at length)—
  Bath Hotel, Cambridge, 6, 170.
  Bell, Edmonton, 45, 49.
  Blue Boar, Cambridge, 15, 19, 168.
  Bull, Bishopsgate Street Within, 8–10, 12, 15, 158, 161.
  Bull, Cambridge, 19, 167.
  Bull, Hoddesdon, 82.
  Castle, Downham Market, 303.
  Chequers, Fowlmere, 115.
  Crown, Downham Market, 276, 302, 304.
  ——, King's Lynn, 321.
  Duke's Head, King's Lynn, 319–321.
  Eagle, Cambridge, 16, 19, 170.
  Falcon, Cambridge, 169.
  ——, Waltham Cross, 67–69.
  Four Swans, Bishopsgate Street Within, 8.
  ——, Waltham Cross, 68.

## INDEX

Inns—*continued*.
   Fox and Hounds, Barley, 107.
   Green Dragon, Bishopsgate Street Within, 8, 12, 15, 19.
   Hoop, Cambridge, 170.
   Lamb, Ely, 256.
   Lion, Cambridge, 14, 168.
   Lord Nelson, Upware, 235–239.
   Lynn Arms, Setchey, 306.
   Pickerel, Cambridge, 170.
   Red Lion, Reed Hill, 120.
   ——, Royston, 14, 120, 125–127.
   Roman Urn, Crossbrook Street, 75.
   Rose and Crown, Upper Edmonton, 51.
   Saracen's Head, Ware, 92, 94.
   Sun, Cambridge, 14, 15, 16.
   Three Tuns, Cambridge, 168.
   Two Brewers, Ponder's End, 53.
   Upware Inn, 235–239.
   White Horse, Fetter Lane, 13, 16.
   Woolpack, Cambridge, 168.
   Wrestlers, Cambridge, 168.
Islington, 326–331.

Kett's Oak, 298–300.
Kingsland Road, 27.
King's Lynn, 4, 34, 306–326.

Lamb, Charles, 36, 47–51, 53, 86.
Landbeach, 177, 180, 189.
Layston, 119.
Littleport, 182, 189, 243, 244, 276–281, 283, 284, 289–292.

Melbourn, 123, 128–131.
Milestones, Early examples of, 103, 110, 136.
Milton, 176, 177.
——, John, 155, 163.
Modney Bridge, 183, 297.

Newton, 115.
Nine Wells, The, 140.

Old-time travellers—
   Cobbett, Richard, 34, 122, 184, 244, 258.
   Gilpin, John, 36, 38, 43–46, 87, 96.

Old-time travellers—*continued*.
   James the First, 36, 46, 71–75.
   Pepys, Samuel, 12, 112–115.
   Prior, Matthew, 82–85.
   Thoresby, Ralph, 76–79.
   Walton, Izaak, 36–38, 43.
Ouse, The, 180, 182, 198, 201, 205, 218–221, 229, 236, 243, 257, 289, 292, 294, 302, 315.

Pasque Flower, The, 121.
Ponder's End, 35, 47, 48, 52–54.
Puckeridge, 102, 117.

Quinbury, 102.

Railways, 22, 28, 32–34, 95, 120, 132, 236, 321.
Rampton, 214.
Roman roads, 34–37, 75, 122, 172, 181–183, 213, 231, 244, 251.
Royston, 4, 7, 117, 119, 120, 122–128.
—— Cave, 124.
—— Crow, 121.
—— Downs, 117, 119–122.
Ryston, 298, 300.

Scotland Green, 42.
Setchey, 305.
Seven Sisters Road, 40.
Shelford, Great, 133, 140.
Shepreth, 131–133, 229.
Shoreditch Church, 10, 34, 35, 48.
Southery, 183, 189, 275, 295–297.
South Runcton, 305.
Spurgeon, Charles Haddon, 179.
Stamford Hill, 34, 35, 36.
Standon Green End, 100.
Stoke Newington, 35.
Stow Bardolph, 304.
Stretham, 182, 253.
—— Bridge, 182, 243, 247–251.

Theobalds, 7, 67, 72–75.
Thetford, 255.
Thriplow Heath, 115.
Tottenham, 36, 38–43.
—— High Cross, 35, 37, 38–43.
Trumpington, 134–136.
Turner's Hill, 75.
Turnford, 80.

Turnpike Acts, 119.
—— Trusts, 119.

Upware, 235–240, 243.

Wade's Mill, 97, 119.
Walsingham, Alan of, 267.
Waltham Cross, 34, 54–70, 79.
Ware, 5, 6, 7, 34, 36, 87–97.
——, Great Bed of, 86, 87, 93.

Waterbeach, 177–180, 189.
West Mill, 117.
West Winch, 306.
Wicken Fen, 198, 233–235, 240.
William the Conqueror, 3, 170–173, 209, 212–215, 217, 221–227, 230, 270.
Wimbotsham, 304.
Witchford, 225, 230.
Wormley, 81.

DA
600
H3

Harper, Charles George
The Cambridge

PLEASE DO NOT REMOVE
CARDS OR SLIPS FROM THIS POCKET

UNIVERSITY OF TORONTO LIBRARY